I Got Rhythm!
THE ETHEL MERMAN STORY

Also by Bob Thomas

NONFICTION

If I Knew Then (with Debbie Reynolds)
The Art of Animation
The Massie Case (with Peter Packer)
King Cohn
Thalberg
Selznick
The Secret Boss of California (with Arthur H. Samish)
The Heart of Hollywood
Winchell
Howard, the Amazing Mr. Hughes (with Noah Dietrich)
Marlon: Portrait of the Rebel as an Artist
Walt Disney: An American Original
The Road to Hollywood (with Bob Hope)
Bud & Lou: The Abbott and Costello Story
The One and Only Bing
Joan Crawford
Reflections: A Life in Two Worlds (with Ricardo Montalban)
Golden Boy: The Untold Story of William Holden
Astaire

FICTION

The Flesh Merchants
Weekend 33

FOR CHILDREN

Walt Disney: Magician of the Movies
Donna DeVarona, Gold Medal Winner

ANTHOLOGY

Directors in Action

I Got Rhythm!

THE ETHEL MERMAN STORY

Bob Thomas

G. P. PUTNAM'S SONS / NEW YORK

G. P. Putnam's Sons
Publishers Since 1838
200 Madison Avenue
New York, NY 10016

Published simultaneously in Canada by
General Publishing Co. Limited, Toronto

Library of Congress Cataloging-in-Publication Data

Thomas, Bob, date.
I got rhythm!

Includes index.
1. Merman, Ethel. 2. Singers—United States—
Biography. I. Title.
ML420.M39T5 1985 782.81'092'4 [B] 85-6309
ISBN 0-399-13041-1

Printed in the United States of America
1 2 3 4 5 6 7 8 9 10

In memory of George Thomas, Jr.

Contents

1.

Merman Remembered

March 1, 1984. Huntington Hartford Theater, Hollywood.

The house lights faded slowly, the curtains parted, revealing a movie screen that came to flickering life with the figure of Frank Sinatra in middle years, resplendent in white tie and tails.

"The songs of Irving Berlin," he said, "have been sung by children in Japan, teenagers in Australia, old folks in France, and pros in London. But nobody sings them any better than the dynamic star Hollywood has frequently borrowed from Broadway. Call her Madam, call her Annie, call her Panama Hattie—she is invariably the First Lady of musical comedy. Ladies and gentlemen, Miss Ethel Merman!"

The figure of Ethel Merman appeared on the screen, her tiny feet planted in the aisle of the Santa Monica Civic Auditorium. The year was 1963, and she was entertaining on the thirty-sixth awards show of the Academy of Motion Picture Arts and Sciences. The twenty-one-year-old kinescope looked faded and grainy, but the Merman voice was vibrantly clear.

"Come on and hear!" she exhorted a man sitting on the aisle.

"Come on and hear!" she insisted to another member of the audience.

"Alexander's Ragtime Band!" She continued her stroll down the aisle, instructing her listeners about "the Best Band in the

Land." Onstage she sang more Berlin songs, ending with "There's No Business Like Show Business." She had sung it thousands of times, but she remained utterly convincing when she proclaimed that "nowhere can you get that happy feeling, when you are stealing that extra bow."

The applause at the Academy Awards presentation was thunderous, and it mingled with the ovation of those who were watching the screen at the Huntington Hartford Theater. They were friends and co-workers of Ethel Merman, most of them unable to believe that her relentless vitality had been extinguished. Two weeks after her death, they had come to a hastily arranged gathering that had none of the aspects of a funeral. It was more of a show, an outpouring of humor and sentiment. Significantly, it was held in a theater.

"That's a tough act to follow," Gus Schirmer said at the end of the Merman solo. He had been her manager in the late years of her career, and he had organized the tribute, along with Carole Cook, who was appearing in Los Angeles in *42nd Street.*

"Among Ethel's proudest possessions in her last months," said the leather-voiced Schirmer, "were communications from the White House. She was a staunch Republican, except for that one lapse in *Call Me Madam.*"

He read a message: " 'Nancy and I appreciated this opportunity to share with all of you our sorrow on Ethel Merman's death and our thoughts on the joy of her life. Ethel Merman was a thoroughly professional performer, and when you needed her, she was there. When Ethel sang, our hearts sang. Ethel Merman bridged this nation's cultural heritage and put her indelible mark on the world of entertainment. . . . With our prayers and heartfelt sympathy to all who gathered for this occasion. Ronald Reagan.' "

Max Showalter, the actor, came to the stage of the Huntington Hartford to reminisce about Merman. In June of 1982, he related, she stayed at his Hollywood house, and he played the score for a musical he was co-writing about Harrigan and Hart, the oldtime musical team. One of the songs extolled the sounds and smells of backstage.

"Honey, that's a song for me!" Ethel exclaimed. "Put it in my key and I'll sing it. What did you say is the name of the song?"

" 'We'll Be There,' " Showalter replied.

"I got news for you," said Ethel. "If I sing it, it's gonna be '*I'll* Be There.' "

Schirmer read a message from Marty Pasetta, who had often directed Merman in television specials. Pasetta recalled his first view of Ethel: strolling down the full length of Forest Hills Stadium in New York, tossing roses to the packed crowd as she bellowed "Everything's Coming Up Roses." He added: "It was then that I realized I was in the presence of a genuine star, because she had everyone in the palm of her hand."

Peter Matz, arranger and conductor, remarked that with Ethel there was never a question about phrasing or tempo—"She told you what they would be." Matz told of introducing his wife to Ethel at a New York concert.

"I know you," said Ethel. "You're a singer."

"I used to be," said Mrs. Matz. "Now I work in psychotherapy."

Ethel pondered for a moment, then said, "That's a sleeper trip." The show-wise audience at the Hartford roared with appreciation.

Matz told another story. After singing a concert at the Metropolitan Opera House, Ethel and Mary Martin posed for photographers, one of whom called, "Mary, take your hand away from Ethel's chin." Ethel muttered, "Shut up, she's holding up my face." More laughter.

Schirmer interjected the story of a Merman appearance on Johnny Carson's "Tonight" show. She instructed the program assistant beforehand: "Have Johnny ask me if I can sing with my mouth full of peanut brittle." Said Schirmer: "Sure enough, Johnny asked her the question on the air. She yanked a box of peanut brittle out of her bag, filled her cheeks with it and sang, 'There's No Business Like Show Business.' "

Carole Cook came to the microphone and cited the Merman dictum: "Honey, make it short, funny, and sweet."

Miss Cook repeated a tale Ethel had related about the time

she went to a dance with the Duke and Duchess of Windsor: "The Duke was just sitting there, and the Duchess was dancing with someone Ethel did not approve of. She turned to the Duke and said, 'Duke, get off your royal ass and dance with your wife!' And he did."

Miss Cook relayed a story from Jerry Orbach, about the days when he was playing Charlie Davenport in the 1966 revival of *Annie Get Your Gun.* Merman felt a strange reaction from the audience during a scene with Orbach. Out of the corner of her eye, she spotted him doing something he hadn't done before. She demanded of the stage manager, "Ask Orbach what the hell he is doing out there." Orbach told the stage manager: "Tell Miss Merman I'm just reacting to her line." Her reply: "Tell that guy, 'I don't react to *your* lines, you don't react to *mine*!' "

Carole Cook related another story she described as Merman's favorite. Ethel and her close friend Betty Bruce, the comedienne, once traveled to Philadelphia to attend one of Mitzi Gaynor's night club openings. At a party after the show, Betty was examining a pair of cuff links in the form of miniature pistols belonging to the night club owner.

"Aren't they interesting?" said Betty, pointing one at Ethel. "Bang, bang, you're dead!" A small report was heard, and a trickle of blood appeared on Merman's ample chest.

"My God," exclaimed Betty, "I've shot my best friend in the tits!"

"Oh, Betty, it's all right," Ethel said calmly. "You coulda pointed it at my face, and I'd be looking at you with one eye."

Sylvia Fine Kaye recalled first meeting Ethel Merman in 1940, "when the world was young." Danny Kaye, with his wife at the piano, was appearing at La Martinique, and Ethel came in every Sunday night, when she was off from *Panama Hattie.* She'd always sing if Sylvia agreed to accompany her, and later Ethel and Danny would sit in a corner and exchange dirty jokes.

Mrs. Kaye spoke of the wartime benefits at which Ethel and Danny performed, of Ethel's unhappy romance with Sherman Billingsley, of her marriage to Robert Levitt.

"Like every bride, Ethel ordered monogrammed towels and

sheets and whatnot," Mrs. Kaye continued. "One day she called me up and said, 'The stuff got here and Bob hates it and he's mad at me. He won't talk to me, and I don't know what's the matter. He just looked at the towels and he got furious.' I said, 'What's on the towels?' She said, 'Just my monogram: E.M.' "

Next came Bob Hope. Before his movie success, he had starred on Broadway with Ethel Merman in *Red, Hot and Blue!* He had come to the memorial with his wife, Dolores, not knowing that he would be called upon to speak. It was a rare occasion when Hope made impromptu remarks to an audience.

After prolonged applause, Hope reminisced:

"We did a show on Broadway with Durante called *Red, Hot and Blue!*, so you can imagine the fun I had. Of all my moments on Broadway, this was the tops. She lived at 25 Central Park West, I lived at 65, and I used to pick her up on the way to the Alvin Theater. We would laugh all the way. In the show we introduced 'It's De-Lovely,' and with Ethel's exuberance and everything, it became such a hit, three or four encores a night. It was a great moment in my Broadway career."

Hope recalled another song—"You've Got Something"—"a low spot for Cole Porter, and a lower spot asking me to sing it." It was a love ballad he sang to Merman, who responded by crossing her eyes out of view of the audience. Hope clowned in return, until he received a note from the composer: "Please sing the ballad straight."

"There were three dressing rooms on the main floor of the Alvin," Hope continued. "I had the little one, Ethel had the second one and Durante had the third, which was a little bigger so it could handle his racing forms. While Jimmy and I were making up, on cue we would run in and attack Merman in her dressing room. You could hear her screams for two or three blocks. We did that about once a week just to keep things boring.

"I don't have many jokes about her that I could remember, but I never had one moment with her that I didn't enjoy. It was solid fun all the way. Up there when she walks into heaven and Crosby and Jolson see her, my God, what she will add to that crew. God bless her."

Mary Martin came to the stage next amid an ovation. In 1938 when she appeared in her first New York musical, *Leave It to Me,* Mary had met Ethel, who was already "the First Lady of Broadway, the Queen of Broadway—and she will always be the First Lady of Broadway, the Queen of Broadway."

They became friends over the years, especially during the period when their children were young. They drew together again in later years, after both had experienced tragedy. Mary talked of their good times together and then of the final, heartbreaking visit just a few weeks before, when Ethel lay dying, her great voice silenced.

Mary admitted that when she heard the news of Ethel's death, "I *had* to be glad that she was gone, because Merman without performing or without sound would never make Merman happy."

She reminisced about their happy times together, drawing laughter from the audience, then turned reflective again, recalling the many friends she had lost—Leland Hayward, Oscar Hammerstein, Noel Coward, her beloved husband, Richard Halliday. She remembered being consoled by a friend who said, "Well, God needed a lot of talent up there."

"That made me feel so much better," Mary remarked. "Because, you see, Merman's up there, with all that talent, and I just hope she's singing [with a haunting replica of the Merman voice] 'Blo-ow, Gabriel, Blow!' "

The speeches over, the theater darkened, and once more the vibrant figure of Ethel Merman filled the movie screen. Once more, with songs from her motion pictures, that irresistibly energizing voice sounded forth, advising her listeners indisputably, "I Got Rhythm!"

That was the Merman that everyone knew: shoulders squared, feet planted firmly on the stage, tossing her defiant heart all the way to the balcony. Only a few at the Huntington Hartford Theater, and a handful more in New York, had ever glimpsed another Ethel Merman: frightened, erratic, explosive, a woman of great sorrows and high achievement. A challenging subject for the biographer's trade.

2.

Ethel Zimmermann of Astoria

When settlers first started coming there in the seventeenth century, it was called Hallett's Cove. After the Revolution, the town grew, and by 1839 it was big enough to be incorporated under the new name Astoria, after John Jacob Astor, the fur-trade monopolist who poured his millions into large chunks of New York real estate. Conveniently located in the northwest section of the borough of Queens, Astoria sheltered those who toiled in Manhattan.

In the second decade of the twentieth century, Astoria became noted for its movie studio. Famous Players–Lasky filmed its motion pictures in a factory-like place with makeshift buildings for interior shooting and outdoor sets that were destroyed by storms every winter. Travel to the studio was convenient for the stars Jesse Lasky and Adolph Zukor lured from the New York stage with high salaries: John Barrymore, Elsie Janis, Ina Claire, Dustin Farnum, Lily Langtry, Lenore Ulric, H. B. Warner. Others who worked at Astoria were celebrities created by the new medium: Rudolph Valentino, Mary Pickford, Gloria Swanson.

Every morning a cluster of young Astorians stood patiently at the gates of the Famous Players–Lasky studio, waiting for a glance at the stars as they reported for work. The most regular of the watchers at 6th and Pierce Avenues was little Ethel Zimmermann, who hurried over from her home, just two blocks away.

She was a skinny kid with long dark hair her mother trained with a curling iron to look like Mary Pickford's. Ethel's best asset was her wide-set dark brown eyes. Otherwise her face, with its long narrow nose and small straight mouth, ranged somewhere between plain and nice-looking. In starched blouse and pleated skirt, she was by far the best-dressed youngster at the studio gate.

"Here she comes! It's Alice Brady!" Ethel cried, and the others strained to see the familiar black limousine cruising down 6th Avenue.

The long shiny car turned into the driveway, and the Japanese chauffeur waited as guards flung open the studio gates for the arrival of the star. The delay allowed Ethel a longer glance at the lone small figure in the backseat. Alice Brady, in her early twenties, was already a brilliant Broadway star under the aegis of her noted father, William A. Brady, a stage and film producer. She also made movies, and Ethel Zimmermann had seen every one of them. To Ethel, Alice Brady was the most beautiful, refined and serene person she could imagine. Among her girlish fantasies was the vision of herself as an actress, just like Alice Brady.

The neighbors on 4th Avenue predicted little Ethel would go places as a singer. Two or three houses away, they could easily hear her singing "By the Light of the Silv'ry Moon" and "Alexander's Ragtime Band" while her adoring father accompanied her on the piano.

She had been born in the third-floor bedroom of her grandmother's house at 359 4th Avenue. The date was January 16, 1908, though in her late years she claimed the year was 1912. Her parents called her Ethel Agnes Zimmermann, Agnes being her mother's first name. Agnes Gardner was a Presbyterian of Scottish descent who had married Edward Zimmermann, a German Lutheran. Perhaps as a compromise, their only child was baptized an Episcopalian at the Church of the Redeemer in Astoria, and she remained an Episcopalian all her life.

Unlike many future stars, Ethel enjoyed a childhood that seemed remarkably trouble-free. In her early years, she was surrounded by loving, supportive relatives. All lived in Grandmother Gardner's house, a rambling three-story place. The lower story was rented out to provide a widow's income. The second floor was occupied by Grandmother Gardner, a daughter and her husband, and their son Claude, who was almost a brother to Ethel. The three Zimmermanns lived on the third floor.

Edward Zimmermann commuted every day to 345 Broadway, in lower Manhattan, where he worked as an accountant for a wholesale dry-goods company. Ethel could hardly wait for him to come home so he could play the piano while she sang. Before she was two, she could sing whole songs, and her father, who also played the organ at the local Masons' hall, bragged that her pitch was absolutely perfect.

Agnes Zimmermann was also proud of Ethel's singing, but she was less indulgent. With her husband gone all day, Agnes provided the discipline, stern but fair. She made sure that Ethel was neatly dressed at all times, applied herself to schoolwork, maintained respect for her elders in the house, learned the rudiments of housewifery: cooking, sewing, cleaning.

Throughout her career, Ethel Merman maintained the image of total fearlessness. But in the autobiography she wrote with George Eells, she provided a glimpse of a frightened little girl:

"I loved [my parents] but was frightened to death of them. I remember that there was a cat-o'-nine-tails on the wall, but it was for show, not for use. My greatest problem was fear of the dark.

"When we lived on 4th Avenue the whistles of the boats and foghorns spooked me. Mom got Communion candles for a night light and sometimes would even lie with me until she thought I was asleep. I wasn't, but I wouldn't let her know it. After she'd gone, I'd silently cry myself to sleep."

At Public School Number 4 in Astoria, Ethel Zimmermann was known as something of a tomboy who could play baseball as well as any of the boys. If one of them dared to pull her long curls, he was discouraged with a bell-ringing whack on the ear. Still, Ethel looked the picture of young femininity when her mother dressed her for church. She attended the Church of the Redeemer four times each Sunday: for the morning service, Sunday school, prayer meeting and Christian Endeavor.

Ethel had a special treat every other Sunday. That was when a family friend she called Uncle Tom took her to the matinee at the Palace Theater on Broadway and 47th Street in Manhattan. Oh, what a marvelous world it was, full of clowns and acrobats and amazingly intelligent animals. Yet the performers who fascinated Ethel most were the female singers. Sophie Tucker, with her bouncy "International Rag" and the saucy "Who Paid the Rent for Mrs. Rip Van Winkle (When Rip Van Winkle Was Away)?"; Belle Baker, with her heartbreaking "Eli, Eli" and the funny Irving Berlin song "Cohen Owes Me 97 Dollars"; the poignant Anna Held, hilarious Fanny Brice, lusty Odette Myrtil; the coolly beautiful Nora Bayes, who held the Palace audience enthralled with "Shine On, Harvest Moon."

When she returned home with Uncle Tom, Ethel did her best to imitate the stars she had heard, not an easy task with her girlish soprano. Her father was delighted, and he began taking Ethel to his lodge, where she amazed his fellow Masons with her loud, true voice.

Ethel sang tirelessly at church socials and weddings, and in 1917 she made what might be considered her professional debut. Army camps around New York were filling with soldiers waiting to be shipped to Europe, and local talent was encouraged to help keep the troops entertained. One day the 4th Avenue neighbors watched with excitement as an army ambulance parked in front of the Zimmermanns' house. Little Ethel and her mother emerged, and the ambulance whizzed off with them for the 25-mile drive to Camp Mills.

"Since Maggie Dooley Did the Hooley Hooley," Ethel sang in a voice that could be heard in the last row by the assemblage of soldiers at the camp. They roared their approval of the precocious nine-year-old, and she felt an exhilaration she had never known before.

The success at Camp Mills led to bookings at other army bases, including Camp Yaphank, immortalized in Irving Berlin's army show *Yip, Yip, Yaphank.* Ethel stirred the troops with Berlin's "Over There" and drew tears with a song she dedicated to her mother, "She's Me Pal," Ethel's version of the popular tune "He's Me Pal."

Agnes Zimmermann soon took over from Uncle Tom and began escorting Ethel to the Palace Theater every Friday night. Although the girl displayed remarkable talent, Agnes could not conceive of a show business career for her daughter. None of the family had been in entertainment, and the odds for success seemed insuperable.

"You're a smart girl, you should teach school like your cousin Agnes," said Mrs. Zimmermann.

Much as she admired her cousin, Ethel couldn't envision life as a schoolteacher. As a compromise, she offered to take a business course so she would always be able to find work as a stenographer. She enrolled for the four-year course at William Cullen Bryant High School in Long Island City. The Zimmermanns were now living in a comfortable fifth-floor walkup on 31st Avenue.

Ethel proved a whiz in the business course, scoring 95 percent or better on all her typing and shorthand tests. She enjoyed her studies, liked the neatness and precision of taking dictation in the quick scrawls of the Pitman Method, then transforming it to type with flying fingers. The whole process appealed to her sense of order.

Singing remained the obsession of her life, however. She knew she was good at it, and she sought every opportunity to perform before an audience, whether it was the Women's Republican Club of Astoria or the annual fundraiser of the Anti-Tuberculosis Society.

After graduation from Bryant High, Ethel applied for work at the Long Island Employment Agency. The business boom of the late 1920s was continuing, and capable stenographers were in demand. Ethel was immediately placed with the Boye-Ite Company, which manufactured anti-freeze for automobiles. Her salary was the respectable sum of $23 a week.

Ethel reported for work each morning at eight o'clock, and performed her chores with enough speed so there was plenty of time to gab with the other girls. At noon the stenographers trooped to a lunchroom on Queens Boulevard, where they met people from other offices. Ethel became acquainted with Victor Kliesrath of the nearby Bragg-Kliesrath Corporation.

"I hear you're a damn good stenographer," he said. "Why don't you come to work for us? I'll give you a five-dollar raise."

"You got a deal!" Ethel replied.

Bragg-Kliesrath, which manufactured the B-K Vacuum Booster Brake for automobiles, soon recognized Miss Zimmermann's talents, and she was assigned to be personal secretary to the president, Caleb Bragg.

He was a brilliant, gifted, erratic man who spent the millions he'd made from his brake invention on large estates, lavish parties and fast cars and boats. He competed in automobile races, and won the Gold Cup with his speedboat, called *Baby Bootlegger*.

Bragg enjoyed the glitter of the show-biz world, and his name was often linked with famous Broadway beauties. Ethel paid special attention when her boss dictated letters to Broadway producers or ordered flowers for stage stars.

She was less efficient with more humdrum business letters. "What did I know about vacuums and boosters and all that stuff?" she told an interviewer years later.

Bragg would peruse her drafts and inquire, "Look, Ethel, didn't I give you more than this?"

"Well, I didn't hear you," she'd reply. "Maybe it's this Pitman Method."

Ethel learned to recognize Bragg's many moods, some of which were violent. At times he became enraged during a telephone call to an automobile plant in Detroit, and he would yank the wire from the wall and hurl the phone against the office wall. Ethel would calmly dial the telephone repair man: "He did it again; come and fix it." Then she disappeared into the supply room until her boss calmed down.

In one respect the job with Bragg was ideal: He rarely came to the office more than two days a week. That helped Ethel pursue her search for a singing career.

She sneaked off and hustled around Broadway, trying to enlist booking agents. Most of them brushed her off when she recited her experience, but a few agreed to "keep you in mind." Sometimes they called to offer singing dates at weddings or parties for $5 or $7.50 per night.

Realizing that a singer had to keep up with the latest, she toured Tin Pan Alley publishers in search of new songs to fit her style. "You mean you pay for 'em?" an agent told her. "Don't be a sucker. Just tell 'em you're a professional singer, and they'll give you song sheets free—for nothing." Ethel soon collected a large library of sheet music.

Her double life required careful management. Often she sang past midnight at a political rally or a wedding anniversary celebration. She would still report for work in the morning, open the mail, dust the office, then retire to the ladies' room. There she would remove her dress, curl up on the sofa and fall soundly asleep.

"The boss is on the phone!" Ethel's slumber would be jolted by another stenographer who kept watch for her. She'd leap into her dress and rush to the office. "Yes, Mr. Bragg," she'd reply breathlessly. After jotting down his instructions, she'd return to her nap.

Ethel took any singing job, sometimes two a night. One New Year's Eve she had one date on Manhattan's 86th Street and another in Brooklyn. She was traveling on the subway to the second party when 1929 began.

Caleb Bragg loved to hobnob with the rich and famous and took little notice of those who worked for him. Not so his partner, Vic Kliesrath, who often treated Bragg-Kliesrath workers to lunch and invited them to dine with his family at his home in Port Washington, Long Island. Ethel would enliven the evening with her songs.

One Saturday afternoon, Kliesrath hosted a company outing at a Port Washington restaurant. Caleb Bragg's houseboat, *The*

Masquerader, was anchored offshore, and he magnanimously invited a few of his employees to join him.

Ethel Zimmermann climbed aboard *The Masquerader* and gained her first view of how the swells lived and played. The boat was shiny and polished, the guests tanned and beautiful. Stewards offered trays of canapés and glasses of champagne. In her big black Milan hat, pleated silk dress and brand-new shoes, Ethel felt perfectly at ease as she mingled with her boss's friends.

"How would you girls like to take a spin in my new speedboat, *Casey Jones*?" Mr. Bragg proposed.

"I'd love it," said Ethel. She and the office telephone operator climbed into the boat, and they went roaring off to the Connecticut shore. On the return trip, the *Casey Jones* hit a piece of driftwood and capsized, hurling the occupants into the water. Bragg sent another boat to the rescue.

"I'm all right," said the miserable Ethel, her outfit ruined and her purse at the bottom of Manhasset Bay. "Just get me out of this."

The two young women were returned to *The Masquerader*, where Bragg outfitted them with silk pajamas and insisted they stay for dinner.

Among Bragg's guests were Arch and Ruth Selwyn, producers of Broadway shows. Ethel recognized their names from reading Broadway columns. Seated next to Mrs. Selwyn at dinner, Ethel explained that although she worked as Mr. Bragg's personal secretary, she was really a singer.

"Y'know, I go to the Palace every week," said Ethel, "and it really burns me up because I know damn well I can sing as good as most of those people up on the stage."

"Really, Miss—"

"Zimmermann. Ethel Zimmermann."

"Well, Miss Zimmermann, if you're as good as you say you are, I'll put you in my next show."

Nothing came of the encounter, but it provided Ethel with two important notions. First, she concluded that Zimmermann was impossible as a stage name. She had realized for some time that it wouldn't fit on theater marquees, but she was afraid to mention a name-change to her father.

She contemplated taking the maiden name of her mother or grandmother. Ethel Gardner or Ethel Hunter would look good in lights. As she expected, however, her father exploded at the suggestions.

"Zimmermann is good enough for me, it's good enough for you!" he decreed.

She arrived at another proposal: dropping the *Zim* and the final *n*. Edward Zimmermann grudgingly agreed that she could take the name Ethel Merman.

The second realization from her conversation with Mrs. Selwyn was the easy accessibility of prominent people who could give jobs to a talented young singer. As Bragg's secretary, Ethel had placed phone calls and written letters to Mr. Bragg's friend George White, who produced the *Scandals*. Would her boss agree to a letter of introduction to the producer? Bragg said he would.

Ethel delivered the letter in person to White's office at the Apollo Theater on 42nd Street. White was unimpressed. His unerring eye for beauty found nothing remarkable in Caleb Bragg's secretary. The legs were shapely, the bust ample, but the face could only be described as nice-looking.

"What do you do?" the producer asked.

"I sing," Ethel replied firmly. "I'm a singer."

"Well, all I can give you is a job in the line. Frances Williams is doing all the singing in the next *Scandals*."

"Nope, not in any line," Ethel told him, ending the interview.

Her next singing job was the best thus far. Little Russia, a night club–speakeasy on 57th Street operated by White Russians, paid her $60 a week to appear nightly. This placed a strain on her work at Bragg-Kliesrath, but her fellow secretaries continued to cover for her. Besides napping during the day, Ethel would sleep for an hour or two at home after work, then arrive by subway at Little Russia by nine o'clock. It was usually three in the morning before she returned to Astoria.

Lou Irwin, an enterprising talent agent, was walking down 57th Street one evening when he encountered an acquaintance, a Broadway character who supplied perfume at wholesale to Flo Ziegfeld, Earl Carroll and other producers.

"How about dropping by that joint, Little Russia?" the man suggested. "A friend of mine owns it, and he needs customers."

Irwin walked into the club just as Ethel Merman was being introduced. He listened in awe. First the girl sang an amazingly accurate imitation of Libby Holman doing "Moanin' Low." She followed in her own voice with "I've Got a Feeling I'm Falling" and "Little White Lies." Irwin had rarely heard a singer so vibrant, so confident, so loud.

Irwin sent his card to Ethel, and she came to his table. She was naturally skeptical of men who claimed they could put her name in lights, but he seemed to be a legitimate agent with clients like Helen Morgan and the Ritz Brothers.

"Come to my office tomorrow and we'll sign a contract," Irwin proposed.

"Well, uh, could I call you in the morning?" Ethel said.

"Why can't we set the date now?"

"I, uh, have another appointment tomorrow, and I'll have to see about it." That was true, but Ethel didn't want to admit that she worked by day as a secretary.

After work the next day, Ethel arrived at Lou Irwin's office with her mother. He was amused to learn that Ethel had a full-time office job. Mrs. Zimmermann had come along to make sure that Irwin would not take advantage of her daughter. Also to sign the contract, since Ethel was not yet twenty-one.

"Archie Mayo, the movie director, is here from Hollywood, looking for musical talent for Warner Brothers shorts," Irwin said. "He's a good friend of mine. I'll line up an audition for you."

Two days later, Ethel brought her music to the Mills music publishing office on 47th Street. Although she had never before been nervous about performing nor was she afterward, she felt her heart pounding as she sang for Archie Mayo. The director nodded approval, as did Lew Warner, son of the company president. Ethel was offered a six-month contract at $200 a week, with options for a longer term at more money.

"When do I start work?" she asked eagerly.

"Don't get excited," advised Warner. "We'll notify you when to report."

At last Ethel considered herself a professional. No more surreptitious naps in the ladies' room. She could quit her office job. She bid goodbye to Mr. Bragg and Mr. Kliesrath, who wished her well, and to the girls in the office, who wept tears of joy. Ethel cried along with them, wondering if she had made the right decision.

3.

The Road to Broadway

Ethel Merman waited for Warner Brothers to call. And waited. The checks came regularly—$200 every week, as stipulated in her contract. But she was never asked to report for work.

The movie industry was in turmoil in 1929—all because of Warner Brothers. *The Jazz Singer*, made two years earlier, had forced all the companies to convert to talkies, with resultant chaos. Musicals were the thing, not only with features made in Hollywood but shorts filmed in New York. Warner Brothers, Paramount and other companies signed dozens of musical personalities from vaudeville, radio and the theater, then hastily tried to devise short films to employ their talents.

Ethel finally made one short, which neither she nor anyone else could remember later. She dimly recalled that it took place in a jungle and she was draped in a leopard skin. She worked two days, then went home to wait for the telephone to ring again.

After more eventless weeks, she called Lou Irwin.

"Listen, Lou," she said, "you gotta get me out of this Warner business. The girls at the office think I'm a kept lady or something. I give up my job and I don't work and I have lots of jack. What good's the money when I lose my reputation and nobody knows I'm a singer? Give 'em back the contract and get me a job singing someplace."

Irwin negotiated a better deal. Warner Brothers agreed to keep her under contract while allowing her to accept singing engagements. When she wasn't working on the outside, Warners would pay her usual salary.

Irwin's first booking for Ethel was at a small night spot on Broadway, Les Ambassadeurs, where Clayton, Jackson and Durante also appeared. The trio had become the sensation of New York night life with their knockabout comedy skits—especially the inspired madness of Jimmy Durante. Ethel did *not* audition for the job, she remarked rather testily in later years. She was hired on the reliable word of Lou Irwin.

Says Fred Astaire: "I heard Ethel Merman sing for the first time at Les Ambassadeurs, a club above the Winter Garden Theater. She had an amazingly large voice and a great deal of personality."

Ray Bolger remembers hearing Merman during the same period: "I took my wife to Les Ambassadeurs, and we were both startled by this young girl who was so brash and loud. I told my wife, 'We're going to see more of this girl.' "

The name of Ethel Merman began popping up in the columns of Walter Winchell, Louis Sobol, Ed Sullivan and others, thrilling Edward and Agnes Zimmermann as well as the secretaries at Bragg-Kliesrath.

Les Ambassadeurs paid Ethel only $85 a week, but she was finally doing what she wanted to do. Ethel's act was at the beginning of the show: She led the chorus line in a few kicks, and later returned in a spotlight all her own to sing "Moanin' Low," "Body and Soul" and other torch songs.

One morning Ethel awakened with her throat in a vise. Tonsillitis again, but worse than she had ever felt it. During most of her teen years she had suffered the pain from time to time, and her father always had the same cure: gargle with iron water, a foul-tasting medicine. "One more gargle of that iron stuff," Ethel said later, "and my teeth would have turned black."

Doctors had always been baffled by her tonsils, which were far down her throat. This time they were diseased and would have to be removed.

Ethel was distressed. She had heard dire stories of singers whose voices had been ruined by throat operations. The surgery meant she would lose her night club job just as she was gaining recognition. Her only consolation was going back on the Warner Brothers payroll, which would help pay for the operation.

Surgery was difficult because of the inaccessibility and diseased condition of the tonsils. Two blood vessels were severed and had to be sewn up. During the recuperation period, the pain in her throat was combined with something not customary for Ethel: depression.

"Will I be able to sing again, doctor?" she asked anxiously. Although she was told that the operation would probably not affect her singing voice, she worried. If she lost her voice, she consoled herself, she could always find work as a secretary.

Two weeks after the operation, she was allowed to try her singing voice. Amazingly, she was able to sing even louder than before.

Lou Irwin decided to book Ethel out of town. She was engaged for six weeks at the Roman Pools Casino, a gambling operation opposite the Roney Plaza Hotel in Miami Beach. The salary was $300 a week, which she augmented with tips from gamblers for whom she acted as a "good-luck charm" at the tables. She used the extra income to splurge on outfits that were the latest in the flapper look—among them two red fox furs.

When she returned to New York Ethel had her first encounter with a legendary figure in the Merman history: Al Siegel.

Siegel was known along Broadway as a kind of miracle man for female singers. Composer-conductor John Green recalls: "He was an extraordinarily gifted man, a brilliant, creative showman with a great nose for a certain kind of talent. He had an uncanny sense for the right songs and how to present them."

Throughout the 1920s, Al Siegel had built the careers of one singer after another. His greatest creation was Bee Palmer, who had been a shimmy dancer until Siegel transformed her into a stylish torch singer who headlined in vaudeville. She was regarded by other singers as the best in the business, earning $2,000 a week. Bee and Al married, and he continued playing piano and conducting for her and devising all her arrangements. Eventually, however, she tired of her career and Al, and she gave up both.

Siegel was on the rebound from Bee and leading a small combo in a 52nd Street club when he met young Ethel Merman at a party. The guests were show people, and many of them got up and entertained the group. Ethel sang "Smile, Darn You, Smile" in an imperative manner, and Siegel was immediately intrigued. He introduced himself, offered his credentials and invited her to his office the following day.

The partnership lasted less than six months, but during that time Ethel Merman was catapulted from an obscure night club singer to the hit of Broadway. Would that have happened if Al Siegel hadn't taken her under his wing? The question has been debated in the delis of Manhattan for decades.

For years after they parted, Siegel claimed to be the genius behind Merman's success. She denied it emphatically: "That stuff about Siegel being some kind of Svengali for me is a lot of crap." As for learning from him how to project her voice: "I *always* had a loud voice." Breathing? "I just sing until I have to stop and take a breath, then I take it and go on singing."

Wolcott Gibbs asked Merman about Siegel during a 1946 interview for an article in *Life*. Her cryptic reply: "I haven't mentioned that Siegel's name for fifteen years."

Most experts agree that Al Siegel did make an important contribution to the Merman career, but not in technique. Siegel was an expert at taking a simple song and converting it into a storytelling experience. Sometimes he wrote his own lyrics to a second chorus that elaborated on the song's message. In the case of "Little White Lies," he added a second chorus that slightly burlesqued the first. Thus the audience participated in the irony of Merman's romantic complaint.

Before Siegel, Ethel had sung love songs in a straightforward manner, yet they seemed out of sync with her loud, lusty voice. Under Siegel's coaching, she could sing the most treacly of ballads with a sardonic twist that became her trademark.

The Merman-Siegel partnership began with a vaudeville date

at the Ritz Theater in Elizabeth, New Jersey. The new material scored with the audience, but Siegel continued perfecting Ethel's delivery. Once he was satisfied, it was as if a song had been carved in alabaster: Ethel performed it without a fraction of variance.

More vaudeville dates followed, then Lou Irwin landed her a Sunday job at the Pavillon Royal in Valley Stream, a Long Island summer resort that attracted the entertainment crowd from Manhattan. Often on Sundays visiting stars volunteered to perform at the club. Ethel loved playing to the well-heeled audience, especially because the Guy Lombardo orchestra provided the accompaniment.

After Merman had become a star, Lou Irwin told an interviewer: "Twenty-five dollars the both of them got at the Pavillon Royal, and they were glad to get it. She was a hit and the next Sunday the pay was seventy-five dollars and the next Sunday it was one hundred and fifty, and did Ethel like that!

"The way it is, three things are important to Ethel. The first is money and the second is money and the third is money, because she is Scotch-German and the Scotch prevails." Ethel had already established a reputation for thriftiness, depositing all her excess money in safe investments and avoiding the extravagances of her fellow performers.

Her Sundays at the Pavillon Royal soon were extended to full weekend appearances, and once more the Broadway crowd was talking about the girl from Astoria with the big voice. Among those who heard about her was Vinton Freedley, producer of hit musicals. He went to see Ethel at the Brooklyn Paramount Theater, where she was singing four times a day between performances of the movie.

Freedley recalled: "She came out in a short black dress all messed up with bows and ribbons and a lot of jet, and her hair was even wilder than it is now, but she was quite a singer."

The producer went backstage and asked Ethel if she would like to appear in a Broadway musical. She accepted eagerly and arrived at his office the following day, dashing over between shows at the Paramount and wearing the same gaudy dress. With some misgivings, Freedley arranged an audition with George Gershwin.

Ethel had to wait for another break at the Paramount before she could pay a call to the Gershwin apartment at 33 Riverside Drive. George and Ira, both at the height of their brilliant careers, greeted her warmly and invited her to sing. George accompanied her on "Little White Lies" and "Exactly Like You," and her voice rang from the apartment walls.

"You're very good," said George, and his brother agreed. They explained that they had created songs for a show called *Girl Crazy* that Freedley and Alex Aarons were producing.

"Would you like to hear what Ira and I have written?" George asked.

"You bet!" replied Ethel.

George played the piano while Ira sang "I Got Rhythm," "Sam and Delilah" and "Boy, What Love Has Done to Me!" Ethel was deep in thought, concentrating not so much on the songs as on how she could interpret them.

"If there's anything you don't like about the music, I'll be happy to change it," George offered.

Ethel was already singing the songs in her mind, and George repeated his offer. "They will do very nicely, Mr. Gershwin," she replied numbly.

Freedley and Aarons gave Ethel a contract to appear in *Girl Crazy* at $375 a week. At Lou Irwin's insistence, Al Siegel was also signed for the show. As rehearsals began, it became apparent that Ethel Merman warranted more than a few walk-ons between her three songs, and so the authors—Guy Bolton and Jack McGowan—augmented her role as Kate Fothergill.

Lou liked to keep his client busy, and during the rehearsal period he booked Ethel for a week at the Palace. It was the culmination of her girlhood dream—to appear on the same stage where she had first seen all the great singers of show business.

Ted Healy was the Palace headliner and master of ceremonies, and he did some knockabout comedy with his Racketeers, later known as the Three Stooges. Other acts included the dancer

Harriet Hoctor and the old-time songster Gus Van. The *Times* reviewer wrote on September 15, 1930:

> From the night clubs to her Palace debut comes Ethel Merman, a comely ballad singer, accompanied by Al Siegel, who is not so new. Miss Merman's torch singing premiere turns out to be an auspicious event in lyric celebration of the broken Broadway heart, and promises well for her debut later in the season on the musical comedy stage.

The *Girl Crazy* company moved to Philadelphia amid expectations that the Aarons-Freedley team and the Gershwins were creating another hit. The male comedy role was in the capable hands of the Broadway favorite, Willie Howard, who had stepped into the show when Bert Lahr bowed out. The leading lady was Ginger Rogers, a beautiful redhead who made an immediate hit with her line "Cigarette me, big boy" in the movie *Young Man of Manhattan*. The leading man was the stalwart of Gershwin musicals, Allen Kearns.

But it was Ethel Merman who was attracting most of the attention in Philadelphia. Audiences fell into a startled hush when she strode self-assuredly onto the stage in a black skirt slit almost to the waist and a red blouse that barely contained her well-developed bust. She leaned against the proscenium arch and began wailing in a Frankie and Johnny vein about a floozy who wasn't choosy and who fell for a swell buckaroo named Sam.

The show's next number was "I Got Rhythm," also sung by Ethel. The song was deceptively simple. George had written a series of ascending and descending notes that somehow became infectious. Ira added a series of shotgun phrases that perfectly summarized a woman's total delight with the assets in her life. The song itself was enough to stop any show. Al Siegel added the topper: On the second chorus, Ethel would hold a single C note for sixteen bars.

"Sam and Delilah" drew a huge response. "I Got Rhythm" brought down the house.

But Ethel's thrill over the Philadelphia reception was tempered by her concern for Al Siegel's health. He had always had a bad cough, but now he was spitting blood, and doctors said he would have to be hospitalized. Al refused. He had brought Ethel this far; he was going to carry through until she was an even bigger star than his ex-wife, Bee Palmer. His determination was spurred by the fact that he stood to gain 25 percent of Ethel's entire earnings.

Girl Crazy had its New York premiere at the Alvin Theater on October 14, 1930. As with all Gershwin openings, the first-night audience included the cream of New York society and the entertainment world. George Gershwin pleased his followers by conducting the pit orchestra. And what an orchestra! It was augmented by members of the popular Red Nichols band, including such future swing greats as Benny Goodman, Glenn Miller, Jimmy Dorsey, Gene Krupa and Jack Teagarden.

The excitement began as soon as Gershwin gave the downbeat for the overture. The melodic standard was struck in the first number, "Bidin' My Time," sung by a quartet of ranch hands. Midway in the first act came a romantic ballad, "Embraceable You," sung by Ginger Rogers and Allen Kearns.

Then came the Merman one-two punch.

"As soon as I sang 'Sam and Delilah,' I knew I was in," Ethel said later. Immediately afterward she had an even greater number. She gazed down with assurance at Al Siegel, who had left a hospital bed to accompany her on the piano on opening night, and began:

I got rhythm,
I got music,
I got my man—
Who could ask for anything more?

When she launched her long note in the second chorus, the Alvin Theater reverberated. It was, Ira Gershwin observed, "a no-nonsense voice that could reach not only standees but ticket-takers in the lobby." Ethel had to perform encore after encore before the first-act curtain could descend.

George Gershwin hurried out of the orchestra pit and dashed up three flights of stairs to Ethel's dressing room. He swung open the door and exclaimed, "Ethel, you've done it!" Then he uttered the line Ethel quoted for the rest of her life: "Never, but never go near a singing teacher."

In the second act Ginger Rogers and Willie Howard performed another great Gershwin song, "But Not for Me." When Ethel Merman reappeared, she was greeted with grateful applause, and she socked across "Boy, What Love Has Done to Me!" Ginger and the chorus were left with the chore of ending the show with "Cactus Time in Arizona."

The applause at the curtain call was tumultuous, and Ethel seemed hardly able to comprehend it all. Along with other members of the cast, she attended a party hosted by George Gershwin, and congratulations were exchanged by all. Ethel's date, a wholesale furniture dealer named Billy Sussman, escorted her to the Central Park Casino for their own celebration.

"Right this way, Miss Merman," gushed the head waiter, leading them to a prize table. Ethel and Billy exchanged smiles of satisfaction. Just a few nights before they had been forced to wait behind the rope until a table was available.

It was almost dawn when Ethel arrived home in Astoria. She slept only a few hours, then rose for a luncheon date with George Gershwin.

"Have you read the reviews?" he asked eagerly.

"What reviews?"

"The reviews in the papers, for God's sake! They loved my songs, the show's a hit, and you're a sensation!"

The New York newspapers were spread around Gershwin's living room, and Ethel read the reviews with wonder and disbelief. The *Times* critic declared that a major asset of the show was Ethel Merman, "whose peculiar song style was brought from the night clubs to the stage to the vast delight of people who go places and watch things being done."

Another reviewer commented that "Ethel isn't mournful, like Libby Holman. She isn't tear-stained and voice-cracked, like Helen Morgan. . . . She approaches sex in a song with the cold fury of a philosopher. She aims at a point slightly above the entrails, but she knocks you out just the same."

Robert Coleman of the *Daily Mirror* wrote: "The big surprise of the evening was Ethel Merman, a young and talented songstress with a peculiar delivery who tied the proceedings up in knots. A graduate of night clubs and motion picture theaters, this girl bids fare to become the toast of Broadway."

The critics wasted little space on summarizing the plot of *Girl Crazy*, a pastiche about a New York playboy who is exiled by his family to Arizona, where he opens a dude ranch equipped with gambling facilities and an abundance of beautiful girls. Merman played the wife of the local saloonkeeper in a story barely substantial enough to support the inspired Gershwin songs, lively dancing and the calculated madness of Willie Howard.

The opening night of *Girl Crazy* marked the end of the professional relationship of Ethel Merman and Al Siegel. He left the Alvin Theater on a stretcher at the end of the first act, and the pianist in the Red Nichols band, Roger Edens, took his place.

Siegel's ailment was diagnosed as tuberculosis, and he was sent to a hospital in Connecticut. When Ethel began receiving offers for night club dates during the run of *Girl Crazy*, she realized she needed up-to-date arrangements. She and Lou Irwin visited Siegel in the hospital and proposed that he write new arrangements for her.

"Okay, but I want thirty-three percent of all your future earnings," he said.

"Forget it," Ethel snapped, turning on her heel and leaving the hospital room.

She continued paying 25 percent of her income to Siegel for a year. Then their contract lapsed, and she paid no more. She erased him from her life, but alas, he kept reappearing like some despised ghost. Al Siegel lived on for many years. He had many friends in show business, and they were quick to assert that if Al hadn't molded her style, Ethel Merman would still be singing in two-bit night clubs and movie houses.

Such talk infuriated Ethel, and she always struck back with colorful language. While promoting his singers, Siegel had cultivated the friendship of columnists, and they sometimes printed his claims about Merman. When Walter Winchell did so, Ethel dispatched a telegram declaring, "I'm telling you that the only thing that Al Siegel ever did was write arrangements. He never taught me anything."

To the end of her life, she was still disclaiming that Al Siegel had been the genius who created Ethel Merman.

4.

New Star on the Great White Way

Ethel Merman was astonished to find herself being hailed as a bright new star of the musical theater. Though she had lived all her twenty-two years only a subway ride from the heart of the American theater, she had never listed Broadway in her catalogue of ambitions. The singers on the stage of the Palace Theater were the stuff of which her girlhood dreams were built. She had once hoped to become a movie star like Alice Brady, but in her maturing years she never envisioned herself as an actress. Her goal had been to establish herself as a solo performer, and that's what many of her co-stars said she remained.

Ethel enjoyed her newfound popularity, and not merely because of the rave reviews and the attention when she entered restaurants. Her success also translated into money, which, as Lou Irwin had suggested, was of primary interest to Ethel Merman.

She had demonstrated, when she shuttled between her stint at the Palace and the *Girl Crazy* rehearsals, that she had enough energy for two jobs. She now instructed Lou to consider all reasonable offers. The most attractive came from the Central Park Casino, which agreed to pay her $1,250 a week for singing less than half an hour nightly.

Ethel could hardly believe her good fortune. The Central Park

Casino was the most fashionable night spot in Manhattan, the favorite of Mayor Jimmy Walker, who had invested some of his own money in it. At every performance Ethel was cheered by a flock of celebrities, from visiting royalty and movie stars to the elite of the New York theater—Ethel Barrymore, Fred and Adele Astaire, Tallulah Bankhead, Helen Hayes, Alfred Lunt and Lynn Fontanne.

Movie companies now sought Ethel. Warner Brothers wanted her to return, this time at $1,500 a week. She declined. She had a better offer: a feature movie for Paramount at the Astoria studio where she had watched the comings and goings of the stars as a girl. Paramount was exploiting the craze for musical talkies by filming Broadway shows.

The best of these was *The Cocoanuts*, which introduced the Marx Brothers to the screen. Less successful was *Follow the Leader*, based on the musical *Manhattan Mary*, with a score by De Sylva, Brown and Henderson. The cast included Ed Wynn, Ginger Rogers, Ethel Merman, Stanley Smith, Lou Holtz, Bobby Watson and Preston Foster.

All this, and *Girl Crazy* too! Ethel never missed a performance, and her fellow actors were amazed at her professionalism. She was always on cue, she always gave the same full-out delivery of her three songs. George Gershwin was fascinated by Ethel, and he liked to slip into the orchestra pit and play the piano himself when she sang "I Got Rhythm."

"The girl's terrific, but she'll never last," he told a close friend. "She hasn't got a cultivated voice. She's using her voice too hard—it'll burn itself out."

Backstage she was always chewing gum, befitting her breezy personality. Sometimes she forgot to remove the gum, and she'd sing her number with a wad in her cheek.

She also had a passion for peanut brittle. Willie Howard once watched with amazement as Ethel consumed a large quantity of peanut brittle while waiting for her cue. "I'll bet you can't sing with that stuff in your mouth," he challenged.

"You're on!" she said, jamming a handful of peanut brittle into her mouth. She sang "I Got Rhythm" faultlessly, including the now famous sixteen-bar C-note.

Aside from the money, Ethel Merman was enjoying another aspect of her newfound career: being courted by handsome, well-heeled men who liked to be seen with the latest Broadway sensation. Her schedule allowed little chance for stepping out on the town, but she accepted offers whenever possible. The man who intrigued her most was Alter Goetz, a Wall Street broker who had managed to survive the Crash. He was in love with Ethel and began taking over her business affairs, scrutinizing contracts and investing her earnings safely. Ethel found Al to be good company, even lovable, but her mother was opposed to the match: Goetz already had a wife, though he was legally separated.

The romance continued until Walter Winchell printed this item: "Al Goetz prefers his wife to Ethel Merman." Ethel was furious with the columnist for using the item and with Goetz for shaming her in public. She vowed never to allow herself to be placed in that position again.

Another movie deal followed, this time with the Paramount shorts department. Ethel was engaged to star in eight short musicals, and her mentor became John Green.

"I was a composer-arranger-conductor at Paramount's Astoria studio when Ethel came there to make shorts," recalled Green, who had already produced a hit song, "Coquette," while a senior at Harvard.

"I had read about her in the columns—how she had been an Al Siegel protégée. She and I hit it off immediately. She made a short called *Roamin'*, in which she played the daughter and shill of a traveling medicine man, and I wrote two songs for her, 'Hello, My Lover, Goodbye' and 'Shake Well Before Using.' "

Ethel was impressed by the young composer's skill in fitting the songs to her style, and she asked Green to make arrangements for her, filling the void left by Al Siegel.

When *Girl Crazy* closed in June of 1931 because of the onset of warm weather (Broadway theaters had no air conditioning), Ethel was booked into the New York Paramount. This time she took along her two favorite pianists-arrangers, John Green and Roger Edens, the brilliant young musician who had supplanted Al Siegel in the *Girl Crazy* pit. At the Paramount, biggest of all the chain's theaters, Ethel shared the bill with Rudy Vallee, the immensely popular crooner she had mooned over as a teenager.

Next, a return to the Palace. Nine months before, she had appeared there as a relative unknown. Now she came back as a headliner.

Lou Holtz was the master of ceremonies, and he was joined in the comedy sketches by William Gaxton. Also featured were Lyda Roberti and a group of songwriters playing their own songs. Among them: Lew Pollack, Harold Arlen and John Green, who played his "Body and Soul."

More than fifty years later, Green recalls Ethel's performance with remarkable clarity:

"Roger and I were seated in white tie and tails at two Steinway baby grands, interlocked. Lou Foreman, the conductor, signaled a big fanfare, and the front travelers pulled aside to reveal a royal blue velvet cyclorama. A pin spot shone on the two pianos, and Roger and I played some cadenzas. Then Ethel entered in a black gown and white ermine cape and began 'Sing You Sinners,' my arrangement.

"She finished to big applause, then went to the pianos and draped her ermine over them. We exchanged a few lines that we had rehearsed, except that Roger and I threw in some filthy words that the audience couldn't hear. We tried to break her up, and did. Then she went into 'Beyond the Blue Horizon.' "

Ethel finished with the song she made famous. Commented the *Times* reviewer: "Miss Merman again admits to having rhythm and daisies in green pastures in the Gershwin song she delivered so effectively in *Girl Crazy,* and it achieves definite success for her act."

Green recalls that Ethel came to the dressing room he shared with Edens and pleaded with them to behave: "Boys, have some mercy. I gotta sell songs out there, and I can't work if you keep making me laugh. Promise you won't do it again. You can be replaced, you know."

"Oh no, we can't," the two men chorused knowingly.

Ethel Merman decided in the summer of 1931 it was time for her to take a vacation—in the manner to which she had never been accustomed. She bought a long, sleek Chrysler touring car, hired a chauffeur and drove with her mother and father to the resort at Lake George. At the end of a long day of sight-seeing, Ethel returned to the hotel and found urgent messages: "Call George White."

"The show's in trouble," White told her, referring to the eleventh edition of his *Scandals*. "Can you and Lou Irwin come down to Atlantic City right away? I need you."

Ethel didn't remind White that his previous offer to her was a spot in the chorus. She agreed to cancel her vacation and go to Atlantic City.

The *Scandals* was inexplicably ailing. White had splurged on costumes and scenery, as was his custom. Clever sketches had been written by Lew Brown, Irving Caesar and White himself. The cast was stellar and diversely talented: Vagabond Lover Rudy Vallee, the most popular singer in America; Willie and Eugene Howard, Broadway's favorite clowns; loose-limbed Ray Bolger; the opera star Everett Marshall; the dancing Gale Quadruplets; Ethel Barrymore Colt of the great theatrical family.

But something was missing. Partly it was the songs. Lew Brown and Ray Henderson were working without their longtime partner, Buddy De Sylva, and their score lacked the surefire hits for which the team was noted. Ethel insisted that new songs had to be written for her.

To obtain Merman's services, George White was required to pay $25,000 to Aarons and Freedley, who had an option for her next show. This was a desperate move by the parsimonious White, and the publicity contributed to Ethel Merman's reputation as a valuable Broadway performer.

White continued tinkering with the *Scandals* in Newark and Brooklyn, and the show finally opened at the Apollo Theater on September 14, 1931.

The eleventh edition of the *Scandals* had something for everyone, including thirty-five beauties for the tired businessman. The opening number was a salute to the Empire State Building, a familiar theme in 1931 musicals. Vallee sang engagingly, Bolger won the audience with an oldstyle soft-shoe, Marshall in blackface intoned "That's Why Darkies Were Born." The Howards performed their famous "Pay the Two Dollars" sketch, and Willie portrayed a fiery Latin lover, a European quack doctor and a big-game hunter who bagged a lion ("I bagged him and I bagged him, but he wouldn't go away").

Ethel would not be overshadowed in this stellar cast. The first solo number was hers, and she made it the hit of the show. It was "Life Is Just a Bowl of Cherries," a sunshiny defiance of the Depression blues. She had another effective song, "Ladies and Gentlemen, That's Love," and a duet with Vallee, "My Song." Brooks Atkinson in the *Times* called her "queen of the singing announcers" and added that she "can draw herself up to a loud note with the hauteur of a real chantress."

The *Scandals*, the only revue in which Ethel Merman appeared, settled down for a seven-month run. It was a happy company, and Ethel enjoyed clowning with Ray Bolger and Willie Howard, her pal from *Girl Crazy*. She was intrigued but not overwhelmed by Rudy Vallee. One night they sat waiting on a backstage bench for Willie and Eugene Howard to finish a sketch. Vallee suddenly leaned over and kissed Ethel on the mouth.

"What did you do that for?" she demanded.

"Because I wanted to," he replied.

"Well, don't do it again," she said indignantly. Laughter and applause signaled the end of the Howard sketch, and Rudy and Ethel strolled onstage for their romantic duet, "My Song," as if nothing had happened.

White was paying Ethel $1,250 a week, but she still sought ways to augment her salary. The Central Park Casino was eager for her to return, and she began another engagement in early 1932. Leo Reisman's orchestra, with Eddy Duchin on piano, accompanied her; the show also featured the dancing of Tony and Renee De Marco.

As always, Mayor Jimmy Walker appeared almost nightly to hear Ethel sing. He enlisted her to sing at political benefits, which she did even though she was a confirmed Republican and Walker a Democrat. He'd send a motorcycle escort to rush her from the Apollo Theater to the benefit and then to the Casino.

When the *Scandals* closed in April of 1932, Ethel returned to the Palace on a bill with Jack Haley, Patsy Kelly and Benny

Rubin. Then she began considering the half-dozen offers she had received for a fall show. She chose the wrong one.

Humpty Dumpty confirmed the Broadway dictum that even the best theatrical talent cannot elevate a bad idea. Buddy De Sylva and Lawrence Schwab proposed a revue satirizing major figures of American history. Holding the skits together was a thin plot involving Lou Holtz as the backer of the show.

De Sylva and Schwab wrote the book, with an assist from Sid Silvers, but their efforts to make sport of Miles Standish, Betsy Ross, George Washington, Alexander Hamilton, Abraham Lincoln et al. failed significantly.

Humpty Dumpty opened at the Nixon Theater in Pittsburgh on September 26, 1932. The Pittsburgh *Press* cited the flatness of the sketches and commented: "There's a Boston tea party wherein the shapers of the musical comedy fall into the dubious practice of putting profane anachronisms into the mouths of beautiful women with powdered wigs. . . . All these things bog down the first act. Generally they're not funny and slow up the show."

Critics recorded only one laugh in *Humpty Dumpty*. It came while Lou Holtz sat in a box watching the revue, which was purposely bad. "Is this lousy?" he asked. The Pittsburgh audience responded with hearty applause, then laughter.

In the minor role of Wanda Brill, Ethel Merman mercifully was spared participation in the plot. The songwriters, Nacio Herb Brown and Richard Whiting, failed to provide her with a show-stopping song. Ethel complained, but to no avail.

"What about 'Eadie Was a Lady'?" suggested Roger Edens, who continued to be Ethel's musical mentor. The song had stemmed from an idea by Buddy De Sylva, a lament for a recently deceased prostitute. Brown and Whiting had composed a song, but Schwab considered it too undignified to include in *Humpty Dumpty*.

With the show teetering, Schwab agreed to allow "Eadie Was a Lady." Edens composed an arrangement, including an important middle passage, and Ethel performed it in a bordello setting with a chorus of sorrowing hookers.

"Eadie Was a Lady" provided Pittsburgh audiences their only

opportunity to cheer during *Humpty Dumpty.* Producers Schwab and De Sylva found themselves $80,000 in the red, with little prospect of recovery. They folded *Humpty Dumpty* in Pittsburgh.

"Rowdiness is a major virtue," wrote Brooks Atkinson of *Take a Chance,* risen from the ashes of *Humpty Dumpty* two months later. It was a raucous spirit, especially as exhibited by Ethel Merman, that transformed a dreadful flop into rollicking entertainment.

The refurbished plot presented Jack Whiting as an Ivy League producer of a Broadway revue and Jack Haley and Sid Silvers as a pair of con men who finance the production. The pair's girl friend is June Knight, who falls in love with Whiting. After a series of misunderstandings, she becomes the star of the revue.

The tableaux satirizing American history had been discarded, along with most of the songs. Vincent Youmans had been enlisted to provide additional tunes. Ethel Merman's role remained minor, but musically she was the bulwark of *Take a Chance.*

"I Got Religion," she bellowed in the middle of the first act, and her revivalist fervor stopped the show. To close the act she sang Youmans' ringing "Rise 'n Shine," another tonic for the Depression gloom.

The second act brought two smash numbers in a row, both holdovers from *Humpty Dumpty.* She combined with Haley on "You're an Old Smoothie," a sophisticated love song ideally suited to their personalities: Merman with her unabashed lustiness; Haley with his moony charm.

The stage directions called for Sid Silvers to be thrown out of a speakeasy at the rear of the stage following the "Smoothie" number. On opening night, he had to be thrown out five times before the audience subsided.

The audience reaction doubled when Merman followed with "Eadie Was a Lady." Decked out in a blood-red satin gown slit up the front and cut low, black boa swinging and hair piled high, she slithered among the sailors and their sweethearts and poured out the mock lament:

Eadie was a lady,
Though her past was shady,
Eadie had class, with a capital K.

"It is a comic ballad in the grand style of sentiment," wrote Atkinson in the *Times*, "and it is a joy to watch Miss Merman toss herself wholeheartedly into the street-corner tune."

The Stage magazine featured two pages of photographs taken of Merman as she sang "Rise 'n Shine." The anonymous writer cited ". . . the fluttering hands; the doubled fist extended toward you, Billy Sunday style, as though to seize your soul and raise it to heaven; the swing of the hips as she walks; the rolling of the shoulders and the accompanying wave of the head; the cocky stride ever so faintly suggestive of the ancient cake walk; the clasping of the quivering hands, imploring the audience to join in glory; the outspread palms, the raised fingers, the hands flinging at you a message of joy; and, at last, the arms stretched up to heaven, and the whole body straining to follow upward, as though one ounce more of faith would give it soaring wings.

"Miss Merman is not a technician. . . . She is, both in singing and pantomime, a natural. But her vitality is so exceptional, and her instinct for emotional expression so impulsive, that she converts her hearers to her plea."

Interviewers often noted how singularly unchanged Ethel Merman had been by her success. Even though she could now afford an East Side apartment, she still lived in her parents' home in Astoria. To the dismay of her sophisticated friends, she dressed much the same as when she had been Caleb Bragg's private secretary. She was easily bored by the smart talk of cocktail parties and preferred to exchange the latest off-color jokes. Unlike some performers who kowtowed to columnists, she made no effort to curry favor. If she felt wronged by a columnist, she fired off a corrective telegram or blasted him in person.

"I'm strictly a meat-and-potatoes woman," said Ethel, who scorned the haute cuisine of Manhattan's fancy restaurants. She bought no expensive jewelry for herself and got rid of her one big extravagance, the Chrysler touring car.

She told a reporter: "It cost me thirty-two hundred and fifty dollars, and a fellow came along and offered me seven hundred for it and I said, 'Take it.' All you can do with a car in New York is keep it in dead storage. I've tried it. You don't get any fun in dead storage."

In September of 1933, a new excitement entered the career of Ethel Merman: a trip to Hollywood to co-star with Bing Crosby.

The impending journey to California brought on a family crisis. Ethel didn't want to go alone, and her mother didn't want to leave her husband. In more than a quarter-century of marriage, Agnes and Edward Zimmermann had never been apart. But he couldn't leave his job at James H. Dunham & Co., and he insisted that Agnes accompany Ethel on the trip west.

Ethel and her mother were greeted at the Santa Fe station by a publicity man from Paramount who asked them to wave as a photographer took an arrival picture. They were driven by limousine to the Ravenswood Apartments on Rossmore Avenue, opposite the Wilshire Country Club.

"Mae West owns this building; she lives on the top floor," explained the publicity man. "It's a great location. You could walk to the studio if you had to."

Ethel unpacked and waited for the studio to call. A few days later she was asked to report for makeup and wardrobe tests. In the makeup department she was seated in a barber's chair while two men in dentists' uniforms assessed her appearance. "Well, at least she's dark enough that she won't compete with Carole," one of them said.

Carole Lombard, Ethel learned, was the prime concern of the studio, being Paramount's biggest female star. She and Bing would play the romantic interest in the film, called *We're Not Dressing*. It was a musical version of James M. Barrie's *The Admirable Crichton*, which Cecil B. De Mille had filmed in 1919 as *Male and Female* with Gloria Swanson and Thomas Meighan.

Supporting Crosby and Lombard were George Burns and Gracie Allen, Ethel Merman and Leon Errol. All were cordial to Ethel and respectful of her achievements in three years on Broadway. The director, Norman Taurog, was an easygoing, roly-poly man, and there was a great deal of kidding on the set, especially between Crosby and Lombard. As soon as the day's work was done, the other actors departed for their homes in Beverly Hills or the San Fernando Valley, and Ethel went back to the Ravenswood and her mother.

Ethel wasn't asked to anyone's house for dinner. No one escorted her to a night club or movie premiere. It was a dismal period for her, following all the attention she had received in New York.

Christmas Eve was the worst time of all. Neither Ethel nor Agnes Zimmermann had ever spent Christmas away from home. Now they found themselves in a cheerless apartment and an unfriendly city three thousand miles away from the one they loved most. They thought of Edward Zimmermann spending an equally grim Christmas Eve in Astoria, and they cried.

Ethel's spirits rose somewhat when the *We're Not Dressing* company moved to Catalina Island for ocean and beach sequences. At least the cast was housed together at the St. Catherine Hotel, shared meals and engaged in the kind of horseplay that helps relieve the boredom of film locations.

Bing Crosby, Ethel discovered, was not the easygoing troubador that he seemed in movies and on radio. He maintained a facile banter, but behind that was an impenetrable barrier. Ethel was amused by the sardonic wit of George Burns and Leon Errol and intrigued to discover that Gracie Allen was shy and withdrawn, totally unlike the dim-witted character she played.

Ethel was fascinated most by Carole Lombard. They were both twenty-five, but the blonde star seemed infinitely more worldly-wise. Ethel thought she'd accumulated a vivid vocabulary from the streets of Astoria and the backstages of Broadway. She was astonished at the way Lombard could cuss, integrating expletives into everyday conversation in what seemed a perfectly natural manner.

Carole was friendly toward Ethel, but she displayed little

interest in women. Men adored her, especially the movie crew, who considered her one of the boys. She was forever devising gags and practical jokes to keep the film company amused.

During the winter season, the St. Catherine Hotel was populated largely by widows and spinsters from the East and the California mainland. They were distressed to find themselves in the fast company of Hollywood film people, and they strained their ears for scandalous gossip they could write back home about.

Irritated by the nosy biddies, Carole decided to give them something to talk about. One morning she called across the hotel dining room at breakfast time: "Bing!"

"What?" Crosby replied.

"Did I leave my nightie in your room last night?"

Ethel realized that since Crosby, Lombard and Burns and Allen were under contract to Paramount, she herself would not receive special treatment. Her role diminished as the shooting progressed, and nearly all the songs went to the studio's hottest star, Bing Crosby. Ethel's only song was "It's a New Spanish Custom," a comedy duet with Leon Errol.

"You'll have to stay over for a couple of weeks, Ethel," Norman Taurog told her as filming neared the end. "The studio thinks we need a big production number to finish the picture."

Ethel was distressed to face two more lonely weeks away from her Broadway pals and her dad. But at least she was finally getting a chance to make an impression in *We're Not Dressing*. She wouldn't have to slink back to New York a failure.

The number was called "The Animal in Me," and Ethel found herself on a jungle set with chimpanzees, camels, llamas and elephants. The delays were tedious as the animals wilted under the hot lights, became fractious and misbehaved in various ways. The biggest problem was the elephants—forty of them. The choreographer wanted them to lift their legs in unison, keeping time to the music like a line of Rockettes. As soon as the final shot was made, Ethel fled back to New York.

For weeks Ethel entertained friends and relatives with stories of her dance with the elephants. When *We're Not Dressing* opened at the Paramount Theater, she wanted to share her Hollywood debut with those closest to her. They included her parents, Gramma Gardner, Aunt Mary and Uncle Harry, cousin Claude, plus a flock of Astoria neighbors.

Ethel sat amid her guests in a reserved section of the mezzanine, and she thrilled as the familiar Paramount trademark appeared on the screen. Then she blushed as friends and relatives applauded the appearance of her name on the screen. They also applauded the number she did with Leon Errol.

"Wait till you see my big number at the end," Ethel said in a whisper that could be heard in the orchestra seats.

It never came. The movie ended without Ethel and the elephants. Her party left the theater amid embarrassment and confusion. The most confused of all was Gramma Gardner, now in her eighties. She wanted to know why she couldn't go backstage to see Ethel, as she had when she saw her granddaughter perform in theaters before.

"What the hell happened to my number?" Ethel demanded of a Paramount executive.

"Oh, we decided it detracted too much from the story, so we cut it out," he replied. Ethel was consoled later when "The Animal in Me" was included in *The Big Broadcast of 1936*, and she was paid again for it.

Following *We're Not Dressing*, Ethel visited Cuba on the first real vacation of her life, then returned to New York. Much as she hated to leave her old neighborhood, she realized it was time to move on. She and her parents took up residence at 25 Central Park West. As she was getting settled, Ethel received an offer to co-star with Eddie Cantor in *Kid Millions*, produced by Sam Goldwyn.

The return to Hollywood proved happier than the *We're Not Dressing* experience. Cantor was warm and friendly, counseling Ethel on how to play to the camera. The cast, which included George Murphy, Ann Sothern and the comedy team of Jesse Block and Eve Sully, was congenial.

Both *We're Not Dressing* and *Kid Millions* made Ethel wonder if she was meant to be a movie star. The directors, Norman

Taurog and Roy Del Ruth, repeatedly told her, "Hold it down, Ethel." She felt constricted by having to quell her natural exuberance for the microscopic camera and the super-sensitive microphone.

Ethel considered herself pretty enough for the screen, but she realized she lacked the kind of beauty that the studios sought in contract players. And without a contract she would never receive the publicity and the prize roles that created stardom. It was then that she decided to concentrate on the musical theater, and in her next Broadway show she succeeded beyond even her own outsized ambitions.

5.

Anything Goes

Anything Goes had a long and historic voyage to its opening at the Alvin Theater on November 21, 1934. It marked the end of the producing partnership of Alex Aarons and Vinton Freedley (who had named the Alvin after themselves), the start of the hit-writing team of Howard Lindsay and Russel Crouse and the first of five collaborations between Cole Porter and Ethel Merman.

The ten-year partnership of Aarons and Freedley, which had produced such musicals as *Lady, Be Good!* and *Funny Face,* foundered in 1933 with *Pardon My English,* a flop despite a Gershwin score. Ill, depressed and broke, Freedley sailed off to Tobago to recuperate. The voyage gave him the idea for another musical: What would happen if a luxury gambling boat were shipwrecked?

Freedley told his idea to Victor Moore and William Gaxton, the great team from *Of Thee I Sing.* Also to Ethel Merman. All were interested. Still confined to a wheelchair because of what might have been a mild heart attack, Freedley sailed off to Europe in search of authors.

Guy Bolton was in England, unable to leave because of tax problems. P. G. Wodehouse declined to desert his tax shelter in France. Cole Porter, whom Freedley wanted to write the songs, was floating leisurely down the Rhine, stopping only at cities with Ritz hotels.

Freedley managed to reach all three, and they agreed to collaborate on a musical to be titled *Hard to Get.* Within a few weeks, Porter came to the producer's London hotel with several songs. Freedley was enthralled.

"I think I could do another song from some background music I did for a show here called *Nymph Errant,*" Porter added. "Perhaps you can buy it back from Charles Cochran." Freedley paid $5,000 for the melody of what would become "I Get a Kick Out of You." Howard Lindsay happened to be in London, and Freedley asked him to direct the new show.

Freedley was distraught, however, when he received the Bolton-Wodehouse script. It had none of the airy humor both writers were famous for. Furthermore, after Septemer 8, 1934, a shipwreck musical was out of the question: The cruise ship *Morro Castle* burned off the New Jersey coast, and 134 passengers and crew perished.

"*You've* got to rewrite the script," Freedley told Lindsay.

"I can't direct all day and rewrite all night," Lindsay replied.

"Then I'll find someone to write with you," the producer said.

The marriage broker for one of the theater's most illustrious teams was Neysa McMein, a magazine artist who was a popular figure among Manhattan's literati. She suggested Russel Crouse to Cole Porter, who relayed his name to Vinton Freedley. Crouse had been a sometime actor, journalist and playwright who was working as press agent for the Theater Guild.

"I had known Crouse at the Players Club," Lindsay remarked in a later interview. "He had written a clever column in the *Evening Post,* and I knew him to be a man of wit and charm. I had said no, no, no to various names Freedley had suggested. I said yes to Crouse.

"Freedley had been looking all over town for Crouse, but couldn't find him. The Guild Theater happened to be across the street from the Alvin. Freedley gazed out of his office window and saw Crouse in a window opposite. He waved for him to come on over."

The Lindsay-Crouse partnership took hold immediately, and the pair began work on *Hard to Get,* which eventually bore the title of a Porter song, "Anything Goes."

"We used about five lines of the Bolton-Wodehouse script," said Lindsay. Within ten days he and Crouse produced a complete script, though they continued rewriting throughout rehearsals and the tryouts.

Equally historic was the meeting of Ethel Merman and Cole Porter. No two Broadway figures could have been more dissimilar: Porter, the Yale-trained son of the rich, paragon of sophistication; Merman, the Astoria stenographer with a taste for thick steaks and dirty jokes. Yet they were mutually fascinated by and adoring of each other's talents. He was ever amused by her brassy frankness, she respected his shy reserve. He found her a joy to write for. No one could sing a rousing song better than Merman, and when she gave way to grudging sentiment—as Porter could never do in his personal life—she reached the heart. After suffering singers who gargled his lyrics, Porter at last had one who could broadcast his words to the galleries.

Porter's biographer, George Eells, reported that the composer did the unthinkable: He submitted the *Anything Goes* score to Edward and Agnes Zimmermann. When Ethel's parents disapproved of two of the songs, he cheerfully discarded them. He even rewrote "Blow, Gabriel, Blow" when Ethel expressed dissatisfaction with the song.

Another national event caused rewriting of "I Get a Kick Out of You." In the original version, Porter had written about not caring for "those nights in the air/that the fair/Mrs. Lindbergh went through." During rehearsals, Bruno Richard Hauptmann was arrested and charged with the kidnapping and murder of Charles Lindbergh, Jr. Porter quickly rewrote the lyric to provide one of his most felicitous phrases:

Flying too high
With some guy in the sky
Is my i-dea of nothing to do,
Yet I get a kick out of you!

Rewriting of the script continued at a frantic pace, Lindsay and Crouse bringing new pages to rehearsal after midnight sessions, sometimes extemporizing on the spot. Ethel proved invaluable on such occasions. She recorded the new lines in shorthand, then typed them for the rest of the company.

The plot was a masterpiece of invention. The show opens in a New York bar where Reno Sweeney (Merman), hostess and onetime evangelist, sings "I Get a Kick Out of You" to a swaggering man-about-town, Billy Crocker (Gaxton). It was daring for director Lindsay to begin a musical with a solo ballad by the leading lady.

Reno is sailing to England, as is Billy's real love, the aristocratic Hope Harcourt (Bettina Hall). Aided by a variety of disguises, Billy stows away on the liner and becomes friends with the fragile Reverend Dr. Moon (Moore). The sweet-faced parson is also in disguise. He is really Public Enemy No. 13, and he carries a tommygun he calls "my little pal putt-putt-putt."

Again Reno expresses her love for Billy, this time in a miracle of hyperbole to which he responds in kind. In "You're the Top," Porter was at his sophisticated best, enumerating those things he held dear: Colosseum–Louvre Museum, Daché bonnet–Shakespeare sonnet, Strauss–Mickey Mouse.

To close the first act, Porter gifted Merman with a third smash hit, "Anything Goes," with total confidence that she could deliver its intricate rhythms and quirky rhymes. How the song became titled is clouded in legend. It may have stemmed from Porter's 1912 Yale theatrical song that included the phrase "everybody knows anything goes."

With a reverend and a former evangelist on board, the situation calls for a revival meeting, and Reno Sweeney volunteers to lead the congregation. Again Porter demonstrated his wide-ranging genius, providing a gospel song suitable for fundamentalist churches, "Blow, Gabriel, Blow."

The *Anything Goes* troupe traveled to the Boston tryout with the last scene still unwritten. Before the final dress rehearsal, Lindsay and Crouse emerged from the men's room with the last lines written on toilet paper. Despite the patchwork nature of the production, opening night in Boston was an absolute triumph. Everything worked. The show moved to New York unchanged.

Opening night at the Alvin Theater defied the Depression.

Society swells paid fifty dollars and upwards for choice seats. White ties and ermines could be seen throughout the house, chinchillas were reported in the balcony. Most society audiences attended first nights for self-display, paying little heed to what happened onstage. But *Anything Goes* drew cheers and gasps of delight.

"A thundering good musical show," announced Brooks Atkinson in the *Times*. He added: "If Ethel Merman did not write 'I Get a Kick Out of You' and also the title song of the show, she has made them hers now by the swinging gusto of her platform style."

The critic for the *Literary Digest* declared: "Miss Ethel Merman, whose incandescent singing has breathed life into more than one faltering play and movie, is entrusted with the best of the Porter inventions, and this feat plus her performance as Reno Sweeney establishes her as the present queen of musical comedy."

The raves for the musical phenomenon called Ethel Merman attracted the interest of no less than Arturo Toscanini. "Who is this singer everyone is talking about?" Toscanini asked his friend, the music critic Samuel Chotzinoff. "I will take you to hear her, maestro," Chotzinoff said.

Tickets to *Anything Goes* were impossible to buy, so Chotzinoff asked Russel Crouse to provide a pair. Toscanini sat motionless, studying Merman with fascination. He admired her total adherence to the Cole Porter songs; always he had lectured his singers to remain faithful to the composer's intentions. At the end of the first act, Chotzinoff asked for his opinion of Miss Merman.

"Castrati! Castrati!" Toscanini exclaimed. He referred to the onetime singers in Italy who were castrated to maintain their clear, pure neutral voices, somewhere in limbo between masculine and feminine. (Many years later, Luciano Pavarotti commented: "Ethel Merman's voice is remarkable. It is all one register. She has no *passaggio* to worry about. She never has to shift gears.")

The *Anything Goes* run proved the most pleasurable in Merman's career to that point, largely because of William Gaxton. A cheerful, warm-hearted man, he demonstrated his goodwill during rehearsals by convincing Victor Moore that they should allow Ethel equal billing.

"Fun?" Ethel enthused to an interviewer. "On the second night Mr. Gaxton sent me some flowers, 'just in case you don't get any,' it said on his card. My Lord, you should have seen my dressing room!"

Gaxton grew more playful as the run progressed. Seeking to break Ethel up in the middle of her song, he would mutter under his breath, "Look at that dame in the third row, the one with the big tits."

The darling of New York society, Gaxton was often visited by notables. One night his good friend Barbara Hutton, newly married to a nobleman, came to his dressing room after the performance. "Hey, Eth, come on over here," Gaxton called. "Princess Reventlow wants to meet you."

"Oh, horseshit, Billy," Ethel replied from her dressing room.

"No, I'm serious," Gaxton insisted. The embarrassed Ethel met Barbara Hutton Reventlow, then joined her and Gaxton for a party at El Morocco.

Producers Aarons and Freedley granted Ethel Merman permission to leave *Anything Goes* before the end of the 420-performance run so she could film another musical in Hollywood with Eddie Cantor. But after she arrived, Sam Goldwyn decided that *Strike Me Pink* was not ready for production. Ethel remained in Hollywood for the most promising film opportunity of her career: repeating her role of Reno Sweeney in *Anything Goes.*

Paramount Pictures had bought the musical as a vehicle for Bing Crosby and W. C. Fields. Since Crosby was popular enough to carry a film by himself, the studio replaced Fields with the bland Charles Ruggles and decided to take a chance on the suddenly available Ethel Merman as leading lady.

With customary studio thinking, Paramount discarded the Cole Porter score except for the title song, "I Get a Kick Out of You" and "You're the Top." Replacing "All Through the Night," "Blow, Gabriel, Blow" and "The Gypsy in Me" were less memorable tunes by studio songwriters.

The Porter lyrics had to be bowdlerized to conform to film industry censorship. Gone was the line in "Anything Goes" about modern authors who once knew better words but now use four-letter ones. And of course, "I get no kick from cocaine" was deleted, as it had been censored from radio.

The movie *Anything Goes* turned into a vehicle for Bing Crosby. The new songs were designed for his voice, and the comedy of the Reverend Dr. Moon was minimized (the clergy could not be an object of ridicule under the censorship code). Hence the movie lacked the sparkling smartness of the stage musical and did little to further Ethel's career in movies.

Nor did *Strike Me Pink* add to her film reputation. It was another Goldwyn concoction patterned to his comedy star, Eddie Cantor, who played a timid tailor with a secret love for a night club singer, Merman. The plot involved an amusement park and gangsters, combining chases with musical numbers by Cantor, Merman and the Goldwyn Girls. None of the Harold Arlen–Lew Brown songs achieved popularity.

Again Ethel Merman retreated to Broadway.

Red, Hot and Blue! was one of those Broadway shows in which the parts were bigger than the whole. Vinton Freedley had sought to reassemble his winning team from *Anything Goes:* Cole Porter, Lindsay and Crouse, Moore, Gaxton and Merman. But Gaxton dropped out to play in *The White Horse Inn,* and Victor Moore was working in Hollywood. Freedley managed to engage one established comic and another on the rise: Jimmy Durante and Bob Hope.

Billing became a problem. Durante's agent, Lou Clayton, demanded that Jimmy's name be placed at the top of the bill. Lou Irwin insisted on the same for Merman.

"I don't give a damn," said Ethel.

"As long as I'm good on stage, it doesn't matter to me," Jimmy remarked.

Neither agent would budge. The impasse was finally resolved by Cole Porter, who suggested to Freedley: "Why not have their names read like a railroad crossing sign?" And so on billboards, in newspaper ads and on the theater program, it read the same:

JIMMY MERMAN
ETHEL DURANTE
BOB HOPE

Lindsay and Crouse created a gallery of raffish characters for *Red, Hot, and Blue!*, as they had for *Anything Goes.* "Nails" O'Reilly Duquesne (Merman) is a former manicurist, now a wealthy widow, who organizes a national lottery as a means of finding the lost love of her hotshot lawyer, Bob Hale (Hope). To further the search, she arranges the paroles of several guests at the posh prison, Lark's Nest. Among them is Policy Pinkie (Durante), who yearns to return to his post as captain of the prison polo team. The search for Hale's childhood sweetheart is made easier by an important clue: When he tried to kiss her at the age of four, she sat down on a waffle iron.

The making of *Red, Hot and Blue!* had none of the bouncy expectancy of *Anything Goes.* Obviously Lindsay and Crouse had provided too much plot, but they kept adding instead of cutting. Freedley complained that Porter's songs needed work, and Porter grew peevish.

Porter had provided the best songs for Merman, and they were all in the first act. The first was "Down in the Depths on the 90th Floor," which contained the line about "my pet pailletted gown." Ethel decided she wanted to wear one when she sang the number.

"But a pailletted gown would cost a thousand dollars!" Freedley protested.

"No gown, no song," Ethel replied.

She got her gown. She adored it except for the comic touch of a lifelike chicken sewn on the rear. Every time she turned around, the chicken seemed ready for flight. "The bird goes," Ethel declared, removing it with scissors. "Any audience gets a laugh outa me, gets it while I'm looking at 'em."

While "Down in the Depths on the 90th Floor" never achieved wide popularity, critics declared it a perfect example of the sophisticated torch song, especially in its sardonic delivery by Merman.

Merman's other hits were the rousing "Ridin' High," which closed the first act, and a duet with Bob Hope. The duet had been eliminated from the movie *Born to Dance*. Porter claimed the title had originated during his around-the-world cruise with his wife, Linda, and Monty Woolley in 1935. All three stayed up to see the dawn over Rio de Janeiro's harbor.

"It's delightful!" exclaimed Porter.

"It's delicious!" said his wife.

"It's de-lovely!" added Woolley.

The Merman-Hope combination on "It's De-Lovely" proved electric, especially as the closing lines accelerated unexpectedly.

"Ethel was the one who taught me to sing out," Hope recalls. "Believe me, you *had* to sing out if you were going to be heard on the stage with her."

With Hope, Merman and Durante in the cast, decorum went out the window. Bob and Ethel tried every means to break each other up. One of his techniques was to adopt the role of Bessie in the wings. Bessie was a little girl with a limitless supply of bawdy jokes, and Ethel was Bessie's best audience.

Opening night in Boston lasted until past midnight. Most of the critical praise was directed at Durante, with Merman being cited for two or three effective numbers. One reviewer commented that Hope "makes a pleasant leading man, delivering his lines and sustaining the comedy as well as the sentiment in satisfactory fashion." But the critics found Porter's songs not up to his usual standard and all said *Red, Hot and Blue!* was far too long. One reviewer, perhaps in jest, proposed that the musical be presented in two sessions, like *Mourning Becomes Electra*.

Freedley continued pressuring Porter for revisions, and Porter became more distant and disagreeable. One day he returned to New York, saying goodbye only to Ethel Merman. After sulking for several days, he agreed to return to the company.

New Yorkers adored Jimmy Durante, and Ethel Merman had become a favorite as well, so the opening of *Red, Hot and Blue!* was eagerly anticipated. Cole Porter's society friends wore their finery to the Alvin Theater on October 29, 1936, and the composer himself arrived with Mary Pickford on one arm and Merle Oberon on the other. Even J. Edgar Hoover, who had met Ethel at the Stork Club, was among the first-nighters. Afterward he told a reporter that he considered the show "a bright entertainment, put over with lots of style."

The rest of the audience seemed to find enjoyment—except for the critics. Most of them, as in Boston, felt that Porter's score fell short of his usual high standard. Richard Watts, Jr. of the *Herald Tribune* observed that "when the incomparable Miss Merman sings a song she does it so magnificently that you are immediately lured into the belief that it is a masterpiece. It is only very careful second thought that leads you to the realization it is less than a classic."

Brooks Atkinson in the *Times* praised the performers but called *Red, Hot and Blue!* "a desperate piece of musical comedy counterfeit." He added: "As for Miss Merman, she is still the most commanding minstrel in the business, wearing her costumes like a drum major, swinging to the music and turning the audience into a congregation of pals for the evening."

The lukewarm reviews helped prevent *Red, Hot and Blue!* from becoming a smash hit, and after 183 performances Freedley moved the show to Chicago. A scenery accident delayed the opening, and Chicago critics were as deprecating as their New York counterparts. *Red, Hot and Blue!* closed after two weeks, and not for many years would Ethel Merman agree to take a musical on the road again.

6.

Encore in Hollywood, Broadway to Stay

Despite overwhelming evidence that she was meant to be a stage performer, Ethel Merman could not totally discard the notion that she had a future in motion pictures. With the closing of *Red, Hot and Blue!*, Lou Irwin brought Ethel a proposal.

"Darryl Zanuck wants you to sign a contract with Fox," her agent reported.

"You mean another one-picture deal?" she asked suspiciously.

"Not exactly. It's one picture *at a time*, with options."

"Which means he can use me for one picture and then say bye-bye, just like Paramount and Goldwyn."

"I don't think so. Zanuck wants to make more musicals, and he's signed people like Jack Haley and the Ritz Brothers. He says he plans to keep you busy."

Ethel was persuaded. That pleased Lou Irwin, who was moving his base of operations from New York to California, where the gold was. At first Ethel seemed pleased too. She found the atmosphere at 20th Century–Fox congenial, and she appreciated the attention she was getting. The hairdressing department suggested that her brown-black hair would photograph better if dyed a soft auburn; she liked the shade so much she kept it ever afterward.

Ethel and her mother took up residence at the Beverly Hills

Hotel, and, unlike on previous visits, they took part in the Hollywood social life. They were invited to parties, and Ethel dated several handsome bachelors, including Cesar Romero.

As a rising young actor in New York, Romero had observed Ethel Merman on two occasions. The first was at the Club Richmond, where her singing failed to impress him. The second came when Romero was making a musical short at the Paramount studio in Astoria. He recalls, "Someone said, 'You ought to come next door and hear this new singer.' I went to the stage and my jaw dropped. It was the same singer, but her whole style had changed."

In Hollywood Romero escorted Ethel to night clubs and movie premieres. Ethel wrote in her autobiography that their "romance" was strictly a device of the publicity department, though Romero was taken in by it. She also portrayed him as a tightwad and fall guy for her practical jokes. "Ethel was unkind to me in her book," says Romero now. "I think the problem was that she was more fond of me than I was of her."

Merman and Romero played sweethearts in *Happy Landing,* her first movie at Fox. The stars were Sonja Henie and Don Ameche, and the plot was an absurd fabrication on which were hung Miss Henie's ice skating routines and several musical numbers. *Happy Landing* enjoyed a modest success, largely because of the ascending popularity of Sonja Henie.

Alexander's Ragtime Band was the kind of movie Ethel had been hoping for. The stars were Tyrone Power, Alice Faye and Don Ameche, and Ethel didn't appear until the second half of the film. But when she did, she was able to deliver some of the excitement she had exhibited on the stage.

Irving Berlin had emptied his catalogue into *Alexander's Ragtime Band,* a period piece about popular music. Ethel, who had met Berlin briefly in New York, was coached by Berlin at Fox, and she impressed him with a syncopation that was ideally suited to his ragtime tunes and with her precise delivery of his lyrics. Among her songs were "A Pretty Girl Is Like a Melody," "Blue Skies," "Heat Wave," "Everybody Step" and "Alexander's Ragtime Band."

For the first time, Ethel believed, she had been given a chance to show her stuff in a movie. Fox exercised its option for another film, but it turned out to be as bad as *Alexander's Ragtime Band* had been good. *Straight, Place and Show* was a B musical that attempted vainly to sustain the careers of the Fox comedy team, the Ritz Brothers. It was a humiliating comedown for Ethel Merman, and she retreated once more to the East.

Merman's next Broadway musical, *Stars in Your Eyes,* began as a spoof of the leftist politics of well-paid filmmakers in the Hollywood factories. J. P. McEvoy's script centered on a much-acclaimed boy wonder whose radical beliefs cause havoc with the studio capitalists. The producer, Dwight Deere Wiman, hired as director Joshua Logan—himself something of a wonder, having directed *On Borrowed Time, I Married an Angel* and *Knickerbocker Holiday* on Broadway while still in his twenties.

Logan saw nothing funny about Reds in lotusland.

"Let's throw all the unfunny Communist stuff out the window and just do a show about the crazy way Hollywood people mix sex and movies," he suggested. Wiman was agreeable. All he wanted was a hit musical to prosper from the influx of tourists for the New York World's Fair of 1939.

Logan launched into the overhaul with McEvoy and with Dorothy Fields and Arthur Schwartz, who were writing the songs. The plot: Jeanette Adair (Merman) is a glamorous star who has inherited Monotonous Pictures from her late husband. She has eyes for the new director on the lot, John Blake (Richard Carlson), but he is in love with the Russian dancer Tata (Tamara Toumanova). Careening through the proceedings is a studio idea-man, Bill, played by Jimmy Durante. Also in the cast were Mildred Natwick and Mary Wickes; the dancers included Dan Dailey, Jr., Alicia Alonso, Jerome Robbins, Nora Kaye and Maria Karnilova.

None of this remarkable talent could save *Stars in Your Eyes.* Opening night in New Haven ran past midnight, and Logan was forced to amputate fifty minutes before the next performance.

The disjointed nature of the show was noted by the Broadway critics.

There were some funny moments, though: Merman's attempted seduction of the drunken Carlson by reading his favorite book, *Alice in Wonderland;* the Merman-Durante duet "It's All Yours," which they interspersed with time-worn vaudeville jokes. But the satire of tribal customs on the West Coast failed to capture New York audiences, and the show closed after 127 performances.

The failure of *Stars in Your Eyes* upset Ethel, who thought she could do no wrong in the eyes of Broadway playgoers. She kept one memento from the show for the rest of her days. On opening night in New York, Logan had presented her with a small silver cup bearing the masks of comedy and tragedy. It was inscribed: "To Sarah Bernhardt, Jr., from Josh."

When Ethel Merman was collaborating with George Eells on her 1978 autobiography, the writer became exasperated by her lack of candor about her early romances.

"Ethel, are we going to try to convince the reader that you were a thirty-year-old virgin?" Eells asked.

"Oh, I was too busy in the theater to do a lot of fooling around," she replied.

"But a lot of people tell me the real love of your life was Sherman Billingsley."

Ethel blanched. "Oh, no! You can't put that in the book! Write about Winthrop Rockefeller. Or Walter Annenberg. Not Sherman Billingsley. He was a married man!"

No man ever captured her feelings as had Sherman Billingsley. Ethel had been through dalliances with Billy Sussman, the wholesale furniture man, and with Al Goetz. She had been introduced to Winthrop Rockefeller by Billy and Madeline Gaxton during the run of *Anything Goes.* Madeline cautioned Ethel: "Now you understand, dear, that Winthrop hasn't been around show business people. So don't shock him with a lot of four-letter words."

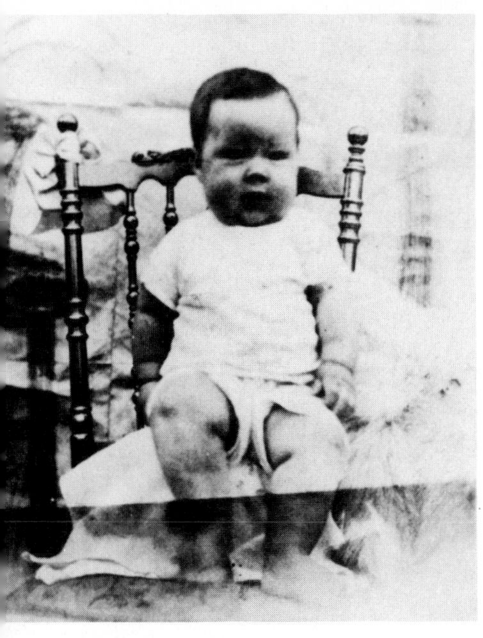

Snapshots from the Zimmermann photo album

Jack Haley, Merman and Jack Whiting in *Take a Chance,* risen from the ashes of *Humpty Dumpty*

Carole Lombard, Ray Milland, Bing Crosby, Leon Errol, Merman in *We're Not Dressing*

"It's a New Spanish Custom" with Errol. Ethel's big number was cut from *We're Not Dressing*

Kid Millions with Eddie Cantor convinced Ethel to return to Broadway

Another co-starring role with Cant
Strike Me Pink

The film version of *Anything Goes*
turned into a Bing Crosby vehicle

Merman as Broadway star in the thirties

Back to Hollywood. On the ice with Sonja Henie, Don Ameche and Cesar Romero

Merman's first experience with Irving Berlin: *Alexander's Ragtime Band* with Tyrone Power, Alice Faye and Jack Haley

The end to Merman's early Hollywood career: *Straight, Place and Show* (with Phyllis Brooks)

Barry Was a Lady was deemed bawdy by
e reviewers

Merman proves she can carry a show on her own broad shoulders: *Panama Hattie*

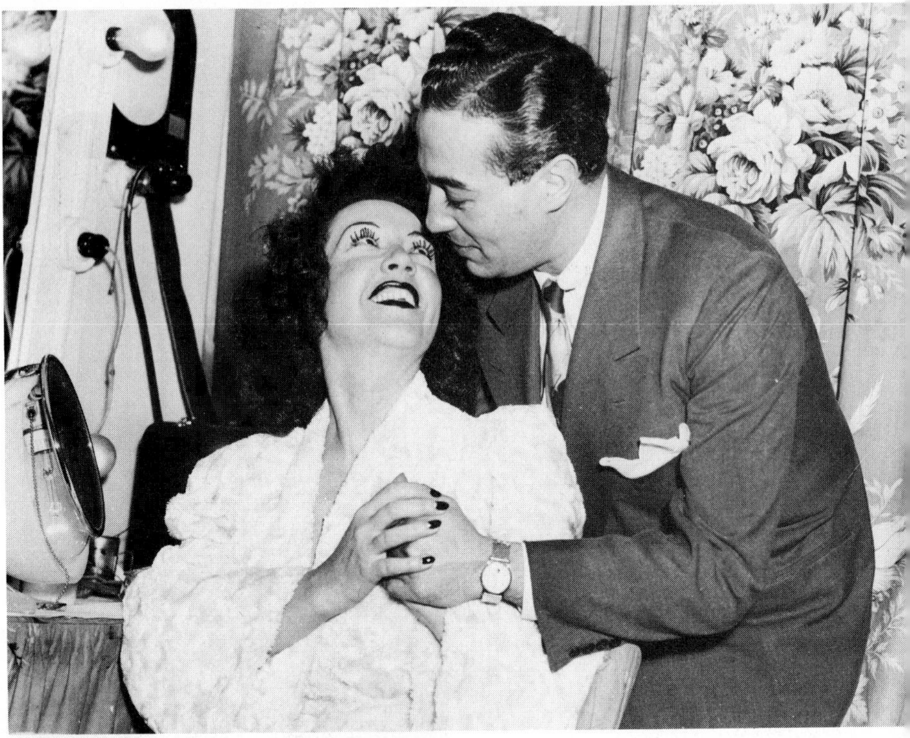

Backstage at *Panama Hattie* with new husband Robert Levitt (AP/ Wide World Phot

"Doin' What Comes Natur'lly"

"Oh, bullshit," Ethel replied. "I'll bring him down to my level."

Rockefeller was immediately intrigued by the brash, plain-spoken musical comedy star, and she was impressed by his polish and wealth. Gossip columnists found great delight in reporting the dates of the incongruous pair.

Walter Annenberg was the next millionaire on Ethel's date list. They met in Philadelphia when Ethel was trying out a show. The Annenbergs had started their fortune during the newspaper circulation wars of the early 1900s, but by the 1930s the family had achieved wealth and respectability as publishers of newspapers, racing sheets and magazines. Walter was the handsome and self-assured heir, and he became enamored of Ethel. He made frequent trips from Philadelphia to New York for quiet dinners with her, and he sent her a variety of gifts, from a gold and diamond bracelet to a cage of white mice.

Ethel becamebored with society swells and returned to beaus who spoke her language. With any man in her life, she demanded complete attention and tolerated no interference. Once she remarked to Madeline Gaxton, "I could never be like you."

"What do you mean?" Mrs. Gaxton asked.

"Well, Billy is always making up to the ladies. That would drive me crazy."

"I never worry. I trust Billy. He would never do anything to hurt me."

"Jeez, Mad, I don't know how you do it. If any dame so much as touched my beau, I'd smack her in the chops."

At least one of Ethel's men found her attitude intolerable. He broke off the affair and explained to Mrs. Gaxton: "Mad, she possesses me, and I just can't stand that."

During the late 1930s, Ethel began wearing a special piece of jewelry, a gold necklace with the letters MERM on one side and SHERM on the other. It was a special gift from the most famous gift-giver in Manhattan, John Sherman Billingsley. He bought perfume and powder compacts by the case. For the smallest occasion or none at all, guests at the Stork Club received champagne, gold cigarette cases, expensive ties. With such largesse, plus incessant publicity and tough management, Sherman Billingsley had built the Stork Club into the most famous night club in America.

He was born on March 10, 1900, in North Enid, territory of Oklahoma. His earliest occupation portended his future: he collected used whisky bottles and sold them to moonshiners. Young Billingsley abandoned schooling after the fourth grade to join his older brothers in operating a string of drugstores in small Oklahoma towns. Ostensibly, the Billingsleys sold cigars and patent medicines, but their major profit came from bootleg booze. The new state of Oklahoma had voted itself dry, but the law went unobserved by cowboys from the massive ranches and riggers of the fast-growing oil fields.

In his late teens, Sherman—he never liked his first name—moved on to new challenges. He never specified why he left his home state, but he sometimes told reporters offhandedly, "I killed a man back in Oklahoma." Trouble followed his travels. In 1916 he was convicted of liquor law violations in Seattle. In 1919 he was arrested in Detroit for violation of the new Prohibition amendment. He was sentenced to fifteen months in Leavenworth and fined $5,000. He served four months, then moved on to New York.

Drugstores offered solace to thirsty citizens during the dry years, and Billingsley soon operated twenty in the Bronx and Westchester County, building apartments and private houses with the profits. A few weeks before the 1929 Crash, he launched his first speakeasy, the Stork Club, on West 58th Street.

"It was the first speakeasy with a carpet on the floor and a canopy out front," Billingsley recalled proudly. The touch of class attracted revenue agents, who shut the Stork Club down. He tried another Stork Club at Park Avenue and 51st Street, then after Repeal moved his operation to 53rd Street just east of Fifth Avenue.

Only four customers appeared for the opening, but Billingsley ordered the velvet rope to turn away latecomers. The technique worked. Customers felt privileged to be allowed inside the Stork Club, and they began coming in larger numbers. Then, the most valuable customer of all.

"It became my fort, my other home," wrote Walter Winchell of the Stork Club, which he termed "the New Yorkiest place in New York." Almost every day in his syndicated column and on most of his radio broadcasts, Winchell referred to the Stork Club in the most glowing terms.

Sherman Billingsley bestowed extraordinary attention on Broadway's biggest musical star. Knowing Ethel's fondness for champagne, he sent cases of the finest French vintage to her dressing room. On opening nights, she found gifts from Cartier's and Tiffany's on her dressing table.

Their friends began to suspect that the relationship of Sherman Billingsley and Ethel Merman went beyond that of restaurateur and star. They were right.

"Sherman *was* the love of Ethel's life," confirms Benay Venuta, Ethel's confidante over half a century. Venuta replaced Merman in *Anything Goes*, and the pair developed a friendship that prevailed, with occasional interruptions, until Merman's death.

Says Venuta: "Ethel was crazy about Sherman, and he was crazy about her. Ethel changed during the time of the romance. Her whole attitude became softer, she dressed in a more feminine way. No other man ever affected her that way."

Aside from physical attraction to Billingsley, which she often satisfied in his upstairs office, Ethel seemed intrigued by the element of danger in his lifestyle.

In 1925, during his bootlegging days, Billingsley had married Hazel Donnelly, a beauty from the Ziegfeld chorus. They had two daughters, Jacqueline and Barbara, and after the success of the Stork Club, the family moved to a Park Avenue apartment. Hazel Billingsley rarely visited her husband's place of business, and during his twelve-hour working days there was ample time for dalliance.

"Ethel, you're playing with fire!" declared Agnes Zimmermann when her daughter confessed she was having an affair with a married man.

"I can't help myself, Mama," Ethel replied. "I love the guy."

"You could ruin everything—your life, your career. Think of his wife. And his two little girls."

"I know, I know," Ethel said. But she couldn't stop seeing Sherman Billingsley.

Du Barry Was a Lady came into being because of Buddy De Sylva's bruised ego. He had departed from the successful songwriting team of De Sylva, Brown and Henderson to become a Broadway producer, then tried his hand at movies. He produced and wrote films for Shirley Temple at Fox and for Danielle Darrieux at Universal. Leaving Universal, he took along a story called *Bachelor Mother,* which he sold to RKO. When *Bachelor Mother* became a hit with Ginger Rogers and David Niven, everyone got credit—except Buddy De Sylva.

Louis (Doc) Shurr, a high-powered agent, suggested that De Sylva reestablish his reputation with the film moguls by producing hits on Broadway. It happened that two of Shurr's clients were available: Bert Lahr and Cole Porter.

Lahr believed that his own movie career had been assured by playing the Cowardly Lion in *The Wizard of Oz.* His fellow actor, Frank Morgan, predicted otherwise: "Bert, you're going to be a great hit in this picture. But it's not going to do you a damn bit of good—you're playing an animal." Despite the success of *The Wizard of Oz,* MGM did not pick up Lahr's option.

De Sylva managed to buy back a story he and Herbert Fields had sold to Paramount, and it became the basis for their script of *Du Barry Was a Lady.* They wrote it with Bert Lahr in mind. But who would be his leading lady?

"Ethel Merman," suggested the ubiquitous Shurr. "With Merman in the show, I'm sure Cole will write the songs. He's crazy about her."

The developments followed the agent's plan. *Stars in Your Eyes* was running down, and Merman was eager for another show to erase a near-defeat. Porter welcomed the chance to write again for the singer who delineated his songs better than any other. De Sylva found a dancer in a vaudeville act Jack Haley was performing in San Francisco during the Golden Gate Exposition. She was Betty Grable, recently dropped from a Paramount contract and divorced from Jackie Coogan. She had signed a contract with 20th Century–Fox, but Darryl Zanuck agreed to release her for *Du Barry Was a Lady.*

The plot, which had originally been designed for Mae West at Paramount, required first-rank performers to pull it off. The show opens in the washroom of the Club Petite in New York, where Louis Blore (Lahr) presides in mock grandeur. He is madly in love with the floor show star, May Daley (Merman), but she has eyes for a married newspaper columnist, Alex Barton (Phil Regan).

When Blore wins $75,000 in the Irish Sweepstakes, he is emboldened to pursue May. He mixes a Mickey Finn for the columnist, but mistakenly drinks it himself. His dreams transport him to the court of Louis XV of France, where he is king and May is Madame Du Barry. The palace romp is ended when the dauphin accidentally shoots an arrow into the royal rear. Blore awakens, pays the columnist to get a divorce, settles his taxes and returns to his washroom duties.

Porter was in peak form for *Du Barry,* supplying one of his most varied and sophisticated scores—outrageous, sniffed a few critics.

"Katie Went to Haiti" provided Merman with a production number in the "Eadie Was a Lady" vein, performed on the night club floor with chorines in fruit headdresses. "Do I Love You, Do I?" was a sweet ballad, and "Well, Did You Evah?" fitted Betty Grable's personality (the song later turned up in the 1956 film *High Society*). "Give Him the Oo-La-La" gave Merman another raucous number.

De Sylva and Fields needed a closing song to soften the blow of May's final rejection of the adoring men's room attendant. Porter concocted a hillbilly tune in which they pledged their platonic devotion to each other. It was called "Friendship," but, as usual, Porter tempered the sentiment with satiric barbs, combining friendship with disdain.

John Lahr in his biography of his father, *Notes on a Cowardly Lion,* suggests that the song coincided with the two stars' feelings toward each other. They respected each other's unique talents, but each had a strongly developed sense of self-preservation. In

Lahr's case it was compounded by a feeling of insecurity seemingly unmatched in show business.

In later years, the comic expressed his wariness of Merman to his son: "She's an individual with a special way of working. There was nothing vicious in what she did, she is a great performer. But she's tough. *She never looks at you on the stage.* She's got her tricks."

Knowing they were dealing with two high-voltage stars, De Sylva and Fields had carefully fashioned the script, dividing the laugh lines equally. But throughout rehearsals Lahr maintained he was being shortchanged. Nobody could convince him otherwise, and on occasion he resorted to a bottle of Scotch for consolation.

Other problems developed. Phil Regan's Irish tenor couldn't reach the balcony, and he was replaced by Ronald Graham. Betty Grable's dance partner was found lacking, and his part was taken by Charles Walters, later a director of MGM musicals.

Opening night in New Haven was joyful. In Boston, tumultuous. The audience demanded encore after encore of "Friendship." Finally Lahr stepped to the footlights and yelled, "That's all there is. Come to Philadelphia."

Du Barry broke a house record in Philadelphia and roared into New York amid vast excitement. The show opened at the 46th Street Theater on December 6, 1939, to a reaction that flabbergasted the performers. The audience, perhaps intimidated by the out-of-town raves, seemed to exhibit a show-me attitude. The comedy sketches drew only scatterings of laughter. The surefire "Friendship" failed to evoke encores. The first-nighters turned frigid during Porter's most controversial song, "But in the Morning, No." During the song Lahr inquired if Merman was good at figures. She answered affirmatively, and he asked if she did double entry. "I do double-entry," she said, "but in the morning, no."

"Dirt without wit," proclaimed the *New Yorker*. Added Brooks Atkinson in the *Times:* "Mr. Porter's ideas are a little skimpy this time, and never more microscopic than in 'But in the Morning, No.' " He complained, "The authors have struck a dead level of Broadway obscenity that does not yield much mirth." Burns Mantle of the *Daily News* agreed that the show was coarse, but he and other reviewers found it enjoyable, principally because of Ethel Merman and Bert Lahr.

The plaudits for Merman were the most enthusiastic she had received. John Mason Brown was moved to write in the *Post:*

"Miss Merman sweeps through the evening with that bright-eyed, shining vitality which is always such a captivating feature of her playing and her singing. She needs no vitamins; she has plenty to spare. Her throat houses as beguiling a calliope as Broadway knows. The Midas touch is upon her tonsils because she can turn brass into gold. She can do more than that. She can keep it brass.

"No one can match her in putting a song across, in trumpeting its lyrics, in personifying its rhythms. All the bright lights of Broadway seem to shine behind her face. Hard-boiled she frankly is, but she makes toughness itself an irresistible virtue. She possesses not only great energy, but a kind of shimmering dignity, too; a dignity born of her poise, her skill, her honesty and her magnificent professionalism."

The coolness of the opening night proved an aberration. From the second night on, audiences were enthralled by Porter's saucy songs, by Raoul Pène du Bois' garish costumes and sets and most of all by the incomparable Lahr and Merman. A hit had been predicted by Louis Shurr on opening night. He told Lahr: "I stopped a couple of critics on the way out, Bert. You'll be here forever."

"Yeah," Lahr replied glumly, "but what do I do next year?"

7.

Stardom and Marriage

Time magazine, which rarely featured theatrical personalities on its cover, did so on October 28, 1940. Ethel Merman's wide smile and flashing eyes appeared on newsstands all over America as her new show was preparing to open in New York. Among the *Time* effusions:

"The undisputed No. 1 musicomedy songstress of these harassed times, pompous psychologists might say that she gives her public vicarious energy which they often sorely need. But the diagnosis would leave out her assured, brazen art.

"A dark, bouncy, oval-faced young woman, Ethel Merman can lay no great claim to great beauty, glamor or 'legitimate' vocal quality, but she is a dynamic baggage with syncopation in every breath and gesture, and a voice with the hard, clarion forthrightness of a jazz trumpet. Where most people hum or whistle for their personal pleasure, Ethel Merman imitates (Ta-ta-ta-ta!) the trumpet part."

The *Time* article helped signal the new status of Ethel Merman in the pantheon of the musical theater.

During a decade on Broadway, Ethel Merman had always been a co-star—with William Gaxton and Victor Moore, with Jimmy Durante and Bob Hope, with Bert Lahr. Now, Buddy De Sylva concluded, it was time for Ethel to star on her own.

De Sylva fashioned a vehicle with the same deft team that had created *Du Barry*. He produced the show, and wrote it with Herbert Fields; Cole Porter composed the songs, Raoul Pène du Bois designed the sets and costumes, Edgar MacGregor staged the book and Robert Alton the dances. It was called *Panama Hattie*.

Merman was type-cast as Hattie Maloney, a case-hardened chanteuse in a Canal Zone bar. She falls in love with Nick Bullett, member of a rich Philadelphia family, serving in uniform on a government mission. Hattie agrees to marry him—if she can win the approval of Geraldine, his eight-year-old daughter from a previous marriage.

Geraldine arrives in Panama and giggles at the gaudy getups that Hattie considers classy. Marriage to Nick seems impossible until Hattie learns of a plot to blow up the canal. She enlists three sailor pals to overturn the plot, becomes a heroine and Mrs. Nick Bullett.

Casting of *Panama Hattie* was crucial, and De Sylva demonstrated his customary skill. From Hollywood he brought James Dunn to play Nick and Arthur Treacher to be Geraldine's snooty butler. For the three gobs, De Sylva took Rags Ragland out of burlesque and Pat Harrington and Frank Hyers from 52nd Street's raucous nitery, Club 18. The jitterbugging Florrie was played by Betty Hutton, recently singer with Vincent Lopez's band. The precocious Joan Carroll became Geraldine.

Even the chorus contained names that would become known in Hollywood: June Allyson, Vera-Ellen, Jane Ball, Janis Carter, Betsy Blair, Lucille Bremer, Doris Dowling.

In early 1940, Cole Porter took a cruise from Cuba to the South Seas and spent extra time in Panama to absorb atmosphere for the new show. He produced a score that was ideally suited to Merman and the tropical setting, though it contained no smash hits. The closest was "Let's Be Buddies," a tear-jerker that signaled the truce between Hattie and Geraldine.

The tryouts in New Haven and Boston brought reviewers' praise and sellout houses, and little repair was needed before the opening at the 46th Street Theater on October 30, 1940.

Ethel Merman's first starring musical was an unquestioned hit.

"Here is Broadway girl-and-music saturnalia at its peak, humorous, tuneful, hard-boiled, sentimental, rapidly paced and handsome, filled with good low comedians and beautiful girls and starring the wonderful Miss Ethel Merman in the leading role," announced Richard Watts, Jr. in the *Herald Tribune.*

"In her finest form, than which there is nothing finer, Ethel Merman sweeps triumphantly through *Panama Hattie,*" began John Mason Brown in the *Post.*

Some of the critics found "Let's Be Buddies" a bit mawkish, and John O'Hara was downright derogatory. Writing in *Newsweek*, he derided the song, as well as "My Mother Would Love You," adding, "Ah, well, [Porter] had a bad riding accident a year or two ago. This ought to teach him to stay in his Brewster-Ford and away from horses."

Porter compensated with a marvelously sophisticated torch song for Merman, in which she lamented her loss of Nick Bullett. "Make It Another Old-Fashioned, Please," she sang in the classic confessional to a bartender.

The New York critics found Betty Hutton too frenetic for their tastes. Richard Lockridge wrote in the *Sun:* "Miss Hutton is so animated she almost comes apart, and I think it would be nice if she would calm down a little—just to the pace of St. Vitus' Dance." Richard Watts, Jr.: ". . . Miss Hutton should be given one number, if that, in the course of an evening and then be permitted to work off her surplus energies elsewhere."

Inevitably, Betty Hutton overextended her energies and her voice during the run of *Panama Hattie.* She was unable to perform, and her understudy, June Allyson, was instructed to go on.

Miss Allyson recalls: "I had been in the chorus, which meant that I dressed on the third floor. Ethel said, 'Honey, we can't have you climbin' those stairs to get changed. You'll miss your cue. You'll use my dressing room.' She cleared off half her dressing table for me to use. She helped me with the makeup and costume, rehearsed with me. She walked me to the wings and cued me for my entrance. She even sent me a bouquet of flowers, the first I ever received."

In less than two years, Buddy De Sylva had produced three great Broadway hits: *Du Barry Was a Lady, Louisiana Purchase* and *Panama Hattie* (*Hattie* would become the first musical to exceed 500 performances since *The New Moon* in the late 1920s). Having established his reputation with the film moguls, De Sylva returned to Hollywood and became head of production for Paramount Pictures. He took along Betty Hutton and made her a star.

The New York opening of *Panama Hattie* found Ethel in magnificent form, and only a handful of close friends were aware of the personal turmoil she was enduring. She was overjoyed at the sight of her name appearing all alone above the title on the 46th Street Theater. But she was also shattered by the realization that she could never share her life with the only man she had ever loved.

During preparations for *Panama Hattie,* the romance with Sherman Billingsley had become an obsession with Ethel and she grew concerned about the consequences. Sherman, after all, had a wife and two children and to all outward appearances was a devoted family man. He claimed that he was in love with Ethel and wanted to divorce his wife and marry her, and for a time Ethel was enamored enough to consider his proposal. Then Hazel Billingsley announced she was pregnant.

"It's over!" Ethel proclaimed. "I'm not going to be a homewrecker, betrayer of a pregnant mother. My God, the Catholic Church would burn me at the stake! I'd be run out of show business!"

Billingsley employed all of his considerable persuasive skill to dissuade her, to no avail. Ethel fled to the New Haven tryout of *Panama Hattie,* insisting that Flo Haley accompany her.

"Sherman was the big love of her life, and she was upset about the breakup," Flo Haley recalls. "She didn't want to be alone, and she didn't want to talk to Sherman. He called her many times but wouldn't leave his name. I knew who it was."

The Merman-Billingsley romance had been an ill-kept secret, inevitably so in view of the public lives both led. Rumors coursed through the theater crowd and café society that Mrs. Billingsley had learned of the liaison and was threatening to expose it to the public. Ethel grew more and more alarmed over the consequences of such a scandal. Only one solution seemed possible: She would have to get married.

Ethel met Bill Smith at the home of Virginia and Arthur Treacher during rehearsals for *Panama Hattie*. He was tall, husky and handsome enough to be an actor, but he worked for a Hollywood talent agency, Feldman-Blum. Like most agents, he had a fast line of chatter, but Ethel detected nothing phony in Bill Smith. He had a sly sense of humor and a slightly satirical view of the entertainment world and its people.

After rehearsing *Panama Hattie* all day, Ethel dined out with members of the company, and Bill Smith went along. He was fascinated by Ethel Merman, and she was intrigued with him. When his business in Manhattan was completed, he returned to California. He and Ethel spent hours on the telephone while she was playing *Panama Hattie* in New Haven and Boston. With her emotions in turmoil over Sherman Billingsley, she considered a solution: Why not marry Bill Smith?

Two weeks after the New York opening of *Panama Hattie*, Ethel Agnes Zimmermann, thirty-two, married William Jacob Smith, thirty-nine, at Elkton, Maryland. On her Sunday off from *Panama Hattie*, the pair had taken the train to Maryland, where no waiting period was required for marriages. Accompanying them were Agnes and Edward Zimmermann and Virginia and Arthur Treacher.

The wedding came as a total surprise to everyone in New York—especially Sherman Billingsley. Broadway columnists scrambled to find out who William J. Smith was. A reporter for the *Daily News* gushed that Ethel "thinks 'My Bill' is the greatest number she's ever met. And 'My Bill' is not a song." Ethel told reporters that following the run of *Panama Hattie* she intended to retire and be a wife and mother.

During the curtain calls on the Monday night following the wedding, Ethel was showered with rice from the chorus and musicians. She radiated the joy of a new bride, another marvel of Merman acting. She already knew the marriage had been a mistake.

"Look, I'm not going to be Mr. Ethel Merman," Bill Smith announced. "Your money is yours. You can take care of the expenses pertaining to your career. I'll pay the costs for us as husband and wife."

It was a brave stand for an agent who was earning no more than $250 a week while his wife was being paid ten times as much. Smith came from a well-to-do Brookline, Massachusetts, family, and he had inherited $300,000. He figured he could afford to pay the household bills, which included a year's lease on an apartment at the Pierre Hotel.

A week after the wedding, Smith returned to California to resume his job. The marriage was conducted over long-distance telephone, with unsatisfactory results. Endearment turned to recrimination, with angry accusations on both sides.

They decided to hold a peace meeting. Since neither could be absent from work, they agreed to meet in mid-continent on Sunday, February 24. Buddy De Sylva had grave misgivings about Ethel's flying to Chicago, but she could not be dissuaded.

The reunion of Ethel and Bill was congenial, even affectionate, but both realized that more than geography stood between them. They agreed that Bill would obtain a divorce in Mexico on grounds of desertion.

Bill Smith returned to obscurity, spending most of his career in the publicity department of 20th Century–Fox studio. He was there in the 1950s when Ethel made two films. They never met, but Ethel said to another publicist, "Tell Bill hello for me; he's a nice guy." Smith died at the Motion Picture Country Hospital in Woodland Hills, California, at the age of eighty-three in 1984, two months before the death of Ethel Merman.

Robert Levitt seemed an unlikely candidate for the role of second husband to Ethel Merman and father to her two children. His background was in newspapers, and he cared little about Broadway musicals. As a matter of fact, they bored him terrifically.

They met at Dinty Moore's, a restaurant next door to the 46th Street Theater where Ethel was appearing in *Panama Hattie*. The occasion was some kind of promotion party for the *Journal-*

American, and the editor, Walter Young, introduced her to Levitt, the newspaper's circulation manager. Ethel was mildly interested in the young man, who was darkly handsome, with the build of a football guard. He was not overwhelmed upon meeting her.

"Let's go out to a night club," suggested Walter as the party started winding down. Ethel, still stimulated after her performance, agreed, and Bob Levitt consented to complete the foursome with her and the Youngs.

The night club visit proved less than successful. Levitt kept glancing at his watch, mindful of his early-morning job. Ethel also had a morning appointment. Since the Youngs wanted to remain at the club, they asked if Bob would escort Ethel home. He said he would.

As they drove through the wintry streets in a taxi, Ethel fumbled in her purse. "Dammit, I'm out of chewing gum," she said. "You got any?"

Levitt admitted he didn't, and she insisted they stop at an all-night drugstore so he could buy her some Wrigley's Spearmint. By the time they reached 25 Central Park West, Levitt's gentlemanly instincts had vanished. Ethel opened the taxi door and found a three-foot snowdrift in front of the entrance to her apartment house.

"Good night, nice to have met you," he muttered, and Ethel tramped her way alone through the snow to the apartment house door.

On the following day Ethel received a package: a carton of Wrigley's Spearmint. She was surprised, because she didn't think she had made any impression on the newspaper guy. She was more surprised when he telephoned and asked for a dinner date. Several times they dined before she had to report to the 46th Street Theater, and she noted that he never mentioned her work. Finally she asked, "How did you like *Panama Hattie*?"

"I, uh, haven't seen it," he admitted.

"Well, did you see me with Hope and Durante in *Red, Hot and Blue!*?"

"Uh, no."

"*Anything Goes*?"

"No."

"What show of mine *have* you seen?"

"None of them. I don't really care for musicals."

"Goddammit, you're going to see *Panama Hattie* tomorrow night. I'll have two tickets at the box office in your name, and you damn well better show up."

Levitt fortified himself with several drinks beforehand and had to force himself to stay awake during the performance.

Any other actress might have been offended. Ethel, oddly enough, lacked the hamminess that afflicts many stars. She was intrigued by the independent newsman whose frank talk contrasted with the usual dressing-room gush. She learned that he was well educated, with a specialty in Middle English, that he was a friend of the Hearst family and was being groomed for important posts in the publishing empire.

The courtship was fevered—and exhausting. Ethel thought Bob loved to stay out late at night spots, and he thought the same about her. Both kept smiling when they could hardly keep their eyes open. Finally she said, "Do you really like to stay up this late?"

"No," he said. "Do you?"

"No." They worked out a schedule whereby she would eat dinner before the show and he would take a nap while she was on stage. Then he would pick her up after the curtain, and they would go out for a snack.

The dates became nightly, and soon they were talking of marriage. The matter of finances came up, and both spoke realistically. He was now promotion director of the *Journal-American*, earning $200 a week, good pay in the newspaper world but far below what Ethel earned in the theater. Obviously Bob couldn't support her status as a Broadway star. They agreed that Ethel would finance matters pertaining to her career, and they would share living expenses as much as he was able.

The wedding took place in Connecticut in the late fall of 1941. Ethel never specified the time or place, for the simple reason that she was already pregnant. Because she didn't want to be separated from her mother and father, the newlyweds moved into a duplex in the same building, 25 Central Park West, where she had lived with them. The place was excessively grand for a newspaperman but befitting a star like Ethel Merman. There were ten spacious rooms on the twenty-first and twenty-second floors, with a huge terrace that afforded views of Broadway as well as the transatlantic liner docks on the Hudson River.

Bob Levitt accepted his new role with equanimity. He grew accustomed to standing in the background while admirers swarmed around Ethel. Nevertheless he barely tolerated some of her more theatrical friends and grudgingly submitted to interviews about his famous wife.

"When these dames come around asking about Ethel," he once complained to Wolcott Gibbs, "I want to tell them to drop dead. But then they work this 'fellow newspaperman' racket on me."

After the United States entered the war in December of 1941, the status of the Levitts changed. He became an army officer, and she took the role of army wife and mother.

By the third month of her pregnancy, Ethel had outgrown her *Panama Hattie* costumes, and she withdrew from the show. Shortly after Pearl Harbor, Bob Levitt enlisted in the army. He graduated from officers' school and drew duty in the Quartermaster Corps at the Port of Embarkation in Brooklyn.

As the celebrated wife of Lieutenant Levitt, Ethel was expected to attend social functions at the base. Except for celebratory champagne, she had never been much of a drinker, but she slugged down enough Manhattans to tolerate an evening at the Officers' Club. She refused emphatically, however, a request from the general's wife to entertain the gathering.

General Homer Groninger, to whom Bob Levitt became aide, fancied himself an expert gin rummy player, and one night he challenged Ethel to a match. He played the old-fashioned kind of gin rummy with cards spread all over the table, and Ethel quickly mastered the game. Much to Bob's chagrin, Ethel trounced the general.

"I tried to explain to Ethel beforehand that he always won,"

Levitt said afterward, "but I guess she didn't get the idea." Ethel, he admitted, was not accustomed to losing.

Ethel grew to alarming proportions, and on July 20, 1942, she gave birth by caesarean section to a seven-pound baby girl. She was named Ethel Merman Levitt and nicknamed Little Bit by her father.

The pregnancy had caused Ethel Merman's longest absence from performing, and although she had vowed to take a full year's vacation, she began listening to offers for a new Broadway show.

A few years later, Bob Levitt remarked wistfully, "I guess I like her best when she's pregnant. Then we could just sit around at home and listen to the radio and play gin."

8.

Something for the Boys

"Mr. Todd, this is Cole Porter."

Mike Todd was startled to be telephoned by the great Cole Porter. Although Todd had made a reputation for himself on Broadway with shows like *The Hot Mikado* and *Star and Garter*, it was largely a negative one. The theater establishment considered him an upstart, a carnival barker (which he had been) who had transferred his slick techniques to Broadway.

"Mr. Todd, I've got a problem," Porter continued. "Dorothy and Herbert Fields have written a show for Ethel Merman, and I have composed the songs. Vinton Freedley is our producer. But Mr. Freedley doesn't like the script or the songs and wants us to make extensive changes. The Fieldses and I don't consider them necessary. Would you like to audition the show?"

"No," Todd replied.

"You wouldn't?"

"I don't have to. If people like you and Merman and the Fieldses are involved, I'll produce the show. Sight unseen."

The show was originally called *The State of Texas*, then *Jenny Get Your Gun*. Dorothy and Herbert Fields, daughter and son of Lew Fields (of Weber and Fields), found the idea in news items and fashioned a script attuned to a nation at war. The items: Three cousins, who had previously not met, inherited a Texas ranch; a person had been able to receive radio transmissions through the Carborundum in his teeth.

Since Buddy De Sylva had gone to Hollywood, the Fieldses and Porter decided their producer should be Vinton Freedley, for whom they had written the Danny Kaye hit *Let's Face It.* Ethel Merman was enlisted as soon as she heard Porter's songs. "Cole, that's the best score you've ever done!" she exclaimed. Her enthusiasm was real, though her judgment faulty.

With Mike Todd supplanting Freedley, *Something for the Boys,* as it was finally called, pushed forward. The plot concerned a chorus girl-turned-war worker, a night club entertainer and a streetcorner pitchman who meet for the first time to claim their inheritance, a desolate Texas ranch with a dilapidated house on the property. It happens to be next door to Kelly Field, and the army takes over the house during maneuvers. Blossom Hart, the factory girl, falls for the sergeant in charge.

After maneuvers, the cousins convert the ranch house into a hotel for servicemen's wives. The sergeant's jealous sweetheart spreads the rumor that it is a house of ill repute, and it is declared off-limits. Blossom's radio-sensitive teeth save the day when she guides a disabled bomber to a safe landing via radioed instructions.

Despite his reputation as a takeover artist, Mike Todd proved remarkably amenable while *Something for the Boys* was being prepared. He insisted on one important addition, however. All of his shows had contained a spectacular scene near the end of the last act. This time he concocted the spectacle of a bomber taking flight in a whir of propellers, later rocking and pitching as it hurtled out of control in a thunderstorm.

Todd had only one serious disagreement with the show's creators. He disliked a large production number that the authors had concocted for a Porter tune. Ethel led the charge to Todd's office, followed by Dorothy and Herbie Fields and Cole Porter. Todd, who had invested over $60,000 of his own money in the show (borrowed from 20th Century–Fox executives Joseph Schenck and Joseph Moskowitz), remained firm.

"I think it's a great number," Merman insisted, and her companions agreed.

"Yeah, it's a great number," the producer replied, puffing on an oversized cigar. "The better it is, the worse off we are. If it stops the show, we have no show."

The argument continued, and Todd threatened to junk *Something for the Boys* and lose his money rather than his control as producer. The others remained equally firm.

"Okay," Todd said, "I'll *prove* it to you and let *you* have the pleasure of heaving it out. If I'm wrong, I'd better go back to selling shoes."

He invested $5,000 in costumes and an elaborate setting. The Boston tryout of *Something for the Boys* proved triumphant—except for that particular number.

"It doesn't work," Todd reiterated. This time his collaborators unhappily agreed. The experience had been expensive for Todd, but he had demonstrated his reasonableness as a producer.

Something for the Boys was scheduled to open on January 7, 1943, at the Alvin, Ethel's good-luck theater. The Broadway crowd was in a state of anticipation. There hadn't been a Merman opening since 1940, and the musical theater had gone hitless for six months.

Mike Todd remained at the back of the house during the performance, pacing nervously, cocking his ear for anticipated laughs, beaming as cheers arose at the finish of Merman's songs. He glowed during the intermission as one well-wisher after another assured him he had another hit.

Todd's tension grew more visible as the second act progressed. He knew *Something for the Boys* was a hit, but it could be a smash if the bomber scene worked. As the scene approached, he spied something that put fire in his eyes. Two of the critics, Burns Mantle of the *Daily News* and Howard Barnes of the *Herald Tribune*, rose from their aisle seats and strode to the rear of the theater. Broadway custom allowed reviewers for morning newspapers to leave shows early so their critiques could appear in final editions.

Mantle and Barnes found Mike Todd blocking the head of the aisle. "You're not leaving!" the producer declared.

"We'll miss our editions!" Mantle argued.

"You'll miss my bomber!" Todd replied. He had stationed ushers on the other aisle to prevent other early departures.

Todd's blockade didn't hurt his reviews. Barnes called the show "definitely a tonic entertainment," adding that "the triumphant Ethel Merman is on hand at every flagging moment of the offering to give it tremendous bounce and vitality." Mantle advised his readers to run, not walk, to the nearest ticket agency.

"Merman Returns and All Is Well," headlined the newspaper *PM*. The reviewer, Louis Kronenberger, proclaimed Ethel "one of the great women of the world" and found her "in high fettle and excellent form."

Most of the critics found the book negligible, however, and the songs disappointing ("Mr. Porter's new songs always sound a lot like Mr. Porter's old songs nowadays"—Wilella Waldorf, *Post*). But they were overwhelmed by the lavish production and especially by Ethel Merman.

"With Miss Merman there, the good time is on both sides of the lights," wrote Lewis Nichols in the *Times*. "For she is truly immense. Ethel Merman in good voice is a raucous overtone to the trumpets of a band; it is a soft trill for a torch song, it is tinny for a parody and fast for one of Mr. Porter's complicated lyrics. Accompanying the voice are the necessary gestures, the roll of the eye or the wave of the hand to suggest friendly ribaldries or separations forever more. . . . It is one of Mr. Porter's lines that sums it up pretty well: she is 'the missing link between Lily Pons and Mae West.' And a credit, of course, to the pair of them."

With *Something for the Boys* acclaimed a solid hit, Ethel settled in for a long run. Her opening night performance was virtually the same as the ones she gave every evening and matinee until the end of the run. Any variance by other members of the cast evoked her disapproval. Any threat to her own lines or business was dealt with severely, as Paula Laurence discovered.

Paula Laurence had been cast in *Something for the Boys* on the recommendation of Cole Porter, who had been impressed with her deadpan singing. *Something for the Boys* was her first

Broadway show, and she had not been educated in the etiquette of musical comedy, nor the self-protectiveness of Ethel Merman.

Their big number together was "By the Mississinewah," in which Merman and Laurence portrayed Indian squaws who shared the same brave. Porter had written a surefire comedy number, which was climaxed by repeating the "iss" in "Mississinewah" eight times. During the tryout Ethel had concocted a piece of business in which she swung the braids of her woolen wig. The audience roared.

Ethel's mind calculated every laugh, every burst of applause throughout each performance. The volume varied only in degrees, depending on the responsiveness of the audience. One night Ethel heard an unexpected ripple of laughter during "By the Mississinewah." Puzzled, she turned around and saw Paula Laurence swinging her braids in imitation of the Merman gesture.

"You tell that broad to stop stealing my business," Ethel shouted to the stage manager. Miss Laurence was warned.

Three weeks later, Ethel heard the same errant laughter during "Mississinewah." She swung around and discovered Laurence with braids flying.

"Out! She's out!" Ethel exclaimed to Mike Todd. The producer gave Paula Laurence her notice. She was replaced by Betty Bruce, who had been playing a minor role in the show.

"Well, she was the star," Miss Laurence commented afterward, "and if she'd wanted me to paint my nose red, I guess I'd have to. And don't think she wouldn't, either."

Over the years, the Paula Laurence incident was cited as evidence that Ethel Merman would quash any threat to her dominance of the stage. Merman detractors claimed that whenever a show-stopping number, especially one by a female performer, developed during a show's tryout, she ordered the number removed. The legend is challenged by the experience of Betty Garrett.

A talented but untried singer-comedienne from St. Joseph, Missouri, Betty Garrett was signed to play a role in *Something for the Boys* and to understudy Ethel Merman. The newcomer's agent insisted she would have her own number in the show, and Cole Porter wrote a lachrymose ballad that opened the second act. It depressed the audience and singer alike.

Cole Porter came to Boston to write a new song. "What do you like to sing?" he asked. "Hillbilly and boogie-woogie," Miss Garrett replied. He asked her for examples, and she sang "Where Have You Been, Billy Boy?" and "The Boogie-Woogie Washer-woman."

Porter composed "I'm in Love with a Soldier Boy," a hillbilly song until the last few bars, when it turned boogie-woogie. The number drew a huge response. Members of the company feared Ethel would order it removed, especially since she had to make her entrance immediately afterward.

"She could have taken it out of the show, but she actually helped me," Betty Garrett says. "When she came onstage to the applause, she looked at the audience, then into the wings at me. If she had started talking, the applause would have died. But she kept looking at me and kept the applause going until she brought me out for a bow."

Betty was surprised during the Broadway run when Betty Bruce told her, "Ethel thinks you're stuck-up. You never come around to her dressing room to say hello." New to the theater, it had never occurred to Betty Garrett that a supporting player would be welcome in the star's dressing room. She realized that stars welcomed contact with their fellow players, and she began calling at Ethel's room. Both enjoyed bawdy stories and colorful language, and the pair became friends.

As a supporting player, Betty Garrett remained offstage for long periods, and she sometimes amused herself as chorus girls did, painting her body with animal faces. One night she decorated her breasts as pigs, the nipples depicting snouts. Betty Bruce saw the artwork and roared, "Ethel's gotta see this!"

Ethel took one look at Betty's front and burst into laughter. "If I did that," she said, lifting her ample bust, "they'd be cows!"

Says Betty Garrett: "Ethel had so much energy onstage, yet she never seemed to exert it. Everyone said she was the greatest opening-night performer but sometimes 'walked through' a show later in the run. I never saw any of that. Maybe she wasn't feeling well and didn't give as much one night. But I never saw her shortchange an audience."

Merman had a reputation for never missing a performance, but after several months in *Something for the Boys*, she fell ill with laryngitis. Rather than cancel the show, Mike Todd decided to have Betty Garrett play the leading role. He was careful not to inform the audience until after the orchestra had played "The Star-Spangled Banner." Then the leading man, Bill Johnson, appeared in front of the curtain.

The speech was carefully worded by Mike Todd himself. The audience groaned, of course, when Johnson announced that Miss Merman would not be able to appear because of acute laryngitis. Refunds would be available, but perhaps the audience would like to stay and see a bright young performer, Miss Betty Garrett. "Who knows," Johnson concluded, "perhaps a star will be born tonight."

Betty was not unprepared. Understudy rehearsals had been held regularly. An old set of Ethel's costumes were hastily taken in. One of the solos was lowered a key to fit Betty's voice.

The audience stayed, and Betty Garrett was cheered at the final curtain. Ethel insisted that Betty use her dressing room and dresser. Ethel called every night during intermission to deliver a pep talk: "Listen, kid, if those people out there could do it better than you, *they'd* be up there, not you." One night a package arrived from Ethel. It was a topaz ring with the inscription: "To Betty, Good Luck, Ethel. October, 1943."

After a week's absence, Ethel returned to *Something for the Boys*, and Betty resumed her role as Mary-Frances. She wore the topaz ring onstage, and Ethel stopped the action to call, "Mr. Electrician, shine a light on that ring."

Something for the Boys came at a happy period for Ethel Merman. She adored being a mother, and she changed her living habits so she could spend maximum time with Little Bit. No more night clubs; Ethel went home immediately after the show so she could play with her daughter in the morning. Instead of resting in her dressing room between matinees and evening performances, she dashed to 25 Central Park West to spend an hour in the nursery. When Ethel was at the theater, her mother and father gave their granddaughter all the attention she needed, and then some.

Ethel, Jr. was baptized an Episcopalian, with William Gaxton and Eleanor Holm acting as godparents. To everyone's surprise, Bob Levitt announced his decision to adopt the Episcopal faith soon afterward. He came from a nonreligious Jewish background, and he reasoned that the family should share the same religion.

Major Robert Levitt continued duty as general's aide at the Brooklyn Port of Embarkation, and he spent most weekends at home. Although she never said as much, having a weekend husband was ideal for Ethel, who was totally occupied during the week as performer, mother and household manager. (Ethel never employed a secretary, typing all her own letters with astonishing speed. And she kept track of all household expenses by using the bookkeeping system she had learned at Bryant High.)

Ethel also kept busy with war benefits. Along with Danny Kaye, Gertrude Lawrence, Helen Hayes, Alfred Lunt, Lynn Fontanne and other Broadway stars, she made frequent appearances at war bond rallies, relief fund dinners, benefits of all kinds. She appeared in the all-star movie *Stage Door Canteen*, and at least once a week sang at the Canteen, which was operated by the American Theater Wing.

Something for the Boys was the ideal wartime entertainment, and it continued doing capacity business into its second year. Then Ethel became pregnant, and she left the show after 422 performances. In April of 1944, she suffered a miscarriage. The tragedy sent her into an unaccustomed state of depression; she grew edgy and irritable. Bob Levitt became the target of her anger and frustration, and after a fierce argument, he stalked out of the apartment. A "trial separation" was announced, but by the end of the month, Ethel and Bob had reconciled.

Ethel wanted to go back to work. She realized that the rhythm of her life was synchronized best when she was in a hit show or pregnant.

Sadie Thompson seemed the ideal vehicle for Ethel Merman.

Somerset Maugham's classic trollop was blood sister to Panama Hattie and the other brassy dames Ethel loved to play. She agreed to appear in a new version of the South Sea tale with music by Vernon Duke and lyrics by Howard Dietz. The script was by Dietz and Rouben Mamoulian.

Ethel began rehearsals on September 18, 1944, and quit twelve days later.

What bothered her were Sadie's lyrics. They were too chic, too clever for her taste. Cole Porter's lyrics were sophisticated, Ethel reasoned, but they also had a down-to-earth quality that fit her style.

One day Ethel stalked into rehearsal and threw her sheet music on the piano. "There's a word here—Malmaison," she said, stabbing a manicured finger at the music sheet. "What does that mean?"

"That's a very famous lipstick color," Dietz replied.

"Yeah?" Ethel retorted. "I never heard of it."

She plodded through the rehearsal, and the next day she arrived triumphantly. "Hey, Howard," she shouted. "That 'Malmaison.' I asked twenty-five other dames and none of them ever heard of it, either. It goes out."

"Oh no it doesn't," Dietz replied.

They were at an impasse. Merman walked out of the show and June Havoc assumed the leading role. *Sadie Thompson* lasted thirty-two performances on Broadway.

Something for the Boys had been the fifth collaboration of Cole Porter and Ethel Merman, and it proved to be the last. Their friendship remained warm and cordial, and Porter always sent Ethel a Christmas present. One year it was a painting, a farm scene with red roosters, one of twenty canvases he had bought from a woman painter he had discovered near his home at Williamstown, Massachusetts. He gave all twenty to friends at Christmastime.

Ethel opened the package and stared at the painting with its bright colors and landscape lacking in perspective. "My kid can paint better than that," she muttered, and she gave it away to a friend.

A few years later, Porter remarked to Ethel: "By the way, how are you enjoying your Grandma Moses?"

"My what?" Slowly she realized the painting she had discarded was the work of one of America's most celebrated artists. For weeks afterward, she asked herself, "Now who in hell did I give it to?" But she never could remember.

9.

Annie Get Your Gun

"How would you like to play Annie Oakley?"

Ethel Merman was in no mood to consider Dorothy Fields' suggestion. Two days earlier, on August 11, 1945, she ad given birth (again by caesarean section) to Robert Daniels Levitt, Jr. Suffering postoperative pain, she listened dully as Dorothy outlined the production.

"Herbie and I will write the book, and I'll do the songs with Jerry Kern. He's agreed to come back from Hollywood to do another show. And Dick and Oscar are going to produce! What do you think, Mermsie?"

"Jeez, Dorothy, I got gas pains," Ethel replied. "How can I think about doing another show? Ask me when I get out of the hospital."

The idea had come to Dorothy Fields one night after she had helped entertain servicemen at the Stage Door Canteen. She was dining with her husband at "21" when she overheard a conversation about a sharpshooter who had won all the prizes in a Coney Island shooting gallery.

"Sharpshooter! Ethel Merman as Annie Oakley!" Miss Fields exclaimed.

The next day, she and her brother oulined the idea to Mike Todd. The producer had an option for the Fieldses to write another show for Ethel to follow their success with *Something for the Boys*.

"A show about a dame who knows from nothing but guns?" Todd replied. "I wouldn't touch it!"

Todd released them from the option. That afternoon Dorothy attended a meeting of the Writers' War Board at which Oscar Hammerstein presided. Afterward she told Hammerstein her proposal. He was enthusiastic.

The following morning, Dorothy and Herbert Fields met with Hammerstein and Richard Rodgers. Agreement was immediate. Rodgers and Hammerstein would produce the show, Dorothy and Herbert would write the book, Jerome Kern would compose the songs to Dorothy's lyrics. Rodgers and Hammerstein never considered writing the songs. After their enormous success with *Oklahoma!* and *Carousel*, they had established the pattern of creating innovative musicals every two years. The Annie Oakley show did not fit the pattern.

By the time Ethel took the baby home from the hospital, she was enthusiastic about embarking on another show. Jerome Kern was harder to convince. His last Broadway show, *Very Warm for May*, written with Oscar Hammerstein, had flopped in 1939, and Kern had been content with the easy life in California, turning out scores for the studios. Rodgers and Hammerstein offered to produce a first-class revival of *Showboat*, thus easing Kern's reentry into the theater. Kern agreed.

Kern arrived in New York in early November of 1945. Three days later he collapsed on the street. Within a week he was dead of a cerebral hemorrhage.

After recovering from the shock of losing a musical giant they both revered, Rodgers and Hammerstein pondered a successor for the Annie Oakley show.

"Why not Irving Berlin?" Hammerstein suggested.

"We're aiming awfully high to try to get Berlin," Rodgers answered.

"What can we lose? The worst that could happen is that he'll refuse."

Berlin was reluctant to follow the great Kern, and he had no desire to write songs for a plot musical. His last had been *Louisiana Purchase* five years before, and he feared that the musical theater had undergone too many changes in his absence. The emphasis now was on fitting songs directly to the plot.

"That hillbilly stuff, Oscar, that's not for me," said Berlin. "I don't know the first thing about that kind of lyric."

"That's ridiculous," Hammerstein replied. "All you have to do is drop the g's."

Berlin agreed to take the script to his Catskill farm over the weekend. He returned with a couple of songs, "They Say It's Wonderful" and "You Can't Get a Man with a Gun." Rodgers and Hammerstein were overwhelmed, and they persuaded the still-reluctant Berlin to undertake the show. The three men quickly worked out the contract details. Dorothy Fields readily agreed to withdraw as lyricist, realizing that Berlin always wrote words and music.

Rodgers and Hammerstein had chosen Josh Logan to direct the Annie Oakley show while Logan was still serving with the army in Europe. The war had ended in Europe though not in the Pacific, but Rodgers wrote that he believed peace would arrive in time for Logan to report for fall rehearsals. The prediction proved correct. His discharge complicated by an eye ailment, Logan worked on the script with the Fieldses between medical examinations.

Berlin astounded everyone with his virtuosity. He had earned a reputation for reaching into his trunk for long-ago songs to fill out a musical's score. This time all of his songs were new, some written with dazzling speed.

A song was needed in front of the curtain during a scenery change. Berlin returned from a weekend with "There's No Business Like Show Business." During a later run-through of the songs, Rodgers noticed that "Show Business" was missing. He asked about it.

"I dropped it because the last time it was being played, I didn't like the expression on your face," Berlin explained. "I didn't think you were happy about it, and I decided not to use it."

"My God, Irving," Rodgers replied. "Don't ever pay any attention to the expression on my face. I love that song. I looked sour only because I was concentrating on where it should go."

During the early stages, Rodgers, Hammerstein, Berlin and Logan conferred in Hammerstein's living room. Logan observed that another duet was needed for the leads, Annie Oakley and Frank Butler, in the second act. "They Say It's Wonderful" in the first act was their only song together.

"But if they're not talking to each other in the second act, how can they sing together?" Berlin asked.

"Could they have a quarrel song or a challenge song?" Rodgers suggested.

"Challenge!" Berlin said with enthusiasm. "Of course! Meeting over! I've got to go home and write a challenge song."

When Logan arrived back at his apartment, the telephone was ringing. It was Berlin, and he sang: "Anything you can do, I can do better; I can do anything better than you."

He finished the song, and the flabbergasted Logan exclaimed, "That's perfect! When in hell did you write that?"

"In the taxicab," Berlin replied. "I had to, didn't I? We go into rehearsal Monday."

In the early stages of *Annie Get Your Gun*, as the show was finally called, Berlin had been worried about the newfangled technique of "integrating" songs into musical plots. He created nineteen entirely new songs ideally suited to the Dorothy and Herbert Fields libretto.

The script elaborated on the saga of Annie Oakley, the backwoods girl whose incredible skill with a rifle wins her a job with Buffalo Bill's Wild West Show. She is entranced with Frank Butler, the show's sharpshooter, and a romance ensues. Buffalo Bill and his manager induce Annie to attempt a spectacular motorcycle act, arguing that Frank will be pleased. But he is incensed at being upstaged by a woman, and he leaves to join the rival show of Pawnee Bill.

Buffalo Bill and his star Annie Oakley stage a triumphant tour of Europe, but come home broke. So does the Pawnee Bill company. The only solution is to combine the shows, allowing

Annie and Frank to reunite. But they quarrel again, and they challenge each other to a shooting match. Annie's friend, Chief Sitting Bull, persuades Annie to "throw" the contest, and Annie gets her man.

Ray Middleton, a rangy, deep-throated singer who had appeared in *Roberta* and more recently in the Air Force show *Winged Victory*, was cast as Frank Butler. The script called for Annie to fall in love with Frank the moment she saw him. In his autobiography, Josh Logan told how he devised the scene:

"I felt the only way I could show such an abrupt change was to have her collapse inwardly and outwardly as if she were a puppet whose strings had been cut quickly. I told Ethel to keep her eyes fixed on Ray but to let everything else in her body and mind go.

"She tried it. Her mouth dropped open, her shoulders sank, her legs opened wide at the knees, her diaphragm caved in. It was an unforgettable effect. Later, we dubbed it the 'goon look,' and it won for me the eternal devotion of everyone, including myself. It seemed to be the catalytic moment—the moment at which the play became a hit."

Annie Get Your Gun took shape with remarkable ease, and none in the company was more confident than Ethel Merman. She and Bob Levitt ordered dinner in their hotel room before the New Haven opening. Ethel's menu: thick soup, steak, French-fried potatoes, two vegetables, salad, coffee and apple pie.

"How can you eat such a heavy dinner?" Levitt wondered. "Aren't you nervous?"

"No, why should I be?" she said with a wave of the hand. "Let the people who've paid four-forty for their seats worry."

The show was acclaimed by the New Haven audience, and everyone in the company was elated. Everyone except Irving Berlin, who told Rodgers, "I'm very unhappy with the orchestrations." Rodgers sent an emergency call to Robert Russell Bennett, who reworked the entire score to Berlin's satisfaction.

It was a complicated production, with heavy scenery and lighting and prop tricks that didn't always work. One scene called for Merman to fire a shotgun into the air and fell a stuffed duck.

In Boston she aimed to the rafters and pulled the trigger. The blank didn't fire, but the bird thudded to the stage floor on cue.

"What do you know?" Ethel ad-libbed, holding the duck by the neck. "Apoplexy!"

Annie Get Your Gun moved to the Imperial Theater in New York amid high expectations. As Richard Rodgers was surveying the stage the day before the premiere, he was startled by a loud cracking sound over his head. A stagehand pushed Rodgers off the stage, and the Imperial was evacuated: The scenery had buckled a girder above the stage. It had to be repaired before the show could go on.

Rodgers and Hammerstein pleaded with Lee Shubert for an out-of-town theater while the Imperial underwent repairs. *Annie Get Your Gun* played two weeks at the Shubert in Philadelphia, selling out after a small ad appeared in the newspapers. A Merman-Berlin show produced by Rodgers and Hammerstein needed nothing else.

Ever eager to believe the worst, the Broadway crowd figured that *Annie Get Your Gun* was in deep trouble. Forget that baloney about the scenery cracking the roof. The show's a turkey. Why else would Dick and Oscar cancel the opening and move to Philadelphia?

At first the opening night audience in New York seemed to reflect this cynicism. Logan and Rodgers agonized as they watched the first act from the rear of the Imperial. The laughs weren't coming. There was no response to the Berlin line "You can't shoot a male in the tail like a quail." Even the "goon look" drew a tepid reaction.

Between acts Logan rushed backstage to commiserate with Ethel. He found her amazingly calm. "You may think I'm playing the part," she told him, "but inside I'm saying, 'Screw you! You jerks! If you were as good as I am, you'd be up here!' "

Everything worked in the second act. The audience found the jokes hilarious, the songs enchanting, the romance touching. By the time the entire company thundered "There's No Business Like Show Business" in the curtain reprise, the first-nighters were ready to cheer.

But the reviews proved as schizoid as the audience.

"Ethel Merman shot a bull's-eye last night," proclaimed William Hawkins in the *World-Telegram*. "For verve and buoyancy, unslacking, there has seldom if ever been a show like it."

"It's a new and exciting Ethel Merman built on the fine and firm foundation of the old one," observed Robert Garland in the *Journal-American*. "She's no longer Miss Merman acting like Ethel Merman. She's Miss Merman acting like Annie Oakley. Something important has been added."

"All that is to be wished for in a musical comedy is to be found at the Imperial," began Howard Barnes in the *Herald Tribune*.

All of the critics praised Ethel Merman. But John Chapman of the *Daily News* found *Annie* a victim of too much advance publicity and "not the greatest show in the world." Louis Kronenberger of *PM* termed the show cheerful but very far from overpowering—"For me, *Annie* is mainly Miss Merman's show, though the rest of it is competent enough of its kind."

Ward Morehouse of the *Sun* agreed that Merman was in her best form but found Berlin's score "not a notable one." The *Times*' Lewis Nichols found the music to be merely "pleasant" but without any great Berlin hits like "White Christmas" and "Easter Parade." Nichols commented: "In any Merman show the other members of the acting company habitually take on the harassed air of losing horses in a steeplechase."

Ethel and Bob Levitt stayed up until dawn to read the reviews. In the morning she called no one to exult over her notices. Instead, she telephoned her grocer.

"Look here," she scolded, "when I paid last week's bill, you charged me for two cans each of pineapple and of grapefruit juice. At the time I told you that you had sent only one of each, and you promised to make good. But you haven't!"

The *Annie Get Your Gun* years were the best of Ethel Merman's life. The show was an unquestioned personal triumph, consolidating her position as the greatest figure in musical comedy. Her Annie Oakley broadened the Merman range immeasurably. From *Girl Crazy* to *Something for the Boys*, she had invariably played the brass-plated dame who knew all the tricks and had heard all the lines.

"Irving Berlin made me a lady," she commented gratefully, citing such songs as "I Got Lost in His Arms" and "They Say It's Wonderful." As the naive country girl who goes gaga over Frank Butler, she displayed a vulnerability that Broadway audiences had never suspected in her.

Ethel was now earning a salary commensurate with her position as Broadway's top star. Rodgers and Hammerstein, who were noted for paying their actors as little as possible, nevertheless granted Ethel 10 percent of the theater gross receipts, which meant $4,700 a week before taxes.

As always, she invested her income prudently. Her only extravagances were the Central Park West apartment—and jewelry. She adored heavy, flashy-looking but expensive pieces, which she ordered from jeweler Lou Freedman. One of her prizes was a bracelet an inch and a half wide with ETHEL A. MERMAN spelled out in baguette diamonds (the period was a ruby). She had Freedman make her a gold cigarette case with the initials EML and a portrait of herself as Panama Hattie done in platinum, diamonds and a ruby. It required six months to create.

Her everyday clothes came off the rack, and she shopped up and down Fifth Avenue for bargains. Her favorite prices for dresses were $39.95 or $49.95, and she rarely bought anything over $100. She would, however, splurge on gowns for public appearances, the expense being tax-deductible. For a singing engagement at the Plaza Hotel, she bought a mink-trimmed chartreuse gown for $550 and a black velvet dress with ermine ascot for $495 (an enormous sum for that time). Ever since *Girl Crazy*, she had patronized the same shop, Wilma's on West 57th Street, which specialized in high-style fashions for entertainers.

Such details were duly reported by *Life*, the *New Yorker*, *Collier's*, *New York Times Magazine* and other periodicals that rediscovered Ethel Merman in the wake of *Annie Get Your Gun*. They disclosed that she was five feet, five inches tall and weighed one hundred and thirty pounds, a dozen pounds over her *Girl*

Crazy weight. That to give herself more height on the stage, she wore very high heels and her black hair swept up in what her daughter called "the bush." That she chewed gum incessantly. That her favorite drink was champagne in a tall glass with ice. That she didn't like to read books or play cards; that conversation was her favorite pastime. That she had a large brown mole on her left arm. That her frequent remark was, "Let's get a big black car and go someplace."

The articles mentioned little about Robert Levitt. He preferred not to participate in interviews or any other part of Ethel's career. He never read the scripts for her new shows, nor did he listen to the songs. When the war ended, Levitt debated whether to return to the Hearst Corporation. He had an offer from his old school, Rollins College in Florida, to teach journalism.

"Supposing we all move down there," he suggested.

"What?" Ethel replied. "Move to Florida? What would I do?"

"You could teach singing and acting."

"Me teach those things? I wouldn't know how. I can't tell other people how I do my stuff."

The conversation was over. Bob Levitt resumed his career with Hearst. His ascent in the corporation was not swift, though, despite his and Ethel's friendship with William Randolph Hearst, Jr. Bob became assistant publisher of the *American Weekly*, Hearst's Sunday supplement; later, when *American Weekly* suffered a decline in advertising revenue, he assumed the role of president and chief troubleshooter.

Bob had learned to tolerate being called "Mr. Merman" and to cope with Ethel's assertive manner. About Ethel's theatrical friends he was less tolerant. With his newspaperman's eye he could penetrate the phoniness and shallowness of those who hovered around Ethel's dressing room in search of favors.

Ethel, on the other hand, did not enjoy the casual cynicism of many of Bob's newspaper friends. As a result, they shared few real friends in each other's fields.

Their children provided the strongest bond between Ethel and Bob Levitt. Bob had never been close to small children before, and he was almost overcome with wonder and pride in young Ethel and Bobby. Ethel approached motherhood as she did her stage roles: with single-minded determination.

The Merman who haunted the Stork Club, El Morocco and other night spots was seldom seen in her old playgrounds now. She had to rise early to attend to Ethel and Bobby. Her daughter was a small girl with serious dark eyes and an independent manner. She proclaimed to visitors: "My name is Little Bit, but they call me Ethel Merman the Second for short."

Her mother sometimes took Little Bit to the theater, though it was evident that the girl was not terribly interested. During rehearsals for *Annie Get Your Gun,* Ethel planted her out front. One day she noticed her daughter reading.

"What are those?" Merman demanded.

"Comic books," little Ethel replied. "Something to do while you're working."

Her mother snatched the books away. "Nobody reads while I'm on stage," she announced.

When the show opened in Boston, little Ethel sat quietly in the audience until her mother shot a bird out of a woman's hat. Then she ran screaming from the theater.

"What was the matter with you?" Merman asked afterward.

"You shot that poor little bird!" cried her daughter.

"That was a phony, for crying out loud. I do it at every show."

Little Ethel, it appeared, was sensitive to noise, including her mother's voice. At times when Merman was holding forth in the apartment, her daughter would say to a playmate, "Let's get out of here. It's too noisy with *her* in here."

The girl was also heard telling her friends, "I got a new fat brother." Indeed, Robert Levitt, Jr. had grown rapidly, much to his mother's delight.

When the boy was ten months old, his mother displayed him to a *New Yorker* reporter, who detected a resemblance to the wrestler Man Mountain Dean.

"Weighs twenty-five pounds, thirteen ounces," Merman said proudly, "and he's had six teeth since he was six months old. He's so big the Kleinert people had to make oversize pants for him." As the boy crawled toward the liquor cabinet, she added, "Anything to eat or drink and he'll go for it."

Merman's early experience with motherhood seemed all-absorbing, but that changed as little Ethel and Bobby began developing wills of their own. A friend recalls approaching her as she was walking the two children in Central Park. The friend observed Merman from behind, but there was no mistaking the stacked hairdo and the forthright voice. It bawled: "You don't wanna go to the zoo. You don't wanna ride the swings. What the fuck *do* you want to do?"

Few performers have ever been so unchanged by wealth and celebrity as Ethel Merman. She never forgot her Astoria roots, and, in fact, maintained high school friendships throughout her life. She found an admirer in Franklin D. Roosevelt, for whom she made an appearance before his nomination for President. After Roosevelt was in the White House, she sang at his birthday celebrations to benefit the March of Dimes. Yet she never abandoned the Republicanism to which she had been loyal since childhood.

Nor could Ethel Merman be overwhelmed by the Duke and Duchess of Windsor. She met them at a gala given by Mrs. William Randolph Hearst, Sr. The Windsors and the Levitts became friends. Ethel called the former King of Great Britain "Eddie English," and occasionally at parties they sang an incongruous duet of "Doin' What Comes Natur'lly."

On the piano in Ethel's living room was a portrait of the Windsors with an inscription addressed to the Levitts, "who raised a family, doing what comes naturally." There were also portraits of President Roosevelt ("To Ethel Merman, Franklin D. Roosevelt") and George Gershwin ("For Ethel—a lucky composer is he who has you singing his songs. All the best, George Gershwin"). Even more prominently displayed were pictures of Agnes and Edward Zimmermann, Robert and Ethel Levitt and their two children.

After two years in *Annie Get Your Gun,* Ethel Merman was bone-tired. Eight times a week she had been singing the equivalent of a full-scale opera, and she wanted to leave the show. Rodgers and Hammerstein pleaded with her to remain, arguing that *Annie* would collapse without her, depriving the rest of the company of jobs. Rodgers became especially insistent, and he and Merman exchanged harsh words backstage one evening.

Ethel finally submitted to a third year, with the proviso that she be allowed a six-week vacation.

The Levitt family traveled by train to Glenwood Springs in the Colorado Rockies, which Ethel had chosen because of Little Bit's passion for horses. The vacation was an idyllic one for Ethel and Bob, their first away from curtain calls and news deadlines. It was the last placid time they would have.

The marriage was slowly deteriorating, in part because of Bob Levitt's thwarted ambitions. He had gone from being a colonel in the army to a middle-level executive position in the Hearst Corporation. He found his work uninspiring, and more and more he sought the raucous camaraderie of newspaper bars. For a few hours over drinks he could escape his role as Mr. Ethel Merman.

10.

Call Me Madam

Call Me Madam had its inception during that summer of 1949 in Glenwood Springs. Among the other guests at the resort were Dorothy Stickney and Howard Lindsay, who had been touted on the place by Ethel Merman.

Glenwood Springs, with its eye-filling vistas of the vaulting Rockies, proved in ideal refuge from the Broadway hurly-burly for the Lindsays. One morning Howard was gazing out his hotel window at the scenery when his eyes fell on the impressive figure of Ethel Merman beside the swimming pool. She was clad in yellow shorts, top and bandanna, and her compact, rounded figure seemed to Lindsay the personification of the strong-willed American woman.

"Put her in a show," Lindsay mused. "Make her the most American American you can think of."

That morning Lindsay had been reading in *Time* magazine about Perle Mesta, the down-to-earth hostess of Washington parties who had been appointed by her friend Harry Truman to be ambassador to Luxembourg. The notion seemed delicious: plunking the breezy, no-nonsense Merman into a tradition-heavy European setting. Lindsay immediately telephoned Buck Crouse, who was vacationing at his place in Anasquam, Massachusetts, and sprang the idea. Crouse was ecstatic.

"Hey, Ethel!" Lindsay shouted down to the swimming pool. "How would you like to play Perle Mesta?"

"Who's Perle Mesta?" yelled Ethel.

After learning who Perle Mesta was, Ethel agreed that a show about her ambassadorship might prove sound. "But I don't want to do any more musicals," she insisted. "I want a good solid dramatic role."

The creator of the leading role in *Life with Father*, Lindsay was a fine actor, and he exerted all his powers of persuasion on Ethel. The ambassadorial role would indeed give her an acting challenge. She would be able to escape the frills and bows and buckskin and wear couturier gowns.

"Well, maybe two or three songs," Ethel conceded.

By July, Lindsay and Crouse had produced a detailed script. They asked Irving Berlin to write the songs, and he was receptive. Following his triumph with *Annie Get Your Gun*, Berlin had provided songs for Robert E. Sherwood's *Miss Liberty*. With Moss Hart directing a musical about the Statue of Liberty, the combination seemed surefire. But *Miss Liberty* was rejected by the critics, and Berlin received the worst reviews of his career.

"I've never been in a tougher spot than I am right now," Berlin told an interviewer. At sixty-two he feared his career was over: "Talent is only the starting point in this business. You've got to keep working at it. And some day I'll reach for it, and it won't be there."

Merman was reunited with Berlin, Lindsay and Crouse, with Leland Hayward as producer. RCA Victor was so dazzled by the prospect of the new show that it provided the entire financing: $225,000.

Ethel forgot about her wish to sing two or three numbers. She did nine. The script called for eight gowns and a negligée, and Leland Hayward chose the high-style designer Mainbocher to create them. Ethel was miffed because Mainbocher barred her mother from the fitting room, but she was thrilled with the gowns. The $11,000 collection included a bouffant dinner gown with sixty yards of red lace and taffeta, a *point d'esprit* pink negligée embroidered with paillettes, a gold lamé party dress and a beige wool going-away dress.

Mainbocher proclaimed that the star was "an angel from heaven to fit" and had "beautiful legs and feet and a trim figure." But as he plotted the conversion of Ethel Merman into a fashion plate, he fretted over her wiry black hair. Ethel had always worn it the same: rising above her forehead in a cascade of tight ring curls, then falling straight to the back of her neck.

"What do you intend to do with your hair?" he asked pointedly.

"Honey, I'm gonna wash it," she replied.

The show took on the title of *Call Me Madam*, and for director Hayward chose the imperious, legendary George Abbott. The role of Cosmo Constantine, the prime minister who wins the ambassador's heart, required an actor with great presence, undisputed charm and a good singing voice. Paul Lukas, the Hungarian who had won the best-actor Academy Award for *Watch on the Rhine* in 1943, had all the physical attributes for the role. But could he sing?

"I don't think so," Lukas replied frankly to Hayward's inquiry. The actor had sung a little tune while appearing with Katharine Hepburn in *Little Women*, and he faintly remembered playing in an operetta as a youth in Budapest. Hayward was undeterred. He asked Lukas to come from Hollywood to New York for an audition with Irving Berlin.

"You have a good barroom baritone," Berlin decreed. Despite Lukas' misgivings, he signed a contract to appear in *Call Me Madam*.

Russell Nype, who had made a good impression in the short-lived *Regina*, the musical version of *The Little Foxes*, was engaged for the role of the ambassador's Ivy League assistant. A Harvard graduate with a clear, sweet voice, he seemed a natural. But his long hair didn't seem right to Hayward. "Get a crew cut," he told the actor. Hayward also noticed that Nype had trouble seeing anything more than six feet distant. "Wear your glasses," said the producer. The crew cut and horn-rimmed glasses became Nype's trademark.

George Abbott discovered Galina Talva at a Manhattan party.

A petite blonde with a mezzo-soprano voice, born in the Bronx to White Russian parents, she seemed ideal as the princess with whom Nype falls in love.

On the morning of August 14, 1950, the principal figures of *Call Me Madam* assembled on the bare stage of the Golden Theater. Paul Lukas bowed to Ethel Merman and kissed her hand. Ethel smiled, stuck a pencil in her hair and a stick of gum in her mouth. From the darkness beyond the orchestra pit came the shrill blast of a policeman's whistle.

"We'll just read through the first act," commanded the dry voice of George Abbott. "No singing, dancing or acting this time."

From opening day no one doubted that Mister Abbott was in total charge. Only once was his authority questioned. One morning when neither Lindsay nor Crouse was present, Abbott changed a few lines of dialogue. It was a natural thing to expect from a man who had been a playwright for thirty years. And so the actors repeated his new lines after Lindsay and Crouse returned.

"Well," Lindsay bristled in his sternest Father Day tones, "I hope we still have the same title!"

"The company is dismissed," Abbott announced. He invited the playwrights into the lobby and explained that his intentions were pure, that he needed a free hand. There must be no argument in front of the actors, he declared. All agreed.

Rehearsals proceeded without contention, but with the customary travails of a Broadway musical in progress. Jerome Robbins began his choreography with an elaborate number of wild mountain men dancing in the village. It was eventually discarded. Lukas continued to fret over his musical inadequacies. His concern reached a peak one night when only he, Irving Berlin, Ethel Merman and a rehearsal pianist were on the stage of the Golden.

Lukas listened as Berlin coached Ethel in a song. Hearing the overpowering Merman voice, the Hungarian cracked.

"In fairness to the company I should resign," Lukas announced. "You should get someone who can do justice to your songs."

"Relax, Paul," Berlin said calmly. "Let me show you how to

do it." With his own high-pitched voice and the aid of the pianist, Berlin led Lukas through "Marrying for Love," phrase by phrase. Tentatively at first, Lukas followed the instructions, imitating the songwriter's delivery, his gestures, his feet movements. By the end, Lukas was performing with the self-assurance of a Metropolitan Opera star. "Wonderful!" Berlin exclaimed. "Now, let's do it again."

Jotting down Abbott's instructions in shorthand, Ethel maintained a businesslike calm throughout the hurly-burly of rehearsals. She was not even fazed when she sprained her thumb in a fall. She put ice on the thumb, wrapped it in a handkerchief and continued rehearsing. She paused only when a doctor arrived to wrap her thumb and wrist in bandages.

By the second week, Ethel knew all her lines, although she continued seeking direction and advice from the director and the authors. A *Collier's* reporter, James Poling, was surprised that she did not fulfill the Broadway rumors that she "goes about backstage equipped with a bullwhip."

She explained: "So far as I know, I only blow my top when someone hurts the show. Up there, I'm a working girl, just as much as I ever was in the old days when I pounded a typewriter from nine to five. If someone fluffs a cue, comes on drunk or misses an entrance while I'm up there beating my brains out—sure, I'll blow. And if I'm shredding my larynx over a song and there's horseplay in the ensemble or if a guy in the orchestra pit is rustling a *Daily Racing Form*, I'll damn well do something about it. I'm up there to work. It's my profession, and I expect everyone else to be professional."

Lindsay and Crouse had decided to insert a notice in the *Call Me Madam* program: "Neither the character of Mrs. Sally Adams nor Miss Ethel Merman resembles any person alive or dead." But, of course, everyone knew that Mrs. Sally Adams was no one other than Perle Mesta, and for a time the show's creators were worried about how she would react to a slightly satirical view of her accomplishments. The publicity-loving Oklahoma millionairess quickly relieved their concern.

During the early stages of *Call Me Madam*, Lindsay and Crouse had written Mrs. Mesta, asking if she objected to being portrayed in a musical. Not at all, she replied. Learning that Dorothy and Howard Lindsay were planning a tour of Europe, she invited them to stay at the American Embassy in Luxembourg. Lindsay declined, since he didn't feel right about satirizing someone whose hospitality he had accepted. But he and his wife visited the Embassy, and he observed how diplomacy was conducted.

A summit meeting of Ethel Merman and Perle Mesta was held in the summer of 1950. It was arranged by columnist Leonard Lyons, who had meticulously selected the guests for this historic dinner meeting, and included Berlin, Lindsay, Crouse, Ray Bolger and Ezio Pinza. Mrs. Mesta would come with Margaret Truman, daughter of the man who had appointed her. Ethel would be accompanied by Bob Levitt.

The guests gathered in Lyons' apartment—except the Levitts. Ethel wouldn't leave home because Bobby was sick and she had to instruct a new nurse. Finally Ethel arrived as the other guests were finishing dessert.

"Say, Perle," she said, "have you ever had the measles?"

Ethel and Perle became immediate friends. Later in the evening, Mrs. Mesta, who had been an amateur singer all her life, was asked if she would sing. She would—if Irving Berlin would accompany her. He sat down at the piano and played his "Always" for Mrs. Mesta's contralto.

"Get a load of that Mesta," Ethel muttered to Margaret Truman. "If Perle's going into my racket, I may ask your dad for a diplomatic job."

Ethel and Perle sat in a corner and chatted about the stage portrayal. What about earrings?

"Ethel, I have short earrings like the ones you're wearing," Perle said. "Maybe I should wear them from now on."

"Oh, no, Perle," Ethel replied. "I have long earrings like yours, and I'll wear them in the show."

"I've got a better idea: When I get to Europe, I'll have my Paris jeweler design a set of black-pearl earrings for you to wear in the show."

"Okay. And we'll put a notice in the program: costumes by Brooks, shoes by La Ray, jewelry by Mesta."

Call Me Madam did not come together as smoothly as had

Annie Get Your Gun. The tryout audience in New Haven clapped and cheered during the first act, then seemed to slip into a coma during the second. Part of the problem was a song that no one in the company liked except Irving Berlin. The songwriter sometimes had fixations about songs he believed would prove hits in the right circumstances; for instance, in 1933 he wrote new lyrics for his 1917 flop, "Smile and Show Your Dimple," and it became the wildly popular "Easter Parade." He had similar faith in "Mr. Monotony." He had written it for a movie, but it had been rejected. Next he tried it unsuccessfully in *Miss Liberty.*

Now he insisted "Mr. Monotony" was meant for *Call Me Madam.* Both Lindsay and Crouse didn't think the song fit. Abbott was doubtful. So was Merman, but she dutifully followed Berlin's wishes. After "Mr. Monotony" failed to ignite the New Haven audience, she announced, "I've gone along, I've cooperated, I've sung the song and it doesn't fit. It's out."

"Free," a flag-waving song in which Sally tries to explain the American way of life to the prime minister, also proved a soggy addition to the second act. Berlin agreed that "Free" had to go.

"We gotta have something to lift the second act," Merman argued.

"You're right," Berlin conceded, and he departed for his hotel room.

While Lindsay, Crouse and Abbott worked on how to cure the malaise of the second act, Ethel retired to her devotions. She found an Episcopal church near her hotel, only to discover that the time for Communion interfered with her next rehearsal. When she explained her situation to the priest, he agreed to give her a private Communion. Afterward she told him, "I'd like to have you come to the show as my guest. You gave me a show, and I'd like to give one to you."

Berlin came forth with a rousing number for the second act, "Something to Dance About." Ethel still lacked a show-stopping number, while Russell Nype was drawing an enormous response with his first-act "It's a Lovely Day Today." The number was so well received that he feared Merman would want him fired from the show. Instead, Merman announced, "I want a number with the kid."

"How about something in counterpoint?" George Abbott suggested. A 1914 Berlin counterpoint, "Play a Simple Melody," had become a 1950 hit record as sung by Bing Crosby and his son Gary.

Berlin once more disappeared into his hotel room. Russel Crouse occupied a room above, and he provided the company with regular reports on Berlin's progress. After two days, Crouse brought the cheerful news: "I think he's got something. I keep hearing the same tune over and over."

One morning Nype received a call in his Taft Hotel room from Irving Berlin. "Come on up, I want to play you a song," Berlin said.

Dressed in pajamas, Berlin sat down at the piano and began playing and singing, "I hear music and there's no one there." Then another melody, "You don't need analyzing." He told Nype, "Now you sing one while I sing the other." The result was a perfect blend.

"Now for heaven's sake, don't tell Ethel that I played the song for you first," said Berlin. "She wouldn't like that at all."

When Ethel heard the number, she crowed, "We'll never get offstage."

The Boston opening was triumphant, the audience demanding encore after encore of "You're Just in Love." But despite nightly evidence that the show was working, Lindsay and Crouse couldn't resist tinkering. During the latter part of the final week in Boston, they proposed adding a few jokes here and there.

"Boys," Ethel announced, "as of right now, I am Miss Birds Eye of 1950. I am frozen. Not a new comma."

Call Me Madam arrived at the Imperial Theater on October 12, 1950, with the greatest advance sale in Broadway history. The critics were rhapsodic about Merman, less so about the book.

"Miss Merman, the illustrious American institution, is one of the joys of the world," announced Richard Watts, Jr. in the *Post*. He termed the volume of her voice, with each syllable unmissed, "indescribably soul-satisfying. In addition, she is a comedienne of rare skill, who combines richness and warmth with her humor."

"Nobody since Alexander the Great has had quite the confidence of Merman," commented William Hawkins in the *World-Telegram.* "You know she's going to deliver."

"It is Miss Merman's show from start to finish," said Robert Garland in the *Journal-American.* "It is her show when she is on the stage. It is her show when she is off. It is her show when Paul Lukas is being charming. It is her show when Russell Nype is being good."

"It is the terrific Ethel who has to hit the homers after her associates have walked or singled," remarked Robert Coleman in the *Daily Mirror.* "And she never lets the team down. . . . She is nothing less than magnificent."

"Her Sally Adams vitalizes a so-so plot immeasurably," declared Howard Barnes in the *Herald Tribune.*

"Miss Merman is her old great self, singing like a boat whistle and leering like a female Valentino, except when that confounded Graustarkian plot slows her down," said John Chapman in the *Daily News.*

Complaints about the weakness of the show's book went unheeded. *Call Me Madam* settled in at the Imperial Theater for another long run.

Ethel herself had never been in doubt. George Abbott had worried about her gold and silver lamé court gown with nine-foot train which she said needed "as much handling as the Super-Chief." During rehearsals Ethel had used a white muslin replica, which became smudged with dirt from the stage floor.

"What's going to happen to your lovely dress once we open?" Abbott asked.

"Aw, that's all right," she replied confidently. "For the first five years of the run I'll wear a lining in it."

The success of *Call Me Madam* stimulated another flood of paeans to the phenomenon known as Ethel Merman. Magazine and newspaper reporters questioned experts of all kinds in their efforts to explain her twenty-year hold on Broadway audiences.

Said Irving Berlin: "Give her a song and she'll make it sound good. Give her a good song and she'll make it sound great. And you'd better write her a good lyric, because when she sings the words, the guy in the last row of the balcony can hear every syllable."

Berlin added, "To me, her great quality as a singer is her genius at socking the whole meaning across. She's a lyric writer's dream; nobody in show business can project the lyric of a song like Ethel. She times a lyric as carefully and brilliantly as a comedian timing a gag. She sings with feeling for the audience and will space a passage when she gets a laugh.

"Her enunciation is perfect. Clear. Sharp. Good. As a technician, she does it with her throat. She's got that rich, creamy something in her throat. She could sing a song deadpan and still sock it over. She is one of the few who can do a double-entendre lyric in good taste. You never have to worry about Merman with a suggestive lyric—she has a way of throwing it away so it brings a nice laugh and still it isn't offensive.

"Give her a comedy song that isn't funny or a rhyme that's bad or a line that's mediocre, and it will stand out like a sore thumb. The audience can always hear what she's singing. Nobody ever has to lean over and ask their neighbor what she said.

"I love to write songs for Ethel. I guess it's a little like a dress designer getting an extra kick when he dreams up a gown for a beautiful woman with a perfect figure."

Cole Porter commented that he enjoyed watching Merman perform during various periods of a show's run: "It was like watching a train hurtle down the tracks, undeviating, the whole performance radiating zest and spontaneity, and yet you knew that it was exactly the same yesterday, and would be the same the day after."

Brooks Atkinson offered this analysis of the Merman style: "She has an overwhelming personality, an oval face, popping eyes, and an alert style of walking and standing. Her sense of enjoyment in what she is doing lights up the stage like an electric sign.

"As a singer, she is unique. She has a razzle-dazzle voice, a perfect sense of timing, and impeccable diction. No one else could have so completely mastered the explosive lyrics of 'You're the Top.' After listening to her whirling performance in one show, a member of the audience remarked, 'She can hold a note longer than the Chase Manhattan Bank.'

"Since she is a natural, she doesn't need to be artful or clever. When she appears in a show, she takes possession of everything in sight—not only the songs but the libretto and the production and the audience. Miss Merman cleans up whenever she sets her vocal cords to vibrating."

While Ethel Merman was again being crowned the Queen of Broadway, feature writers also lavished attention on Russell Nype. "A Star Is Born" heralded a New York daily in a three-column headline. "That caused a bit of ice on Ethel's part," Nype recalls. The young actor was careful to defer to the star at all times. While she sang their duet directly to the audience, he directed his focus at her, even during the applause.

"Goddammit, you'd better start looking at the audience," she told him after a few months of the run. "People are writing me letters: 'You dirty bitch, you're not letting that boy take any of the credit!' "

Nype learned to accustom himself to the Merman style: "She was a bit of an automaton on stage. Once she learned the role, she never changed. She didn't 'walk through' a performance, but she did it the same every night. After one of her big numbers, she would tell me, 'I was thinking of my laundry list.'

"I was entirely different; I loved the audience reaction. 'Who cares about the audience,' she said. 'It's a job, that's all. A job.' "

Thus, the Merman paradox. She communicated to Broadway audiences as did no other star. They adored her, reveled in her brassiness, gloried in that voice that seemed to be the sound of Manhattan. Yet she remained untouched by the adoration. The approval of the crowd wasn't needed to sustain her ego. She was what she was: Merman. They could take it or leave it.

11.

Hollywood and Marriage Again

"I know Ethel gets terribly cozy with the audience," one of her colleagues told Wolcott Gibbs, "but you can't help feeling that she's never been introduced to the cast."

The observation was overstated but apt. Ethel Merman's rapport with audiences was legendary. Directors soon learned why: It had to do with the Merman policy about positioning on the stage. A director once placed the chorus at the footlights during a Merman number. She vetoed that, saying, "Nobody gets between Merman and the audience."

According to legend, Bob Hope once sprawled on the stage and made faces at Merman during one of her songs in *Red, Hot and Blue!* The story goes that Ethel bawled to the stage manager: "If that sonofabitch does that again, I swear to God I'm going to sit right down on top of him!" (If it happened, Hope doesn't remember it.)

One of Ethel's co-workers told a *New York Times* reporter: "Ethel's natural fault, if it is a fault, is the feeling that she is infallible. It's just that that makes her so good, but it also has some repercussions that can be irritating.

"When a show gets set, she doesn't want to rehearse anymore. Maybe she's right. Look how long *Annie* ran. If she gains weight and the costumes are tight, then it's the costumes that have shrunk. She won't try something new if she's convinced it isn't right for her, but you've got to admit she's right 90 percent of the time."

During the second year of *Call Me Madam*, Paul Lukas committed the unpardonable sin: He upstaged Ethel Merman.

Lukas had never overcome his discomfort at being cast in a singing role. Whether by accident, because of boredom or simple devilishness, he retreated upstage during a key scene, forcing Ethel to turn her back on the audience. She protested vigorously to the stage manager, but the offense was repeated.

Ethel realized she couldn't force the firing of Oscar winner Paul Lukas, as she had with Paula Laurence. So she decided on another tactic: She would ignore him.

George Abbott recalled: "Night after night I would have to go backstage and give her notes telling her that she ought to look at her leading man during love scenes. She would agree blandly and would look at him for a couple of performances, but when I returned the next week I'd find her standing there talking to the audience and leaving Lukas out on a limb by himself. The audience didn't seem to mind, however; only the theater-wise knew the difference."

Toward the end of the second year, Lukas had an offer to appear in *Flight into Egypt*, and he seized it as an escape from his miserable situation. He gave notice, and Leland Hayward searched for a replacement. He sent for Richard Eastham, a tall, handsome, strong-voiced actor who had toured in *South Pacific*.

Though reluctant to play yet another role as a middle-aged foreigner, Eastham appeared for an audition before George Abbott, Jerome Robbins and Howard Lindsay. The actor noticed a shadowy figure at the back of the house. It was unquestionably Ethel Merman. Halfway through the reading, Abbott asked Eastham: "When can you start in the show?"

Eastham began rehearsals with Elaine Stritch, the understudy for the role of Sally Adams. One day the stage manager told him: "Miss Merman is coming in today. There are a few things you should know about working with her."

"Yes, I've heard about her," Eastham said. "Don't upstage

her. Always stand downstage and direct the lines to her upstage. Right?"

Ethel was pleased with her new leading man, and the tension that had surrounded the *Call Me Madam* company for so long began to dissipate. Richard Eastham felt emboldened to suggest a change in stage directions.

During the scene in which he presents Sally Adams to the prime minister, four actors stand abreast. Eastham suggested to the stage manager: "Wouldn't it be better if I just stepped back, since I have to make my exit anyway?"

The word came back from Miss Merman: "Of course—that makes sense." At the next performance, Eastham introduced Sally Adams, then stepped back. The Merman instinct was too strong; she also stepped back to avoid being upstaged.

"Oh, shit! I did it, didn't I?" she muttered to Eastham between her teeth. Only by supreme concentration was she able to avoid retreating at subsequent performances.

Ethel allowed nothing to interfere with the smooth flow of the performance. Once she grabbed an actor by the lapels when they exited into the wings. "I smell liquor on you!" she exclaimed. "Who do you think you are, trying to ruin this show? I work hard, and you damn well better do the same. No more drinking!"

A young actress in the *Call Me Madam* cast happened to be a protégée of Richard Rodgers. Whether by inexperience or overconfidence because of her sponsor, the actress became sloppy in her stage deportment. During a performance she was late for her cue, leaving Ethel standing alone on the stage.

"Goddammit, I want that bitch fired!" Ethel stormed afterward. "How dare she leave me out there with egg on my face?"

The stage manager cleared his throat and remarked, "You know, Miss Merman, that Richard Rodgers is very much interested in the girl's career."

"I don't give a damn. She's lousing up the show. If she's late one more time, out she goes!"

Ethel had no fear of Rodgers, though he and Oscar Hammerstein were the most powerful figures in musical comedy.

She remained angry at Rodgers for trying to force her to return from a vacation when the box office for *Annie Get Your Gun* started sagging. The publicity had made it appear that Merman was the villain in threatening the jobs of the other members of the *Annie* company.

The young actress did it again—left Ethel waiting on stage. "That's it! Out! Out!" Ethel exploded. "She goes!"

The stage manager warily bore her ultimatum to Richard Rodgers. "Tell that bitch to go to hell," Rodgers said.

Ethel's instructions to the stage manager: "You tell Richard Rodgers to go fuck himself. That dame is fired."

Ethel Merman and Richard Rodgers did not talk to each other for many years thereafter. Their paths crossed one night in Sardi's late in both their careers.

"Let's bury the hatchet, Ethel," Rodgers suggested.

"It's okay with me," she replied. As long as Rodgers made the overture, she acquiesced. But never would she take the first step to end a feud. That was not the Merman code.

Ethel's bad humor during much of the run of *Call Me Madam* stemmed from the misery of her foundering marriage to Bob Levitt. His own life, so full of hope and promise when the war ended, had turned to ashes. He had failed in his work at the Hearst Corporation and was fired. His only achievement, it seemed, was marrying Ethel Merman. He drank more heavily and stayed away from home often. When he returned, there were dreadful scenes with Ethel.

Both of them were concerned over how their fights would affect the children. Ethel sought counseling from her minister at St. Bartholomew's Church. She unburdened herself to friends. Finally the situation became intolerable, and she ordered Bob out of the house. The marriage was over.

In later years she idealized the marriage to Bob Levitt. "He was the only guy I ever deeply loved," she wrote in her autobiography. Friends who witnessed the turmoil of the late years of their marriage considered that sentimental exaggeration. "Bob

Levitt was never a match for Ethel," said one of them. "She steamrollered him."

The separation liberated Ethel socially. The Duke and Duchess of Windsor adored *Call Me Madam,* and they drew Ethel and Russell Nype into their social circle. The Duchess showed extraordinary interest in Nype while Ethel found an admiring escort in Charles Cushing, a millionaire investment banker. Ethel began to spend many weekends in the country at the mansions of the very rich. Her new friends were delighted with Ethel, who adopted none of their airs. She never lost her Astoria earthiness.

Another new friend was General Dwight Eisenhower. After the war Ike and Mamie had attended *Annie Get Your Gun,* and Ike told Ethel it was the first Broadway show he'd seen in thirty years. The Eisenhowers also came to *Call Me Madam* while Ike was president of Columbia University, and he was visibly pleased with the "They Like Ike" number. Irving Berlin, an Eisenhower fan, had designed the song for political purposes, and after Eisenhower declared for the presidency in 1952, "I Like Ike" became the Republican rallying song. Ethel Merman, ever the fervent Republican, sang it at the party's national convention in San Francisco.

On October 20, 1951, Ethel's third husband entered her life. The occasion: a supper party at L'Aiglon to celebrate the first anniversary of *Call Me Madam.* Leland Hayward invited celebrities, socialites and press to a gala party to create renewed publicity for the hit show. Among the guests was Robert Foreman Six, a mountainous, smooth-talking man from Colorado. Ethel met him during her rounds of the restaurant tables. She learned that he was president of Continental Airlines and maintained headquarters in Denver but was a frequent visitor to New York.

Bob Six's date somehow drifted elsewhere, and he and Ethel went out for a hamburger after the L'Aiglon party. They talked until dawn, and Ethel learned a great deal about the forceful, ruggedly handsome man from the West.

He was forty-four years old, a year older than Ethel. He had been born in Stockton, California, the son of a surgeon. To his father's dismay, young Bob had little interest in education and he left high school in his second year to become a rural bill collector for Pacific Gas and Electric. At the very beginning of his business career, he demonstrated a cool directness that was to mark his later years as a top executive. When farmers showed an unwillingness to pay their electric bills, the young man climbed the power poles and snipped their lines.

Like many young Americans, Six was inspired by Charles Lindbergh's 1927 flight across the Atlantic Ocean. He was fired by Pacific Gas and Electric when his boss discovered the bill collector was learning to fly on company time.

Six drifted around the world for a few years, flying for a Chinese airline from Shanghai to Chungking, moving on to Spain and France. He returned to San Francisco to become a district circulation manager for the *Chronicle*, and in 1934 he married a divorcée, Henrietta Earhart Ruggles, daughter of a pharmaceutical millionaire. Six branched out as dealer for Beechcraft airplanes in northern California.

In 1937, Bob Six found an opportunity of great promise. The Southwest Division of Varney Speed Lines needed money. It was a tiny operation with three four-passenger, single-engine planes, fifteen employees and a mail route from Pueblo, Colorado, to El Paso, Texas.

"It's small now, but it has a great potential," Six reasoned with his father-in-law, chairman of Charles Pfizer and Company. Charles Earhart agreed to lend Six $90,000 to buy a 40 percent interest in the airline.

Bob Six started moving his new company with a swiftness of decision that characterized his business career. He changed the name to Continental Airlines and wangled a route to Denver. As Continental's president, Six built the company into a solid regional airline, then after World War II began expanding its horizons. By 1955, Continental was flying to Chicago, Kansas City and Los Angeles. Short on cash, Six convinced aircraft manufacturers to sell him planes with nothing down, payment later. His methods and outspokenness angered executives of larger airlines, especially Pan American, which he disparaged as "the blue meatball."

Continental employees became familiar with the six-foot-four, 210-pound figure of their boss. During a flight he would turn up all over the plane, counting pillows, tasting food, checking china for chips. He was a devotee of the vigorous life and once broke his tailbone while playing musical chairs on horseback. His associates also noted an affinity for show business. Six organized and was a member of a company fast-draw team that challenged other teams throughout the West.

"By the way," Bob Six told Ethel Merman, "I'm separated from my wife."

"Whaddaya know?" she replied. "I'm separated from my husband."

Ethel invited Six to lunch at her apartment before he departed for Denver. He telephoned her from wherever he traveled, and during his monthly visits to New York escorted her to the restaurants and night clubs Ethel loved but saw little of during her marriage to Bob Levitt. Walter Winchell reported: "Eth Merm's current dinner escort is Continental Airlines' biggie, Bob Six. Sech muscles!"

All this attention from Bob Six flattered Ethel, and she enjoyed having columnists report that she was being wined and dined by the dynamic airlines boss. When he wasn't in town, she continued dating Charles Cushing and others, but she admitted to friends that Bob Six was a very persuasive man.

Ever since *Red, Hot and Blue!* Merman had refused to take a show on the road. After a year or two in one role—three years as Annie Oakley—she had no desire to repeat it in the "sticks." Especially after her children were born, Ethel was adamant about not leaving them for a tour. But she couldn't resist opening the national tour of *Call Me Madam* in Washington, D.C., where the show was certain to attract a whirl of publicity.

The Washington opening brought out most of the capital's famous names—with the exception of President Truman, who was amused neither by Ethel's "Hello, Harry" speeches nor by the show's hymn to Dwight Eisenhower, now campaigning for the presidency as a Republican. Ike's rival, Robert A. Taft, was in the National Theater audience and was ruffled by the line that he "has a mind like a steel trap that closed twenty years ago and hasn't opened since." On the other hand, Secretary of State Dean Acheson was pleased with his portrayal and told Leland Hayward: "If you need a replacement, I think I'll be available soon."

The opening night audience cheered Merman and the show, and afterward the distinguished guests were invited to a supper dance in her honor hosted by—Bob Six. Ethel basked in the adoration of the biggest names in politics, and she gave them an impromptu concert in the early morning hours. The party, along with Bob Six's constant attention, convinced her that he would be her next husband.

In June of 1952, Merman relinquished the role of Sally Adams to Elaine Stritch and flew to Mexico for the divorce from Levitt. She went first to Mexico City, where she told reporters the divorce would be sought on grounds of incompatibility.

"It's all amicable," Ethel remarked. "I'm not asking alimony, and I already have custody of our two children."

She had planned to obtain the divorce in Cuernavaca, a fashionable place for visiting celebrities to shed their mates. But a reform government was doing away with quickie marriages, and Ethel flew to Juarez. A Mexican judge granted the divorce a half hour after the suit was filed by Paul O'Dwyer, brother of the American ambassador to Mexico, William O'Dwyer. When Bob Six appeared in Juarez, reporters sensed Ethel Merman was going to marry a third time.

"We're just good friends, there's nothing like a romance going right now," Ethel lied to the press on her return to New York. "It was all a mistake. Mr. Six flew from Denver to Juarez to see a bullfight, not me."

Ethel and Bob Levitt remained on good terms, and he was an unswervingly attentive and loving father to Little Ethel and Bobby. In later years Ethel regretted that she had obtained the fast divorce and succumbed to the relentless persuasion of Bob

Six. Perhaps, she sighed with an excess of sentiment, she and Bob Levitt might have resumed their marriage.

Bob Levitt's life seemed to enter a downward spiral after his divorce from Ethel. He had a brief, disastrous marriage, and he moved from Screen Gems to California National Productions, but seemed unhappy in the world of business. In October of 1957, he married again, and Ethel gave permission for their two children to attend the wedding.

Three months later, Little Ethel and Bobby visited their father and his bride for a weekend at his house in East Hampton. "You go back to town, and I'll join you this evening," he told the others on Sunday afternoon.

After they had gone, Levitt sat down at his desk and wrote a letter beginning "To whom it may concern." In straightforward language he said he had taken an overdose of barbiturates. He gave instructions about the disposition of his property. The jewelry would go to Ethel.

Folding up his topcoat as a pillow, he lay down on the den couch. That's how he was found the next day, as if in a deep, restful sleep.

It was the first great tragedy of Ethel's life, and she was filled with sadness and remorse. Now she remembered only the happy times with Bob, not the late years when his bitterness poisoned their marriage. He had willed his jewelry to Ethel, and she had his cuff links and studs made into a bracelet that she wore. And she was never without the gold Omega watch that bore his initials.

At last there was a movie for Merman.

One of Ethel's constant irritations over the years had been the way Hollywood ignored her when casting movies from her hit musicals. Except for *Anything Goes*, the roles she had created had always been awarded to other actresses: Kitty Kelly in *Girl Crazy;* Lillian Roth in *Take a Chance;* Lucille Ball in *Du Barry Was a Lady;* Ann Sothern in *Panama Hattie;* Betty Hutton (replacing Judy Garland) in *Annie Get Your Gun.*

Darryl Zanuck bought the rights to *Call Me Madam* for 20th

Century–Fox, and Irving Berlin persuaded his good friend that Merman was the only star who could play Sally Adams in the movie. Merman had failed as a romantic star in films, but there could be no objection to her as a middle-aged woman in a dynamic role. Zanuck agreed. He also agreed to cast Merman in a second film, another compilation of Irving Berlin hits.

This time Ethel came to Hollywood in style. She was greeted at the studio by producer Sol Siegel and director Walter Lang and escorted to her dressing room, formerly occupied by Betty Grable and redecorated in lavish style. She met her co-stars, George Sanders, Donald O'Connor and Vera-Ellen. She viewed sketches of her gowns, designed by Irene Sharaff. Publicity chief Harry Brand offered all the facilities of his department.

The studio rented an apartment at the Beverly Hills Hotel for Ethel and provided a nursemaid and a hotel bungalow when Little Ethel and Bobby arrived. A chauffeured limousine was available at all times. "I think I'm going to like the movie racket," Ethel gloated.

Ethel was determined to succeed in her return to films after fifteen years. Many stage stars declined to review their rushes, agreeing with Ethel Barrymore's comment, "I never saw myself on the stage, why should I see myself on the screen?" Merman thought otherwise. She studied every foot of the previous day's scenes. "How else can I tell what's wrong?" she reasoned.

She had total faith in Walter Lang, the low-key, methodical director of Fox's most successful musicals and comedies: *State Fair* (1945 version), *Mother Wore Tights*, *Sitting Pretty*, *Cheaper by the Dozen*, *With a Song in My Heart*. "If Walter Lang asked me to sing standing on my head, I'd do it," Ethel told Hedda Hopper.

Donald O'Connor recalls Lang's methodical technique: "Ethel and George Sanders were doing a scene together, and they seemed to be sparking to each other. All of a sudden, Walter called 'Cut!' The second shot didn't seem as good as the first one, and I asked Walter why he had cut while the scene was going beautifully. He told me: 'Oh, I forgot my lines. You see, I memorize all the lines of every scene. I got lost and I had to cut.' When I told this to Ethel, she said, 'I sure hope he doesn't forget how to direct!' "

O'Connor also learned the peril of recording a duet with Ethel Merman: "I had talked to the music director, Alfred Newman, about recording 'You're Just in Love' with the full orchestra instead of singing in an isolation booth. I felt the sound was much better that way. I tried it with the orchestra, and Al agreed that it sounded good. Then Merman came in.

"We started singing 'I hear music . . .' She was six feet away and my eardrums were vibrating. We finally recorded the song with me in an isolation booth and her in the studio with the orchestra. When we filmed the song to the playback, I wore ear plugs."

Robert E. Sherwood, the playwright, was working on a Fox script during the filming of *Call Me Madam.* He telephoned Ethel: "My office is about three blocks away from your rehearsal hall, and I want you to know that you're coming in just fine."

Walter Lang allowed Ethel to be her own strong, assertive self in scenes, and he and cinematographer Leon Shamroy took special care to avoid unflattering camera angles. Lang also was on the alert for humdrum readings of lines Ethel had repeated more than six hundred times on the stage.

One of the musical's biggest laughs came when Sally Adams makes a deep curtsy while meeting royalty, then falls on her behind. Lang rehearsed the scene with only the curtsy. When Ethel did her pratfall during the take, the cast provided the spontaneous reaction that Lang was seeking.

To friends who visited her on the set of *Call Me Madam,* Ethel said, "You gotta meet my new beau, Bob Six. He's a real man's man." Six made frequent visits to Los Angeles to see Ethel, and the Hollywood columnists reported that a marriage seemed imminent.

Ethel remained in Hollywood after the filming of *Call Me Madam* to see the final assembly of the film. She emerged from the projection room with cautious optimism. She believed in her heart that her return to the screen was a triumph, but she was careful not to build her hopes up too high. Hollywood had betrayed her too many times.

As the premiere of *Call Me Madam* approached, Six stepped up his campaign to convince Ethel to marry him. In March of 1953, they were in El Centro, California at the ranch of Paul O'Dwyer, the attorney who had arranged Ethel's Mexican divorce from Bob Levitt.

"Calexico is just across the border," said O'Dwyer. "You could drive over there, get married and nobody will know about it."

"Why don't we?" said Six. Ethel agreed. She also followed his wishes to keep the wedding quiet, though at the time she didn't understand his reasons.

They were married March 9, 1953, and three days later the newlyweds attended the premiere of *Call Me Madam* in Miami. Ethel sidestepped reporters' questions about a marriage to Bob Six. Not until June 6 was the marriage made public. A Denver reporter learned that Six was negotiating to buy an estate in Cherry Hills Village near Denver. Was he planning it as a honeymoon home with Ethel Merman? Six at first denied the suggestion, then his office confirmed it.

"Yes, it's true," Ethel told the press in New York. "Bob Six and I are married. I'm going to make *There's No Business Like Show Business* in Hollywood this summer, then Colorado will be my home. It's bye-bye Broadway."

12.

Colorado Interlude

"Television? What the hell do I know about television?"

Ethel Merman was responding to a proposal in early 1953 by Leland Hayward. The producer had been commissioned by the Ford Motor Company to stage a two-hour television spectacular to salute Ford's fiftieth anniversary. Hayward wanted Ethel to join the all-star cast.

She argued that television would be too constricting for her freewheeling style. Hayward countered that she could move as much as she wanted and the camera would follow her.

Ethel remained skeptical, then Hayward, one of the most adroit persuaders in show business, played his trump card: "You'll be in total control, Ethel. If you want something, you get it. If you don't like something, out it goes. That's the way it will be."

"Well, if you put it that way, okay, I'll do it," Ethel said.

"Oh, by the way," Hayward added, "I've got an idea for the show. How about you and Mary Martin singing a duet?"

"Hmm, not a bad idea. If it's okay with Mary, it's okay with me."

The Broadway crowd could scarcely believe the news that Ethel Merman and Mary Martin were scheduled to sing a duet on television. It was thought Merman resented Martin for threatening her position as grande dame of the Broadway musical. Fireworks were predicted.

Hayward assigned Jerome Robbins to stage, and possibly mediate, the duet. Robbins reasoned that with two such massive talents on stage, nothing else was needed, except a couple of swivel stools on which the singers could sit.

Merman and Martin plunged into the production with the zest of schoolgirls planning a May Day musical. Mary remembered a trick she learned while singing in the Hollywood Roosevelt Hotel bar as an unknown. A zany pianist would play "Stormy Weather" while she was singing "Tea for Two."

"It sounds crazy," Mary remarked, "but somehow the counterpoint works." Martin and Merman singing two different songs at the same time proved surprisingly effective.

"How about singing a bunch of 'I' songs?" Ethel suggested. "You know, like 'I've Got You Under My Skin,' 'I Cried for You,' 'I'm Always Chasing Rainbows,' 'I Love a Parade.' "

They rehearsed all day and into the night, making minute changes to perfect the timing. "Don't worry, I'll type up all the changes and have copies for everybody in the morning," Ethel said.

Ethel felt comfortable because the orchestra was conducted by Jay Blackton, who had led the pit orchestra for *Annie Get Your Gun* and *Call Me Madam.* Mary was reassured because the pianist was her favorite accompanist, Johnny Lesko.

"The Ford Fiftieth Anniversary Show" was scheduled to be broadcast live on both the CBS and NBC networks on June 15, 1953. As the show date neared, both Merman and Martin felt confident they could master the split-second cues and changes of lyrics. Dress rehearsal was held in the massive Center Theater at Rockefeller Center before an invited audience a few hours before the actual broadcast.

Shortly before the dress rehearsal, Hayward brought the bad news to Ethel and Mary: neither Blackton nor Lesko could work on the show. They didn't belong to the television union.

"We can't do the show without them," Mary wailed.

"It'll be a disaster," Ethel predicted. She was right. The unfamiliar conductor and pianist couldn't duplicate the precise timing of the rehearsals. Cues were missed, and the counterpoint sounded like two radios playing at the same time.

The impressive talent behind *Call Me Madam* (from left): Raoul Pène DuBois, Leland Hayward, Howard Lindsay, George Abbott, Russel Crouse, Merman, Irving Berlin, Paul Lukas

Ethel went glamorous with Mainbocher designs in *Call Me Madam*

Singing "You're Just in Love" with Donald O'Connor in the film *Call Me Madam*

With Ethel, Jr., ten, and Bobby, seven, at New York event in 1953 (AP/Wide World Photos)

Marilyn Monroe was missing when the cas *There's No Business Like Show Business* posed for this shot: O'Connor, Merman, D Dailey, Mitzi Gaynor, Johnny Ray

In the script Ethel disapproved of son Donald's romance with Marilyn

all Her Madam Now" read the headlines
en Ethel announced her marriage to airline
s Robert Six in 1953 (AP/Wide World Photos)

Ethel and Fernando Lamas force smiles on opening night of *Happy Hunting* (AP/Wide World Photos)

Ethel appears with her co-star from *Red, Hot and Blue!* in a Bob Hope television special

A sad parting with Jack Klugman in *Gyp*

As Mama Rose with Uncle Jocko (Mort Marshall), Baby Louise (Karen Moore) and Baby June (Jacqueline Mayo)

Madam Merman and girls, *The Art of Love*

Wedding day for Ethel and Ernie, with daughters Ethel Geary, twenty-one, and Nancy Borgnine, twelve (AP/Wide World Photos)

The official Merman photograph

dward and Agnes Zimmermann with
aughter at the opening of *Hello, Dolly!* in
970 (AP/Wide World Photos)

shots: with opera singer Sherrill Milnes
oof-garden party; with Anthony Newley
airport after a Monte Carlo gala (Robert
ner)

Back on Broadway—together! Mary Mar
and Ethel Merman

One of the last photographs (Max Showalte

The two singers retired in terror to their dressing rooms. In three hours they would face millions of Americans and sound like amateurs. Mary and her manager-husband Richard Halliday wanted to cancel the number. Ethel was resigned to making the best of a bad situation, even though, she said, her contract gave her final approval.

"What?" said Mary. Her contract read the same. They discovered that Hayward had also pulled the same line: Wouldn't it be fun to do a duet—with your final approval, of course. The two women laughed at their own gullibility and agreed to try to make it through the duet. Shortly before curtain time, they were relieved to learn that Blackton and Lesko had been returned to their positions through special payments to the union.

In one evening Ethel Merman and Mary Martin played to more people than they could face on stage throughout their lifetimes. Although Marian Anderson, Eddie Fisher, Rudy Vallee, Kukla, Fran and Ollie, Edward R. Murrow and others appeared on the show, all the reviews focused on the Merman-Martin duet. "Terrific! Terrific" began the *New York Times* review. A Decca album of the duet sold 100,000 copies in the first ten days.

"The Ford Fiftieth Anniversary Show" attracted a phenomenal sixty million viewers and paved the way for Sylvester (Pat) Weaver's 1954 launching of the television spectacular—known today as a special. And ever afterward musical performers would do their work on stools.

When I interviewed Ethel Merman in December of 1953, she claimed to be pleased with her new life.

"I love Denver," she said with customary emphasis. "I don't think I've ever been happier in my life. The air is simply wonderful; it's the mile-high city, you know. I was in New York last week, and oh, it was terrible. The 'smaze' or 'smog' or whatever you call it. You can hardly breathe. Yes, I miss the theater a little, but happiness is more important. My kids, Ethel and Bobby, love Denver. They're going to public schools now, instead of the private schools they went to in New York. Ethel likes that much better, because she's in a school with boys now."

No more Broadway shows, she vowed. Leland Hayward had tried to entice her with a show based on the book *The Last Resorts*. She'd have the same crew from *Call Me Madam*—Howard Lindsay and Russel Crouse to write the book, Irving Berlin for the songs. Berlin even played a couple of the proposed songs when she visited New York.

"Sorry, boys," she replied, "my family is more important."

Ethel was in Hollywood for a television show with her old pal Jimmy Durante, and she recalled her heartbreak over dropping out of her appearance with Clayton, Jackson and Durante in 1929 because of her tonsillectomy.

Part of Ethel's buoyance was due to the unqualified success of the movie *Call Me Madam,* with critics as well as the public. She believed that at long last she had made her breakthrough on the screen, and she placed an almost mystical faith in Walter Lang.

"I was never happy with the things I did in pictures before," she told me. "They always said I was too brassy and too loud for movies. I had to hold myself back, and I'm not that kind of a girl. The last picture I did was *Alexander's Ragtime Band* in a featured role." (She had mercifully forgotten the Ritz Brothers movie.)

"I loved Walter Lang," she continued. "He told me to let myself go. He reasoned that people were expecting the Ethel Merman of the stage, and that's what we should give them."

Lang had been scheduled to direct *There's No Business Like Show Business* the previous summer, but he had suffered a serious illness. A substitute director had been proposed, but Ethel said, "I'll wait for Walter."

Filming of the movie finally began in June. Darryl Zanuck had assembled a sterling cast for the Irving Berlin musical: Ethel Merman, Dan Dailey, Mitzi Gaynor, Donald O'Connor, the new singing sensation Johnny Ray and—Marilyn Monroe. The Fox publicity department poured forth reams of copy, much of it directed toward the studio's new star, Monroe. At the outset

Merman was philosophical. "Hell, *she's* the one we need to sell this picture," she told a friend.

Ethel entered *There's No Business Like Show Business* with gusto, determined it would consolidate her film career. She and Dailey were cast as veteran entertainers with a family of performers—O'Connor, Gaynor and Ray. The principals were invited to a pre-production get-together in the office of the producer, Sol Siegel—Marilyn never arrived—and Ethel regaled her new family with some of her bawdy stories.

"Did you hear about the two maids who were sitting on a porch?" Ethel asked Mitzi Gaynor. "One of them said, 'Do you remember the minuet?' The other one said, 'Hell, I don't even remember the men I fucked.' "

The rapport between Merman and Gaynor was immediate. None was ever established between Merman and Monroe.

Marilyn had been an unwilling recruit to *There's No Business Like Show Business*. She thought the script was shallow and her own role meaningless. She consented to join the production only when Zanuck promised her next film would be *The Seven Year Itch*, directed by Billy Wilder.

It was a difficult period for Marilyn. She had married Joe DiMaggio six months before, and already their relations had become strained. He detested her Hollywood friends, and she had no basis for communicating with his baseball and hunting buddies. The fame that had earlier seemed so alluring to Marilyn now threatened to crush her. She was beset with self-doubt, resulting in chronic tardiness and reliance on her ever-present dramatic coach, Natasha Lytess. Such behavior was not destined to find a sympathizer in the fiercely professional Merman.

Ethel maintained her composure nonetheless. She remained unruffled when Marilyn failed to appear for a group portrait with the other cast principals. The other five stood in their evening clothes and posed smilingly, leaving a gap where Marilyn's portrait would be inserted later.

"The group shot was to be used in the ads," Johnny Ray recalls. "All the stars had equal billing, but Ethel's contract provided that her name come first. One morning the *Hollywood Reporter* ran the photograph in a double-truck ad that listed 'Marilyn Monroe, Dan Dailey, Ethel Merman, etc.' I showed the ad to Ethel and said, 'What do you think of that?' She read it but didn't say a word. I could tell when she was angry. Her eyes became steely and her fists clenched. I don't know what she said to the studio manager, but the billing error was never repeated."

With her domestic situation worsening, Marilyn Monroe became more difficult on the set of *There's No Business Like Show Business.* She refused to wear the clothes designed for her by Miles White and insisted that Bill Travilla design her costumes. She argued repeatedly with the choreographer, Robert Alton, and demanded that Jack Cole stage her "Heat Wave" number. Three times she reported to the studio that she was ill, and the schedule had to be rearranged.

The rumors of trouble in the DiMaggio-Monroe marriage persisted, and Marilyn complained to columnist Sidney Skolsky that they slept apart: "This separate bedroom deal is not in the American tradition. In the pioneer days, did you ever hear of a man and his wife sleeping in separate covered wagons?"

To quell the rumors, DiMaggio agreed to pay a visit to the set. But he refused to have his photograph taken with his wife. Instead, he posed with Ethel Merman. "She's my favorite star," declared Joe as he stood beside the beaming Merman.

The incident worsened Marilyn's conduct on the set. She complained to producer Siegel that Donald O'Connor, her romantic interest in the picture, looked so young that she could be taken for his mother. She objected to playing their scene together shoeless—but with high heels she would have towered over O'Connor. Marilyn ignored Walter Lang and listened only to Natasha Lytess. Johnny Ray once overheard the dramatic coach instruct Marilyn: "In this scene you are a bubble, and you float."

Marilyn's tardiness grew more acute, and Ethel's patience wore thin. "I found a way to keep Ethel cool," says Mitzi Gaynor. "Whenever Marilyn wouldn't come out of her dressing room, I gave Ethel a wink, hinting that something naughty was going on in there. Of course that wasn't true, but if Ethel thought maybe some hanky-panky was going on, she could enjoy the situation."

There's No Business Like Show Business was finally completed with Marilyn working seven days a week to make up for lost time and to release her for *The Seven Year Itch.* Ethel returned to Colorado with the expectation that the film would prove her best work. For the first time on the screen, she had played emotional scenes. She had sung the Berlin repertoire from "Play a Simple Melody" to "A Pretty Girl Is Like a Melody." She had even done a creditable time step in a dance number with Mitzi Gaynor.

Despite the lure of Marilyn Monroe and the stellar cast, *There's No Business Like Show Business* failed to match the success of *Call Me Madam.* Reviewers grumbled that the show-biz family saga was old hat and that the Berlin library, already exploited in *Alexander's Ragtime Band, Blue Skies, Easter Parade* and the recent *White Christmas,* deserved a rest.

In early 1956, the *Saturday Evening Post* presented seven autobiographical articles by Ethel Merman as told to Pete Martin of the magazine's staff. Later that year Doubleday published the articles as a book, *Who Could Ask for Anything More?* The familiar Merman saga was told in breezy, pseudo-tough style, with some aspects of her life glossed over or ignored completely. Al Siegel received cursory treatment, and no mention was made of the romance with Sherman Billingsley. Curiously, Ethel referred to her husbands by their last names only: "When I met Smith, he was an actor's agent . . ."; "Levitt and I had a strict policy about not letting the kids participate in my career"; "While I leave the steaks to Six, I have my own ideas about how to give a party."

In *Who Could Ask for Anything More?* Ethel bragged about Six's skill as a barbecue chef and how he outshone Clark Gable, Tyrone Power and other guests when he cooked steaks at a dinner party given by the Walter Langs.

"He does everything for me," Ethel said of her husband. "Last summer when I thought my appendix was about to burst, he took care of me like a male nurse. And he takes an interest in my work. He doesn't expect anything out of it; he's just interested in me and in what happens to me. I don't want to sound girlish about it, but I simply adore the guy." (Ethel was to write a different kind of story in her 1978 autobiography, as we shall see later.)

Though she missed seeing her parents, Ethel professed to adore living in Cherry Hills, which was close enough to Denver to keep her from feeling she was living in the sticks. Denver, after all, did have one night club, the Emerald Room in the Brown Palace Hotel, where pals such as Kay Thompson and Mary McCarty appeared. The Sixes bought a twenty-eight-room house on six wooded acres for $79,000, and Ethel set about decorating its carved-oak interior with "lots of colorful chintz."

Her New York friends viewed the transformation in Ethel with astonishment. Merman as hostess of a baronial mansion in the middle of nowhere, serving canapés to bankers, realtors and politicos. Merman, the indoor girl, camping out in the Rockies. Merman climbing into bed at nine o'clock, the time she was usually belting out her first big solo.

Young Ethel—she no longer would allow herself to be called Little—adored the Colorado life from the start. Like most teenage girls, she loved horses, and now she could have one of her own, with endless miles of open country to ride in. Bobby also adjusted well to the changed pattern of living, and he enjoyed the fishing trips with his new stepfather.

Ethel made occasional trips to New York to see her parents and appear on television. Leland Hayward produced a one-hour version of *Anything Goes* for NBC, with Ethel in her original role and Frank Sinatra and Bert Lahr in the William Gaxton and Victor Moore parts. In 1956, she realized her ambition to play a nonsinging role, taking the Tallulah Bankhead part in *Reflected Glory* for "G.E. Theater." She starred in another drama, *Honest in the Rain*, for the "U.S. Steel Hour."

Wherever she went, Ethel told reporters how much she liked Denver: "There's no humidity, even at ninety-five degrees, and you can breathe the air at all times. It's where I plan to stay forever." She was also effusive in her praise of Bob Six: "He's not only president of an airline, he's also director of a bank and an oil company. He thrives on excitement. He's in Denver one day, in New York the next, three days later in Los Angeles." Ethel extolled the joys of Colorado living and her happiness as Mrs. Robert Six to the entire nation in late 1955 when Edward R. Murrow sent his cameras into her Cherry Hills house for his "Person to Person" program on CBS Television.

In later years, with the luxury of hindsight, Ethel perceived bits of evidence that the marriage to Six was not all it seemed. The gala Washington party in her honor, she discovered long afterward, had been financed by Continental Airlines as a public relations event—"it was all publicity to put Bob Six on the map."

The news of their marriage, she observed belatedly, had been released by Continental's public relations department with references to the airline and Six's "extensive oil properties in Colorado, Wyoming and Utah." Merman's latest movie, *There's No Business Like Show Business*, went unnamed.

Then there was the matter of finances. Ethel and Bob had agreed from the outset that they would split mutual expenses fifty-fifty. Ethel, who had always scrutinized her own expenses with a bookkeeper's eye, received a monthly report of household costs. Although she and Six paid equal amounts for the four servants' salaries, she alone was required to pay the gardener. When Bobby flew from California to Colorado on Continental Airlines, Ethel was billed for his fare—at no discount. Every household bill was divided, and not always equally, Ethel noted. "Six even put a bill for fifty cents on the ledger," Ethel once told a friend. "I paid my half—twenty-five cents."

13.

Back to Broadway

"What I didn't realize was that he wasn't interested in me as Ethel Zimmermann," she wrote in her memoirs. "He was interested in ETHEL MERMAN, the public personality, the star."

That realization came hard. As with any role she undertook, Ethel played Mrs. Robert Six to the hilt. She accompanied her husband on inaugural flights. She sang at company dinners. She played hostess to businessmen and politicians Six was courting. She participated in local charities and dined at his country club.

Except for occasional television shows, Ethel declined most offers for appearances, explaining that she preferred to remain in Denver with her husband and children. She had earned $6,000 a week in *Call Me Madam* and $150,000 per picture at Fox. Now her income had dwindled to almost nothing. With her share of the household expenses ever mounting, Ethel was forced to dip into her hard-earned capital, something it pained her to do. She had even paid all of the $10,000 down payment on the Cherry Hills house at Six's request. He gave her a note for his $5,000 but didn't repay it until she insisted.

In early 1956, Bob Six began spending long periods in New York. When Ethel complained that he didn't telephone as he had promised, he responded angrily. For the first time, Ethel realized her third marriage was in trouble.

Although bewildered and hurt by Six's behavior, Ethel was determined to preserve the marriage. She reasoned that since her husband was spending so much time in New York, their lives might become more compatible if she returned to Broadway. She proposed the idea to Six, and he readily agreed. Instead of taking a highly taxable salary, he argued, Ethel could invest in the show through their company, Mersix Incorporated.

Having said no for three years to offers of a Broadway show, Ethel now said yes to Howard Lindsay and Russel Crouse. The remarkably prolific pair sought once more to place the ultra-American Merman amid European aristocracy. Lindsay and Crouse aimed to capitalize on the intense public interest in the 1956 wedding of Grace Kelly of Philadelphia and Hollywood and Prince Rainier of Monaco.

Suppose Ethel is a rich Philadelphia widow who doesn't get invited to the wedding, Lindsay and Crouse proposed. Suppose she seeks revenge by trying to marry her daughter to the pretender to the Spanish throne. And suppose she succeeds but falls in love with the guy herself.

Musical comedies have been constructed with flimsier librettos, and Ethel agreed to go along with the team that had provided her with *Anything Goes, Red, Hot and Blue!* and *Call Me Madam.* She also had faith in the producer, Jo Mielziner, who had designed *Something for the Boys* and *Annie Get Your Gun,* and in the director, Abe Burrows. However, she had less confidence in the songwriters, Harold Karr and Matt Dubey.

The casting of the Duke of Granada, the penniless Hapsburg, was crucial. The show needed an actor like Paul Lukas who could impart immediate Continental charm but who would be of indeterminate age so he could plausibly woo both the Philadelphia widow and her daughter. The choice: Fernando Lamas.

Lamas was an Argentine with strong features, a virile build and total self-confidence that was often mistaken for arrogance. An intelligent man with a devilish sense of humor, he had acted in Argentine and Mexican films and fell into a Hollywood career more or less by accident. He appeared opposite Lana Turner in *The Merry Widow,* and their offscreen romance was widely publicized. By 1956 his film career as a Latin lover (a term he detested) had ended, and he welcomed the chance to appear opposite Ethel Merman in a Broadway musical.

The first rehearsal of *Happy Hunting* set the tone for the entire engagement. Abe Burrows began it with only Merman, Lamas and a few other members of the company on the bare stage of the Majestic Theater. The two stars greeted each other with a degree of formality and immediately began reading their first scene together. After ten minutes, Lamas held up his hand to halt the proceedings.

"Excuse me," he said in his mellow Argentine accent, "but I would like to ask a question. Is this the way it's going to be?"

"Is what the way it's going to be?" Burrows asked warily.

"What I mean is, am I going to read my lines to Miss Merman while Miss Merman reads hers to the audience?"

A sudden hush enveloped the theater, and the onlookers glanced at Merman to see her reaction. Her eyes narrowed, her jaw tightened.

"Mr. Lamas," she began, her voice growing edgy, "I want you to know that I have been playing scenes this way for twenty-five years on Broadway."

"That's doesn't mean you're right," Lamas replied. "That just means you're old."

A witness to the exchange comments: "From that moment on, it was World War III."

Thenceforward, neither Merman nor Lamas would speak to each other except when necessary for their mutual endeavor. Abe Burrows struggled to establish some form of rapport between the two stars, but it was impossible. Just when things were going smoothly, Lamas would utter a wisecrack that made Merman seethe.

Howard Lindsay and Russel Crouse came as peace ambassadors to the brownstone flat Lamas had rented for the duration of *Happy Hunting*. "Fernando," Lindsay began in his most avuncular manner, "you've got to help us for the good of the show. You're driving Ethel crazy. Every time we get her settled down, you make another crack and she hits the ceiling. You really should be more respectful. After all, she *is* the First Lady of the musical theater."

"I know all that shit," Lamas replied. "I'm sorry, but I can't help myself. I can't stand anybody who doesn't have a sense of humor."

"We can't change Ethel now," Crouse remarked. "We've got to put up with her the way she is. Please try to be nice to her."

"I'll try," grumbled Lamas.

An armed truce prevailed through the tryout period. *Happy Hunting* had its Broadway premiere on December 6, 1956, amid a chorus of hosannas for the return of Ethel Merman.

"She is monumental, magnificent, and miraculous," proclaimed Tom Donnelly in the *World-Telegram and Sun*. "Can anyone else touch her when it comes to demonstrating the absolute mastery of the musical stage? Certainly not. Can anyone think of a new way to describe the glory of her voice, a way which would not involve the standard comparison to a brass band? I wish I could."

Walter Kerr in the *Herald Tribune* rhapsodized: "How can you resist an un-ladylike Kewpie-doll with sunrise eyes, tadpole eyebrows, and rhinestones all over her toes—who rolls in from the wings, winds up her head like a pitcher getting ready to win the ball game, and fixes you with a blinking stare that's like something seen at night in a very dark forest? Owls can't do it, but Miss Merman can. . . .

"The thing about Merman is that she doesn't need comedy because she just naturally drips comedy the way some trees drip maple syrup. Lines? Who needs lines? Her tone is funny, her attitude (whatever it may be at any slapdash moment) is funny, her simple presence in the neighborhood is humor itself."

Indeed, Merman was able to draw laughs from Lindsay and Crouse's limpest lines. Learning that Prince Rainier is referred to as "His Grace," Merman replied, "Is his name Grace, too?"

Critics nevertheless found the book pedestrian and the songs, except for "Mutual Admiration Society," undistinguished. The superlatives were saved for Merman.

Robert Coleman, *Daily Mirror:* "La Merman is one of the

theater's titans. She's a real take-over gal with the drive and authority of a five-star general."

Brooks Atkinson, *Times:* "The explosion in Forty-fourth Street last evening was nothing to be alarmed about. It was merely Ethel Merman returning to the New York theater and being welcomed by her friends."

Richard Watts, Jr., *Post:* "The star even does a number with a trained horse, which is not only swaggeringly courageous of her but works out well. . . . With or without her horse, Miss Merman is dynamic, humorous, immensely likable and even rather touching."

John McClain, *Journal-American:* " 'Big Merm' just simply gets out there and takes charge, she swaggers and struts, her numbers can be heard comfortably in Hohokus, N.J., and when she delivers a joke line she will come down in the audience and hit you with a juvenile if you don't laugh. She is plainly the greatest."

Merman was back, and ticket brokers were gladdened. Despite the critics' reservations about the show itself, *Happy Hunting* amassed an advance sale of $2 million.

After the first few weeks of the run, the Merman-Lamas imbroglio resumed. She accused him of the unthinkable: upstaging her. She claimed that during their love duet, he kept retreating behind the chair in which she was sitting. Rather than turning the back of her head to the audience, she continued directing her romantic lyrics to the place where he had been.

When he was late for his entrance, she muttered under her breath, "You missed your cue." He replied sotto voce, "My zipper was stuck." Ethel sputtered her next line.

During one scene, Ethel yanked angrily at a dresser drawer and the entire dresser fell on her, scattering clothes all over. Lamas thought it was so funny that he sat down on the floor and pounded the carpet. The audience was equally convulsed.

"You sonofabitch, help me!" Merman hissed, trying to extricate herself from a mass of lingerie.

"You look terrific in pink," Lamas said, and the audience roared.

The *Happy Hunting* management had tried to keep news of the feud out of print, lest it destroy the onstage illusion of romance. It was The Kiss that caused the star war to go public.

A climactic moment in the show comes when Liz Livingstone and the Duke of Granada kiss and realize they are in love. As the months of acrimony wore on, both Merman and Lamas found the kiss more and more painful. "Can't I kiss her on the cheek, not the mouth?" Lamas implored Abe Burrows.

"If you want it that way—*you* tell her," Burrows said prudently. "I'm not going to."

The kiss remained. One night Lamas was particularly exasperated with Merman. After they had kissed, he walked to the footlights and wiped his mouth with the back of his hand.

The New York newspapers reported the incident the next day, and Ethel was naturally furious. The situation worsened when Fernando appeared on Mike Wallace's television interview program. When Wallace asked him about the kiss incident, Lamas replied, "Have you ever kissed Ethel Merman?"

When Wallace admitted he hadn't, Lamas remarked, "It's somewhere between kissing your uncle and a Sherman tank."

Merman yelled "Foul!" and filed a protest with Actors Equity. The union reprimanded Lamas, and Ethel felt vindicated.

She then became embroiled in another dispute with a cast member, prompting the Broadway crowd to wonder if Merman, who was nearing fifty, had become cantankerous in her late career. A night club performer, Gene Wesson, had been playing the relatively youthful role of Harry Watson. One night Merman, who did not like her concentration disturbed, was startled to see a gray-haired Gene Wesson.

"What the fuck is he doing with gray hair?" she demanded of the stage manager.

Wesson explained that he had tested for the role of John Barrymore in the film version of his daughter Diana's confessional book, *Too Much, Too Soon.* Wesson was certain he was going to land the part (in fact, Errol Flynn did), and he refused to dye his hair back to its original color. He was fired.

The firing provided a series of items for Broadway and Hollywood columnists, especially when Wesson filed charges with Actors Equity against Merman. He told a reporter: "I feel I will have no trouble proving that Miss Merman was behind my firing. She dictates to management—tells them what to do, approves all the hiring and firing." Again, Ethel's side of the argument was upheld by Equity.

The feud with Lamas did not end. She accused him of blocking her path at the curtain call, of ruining her laugh lines. The two stars continued sniping at each other until the last of the 412 performances.

In later years, Lamas claimed that Merman robbed him of what could have been the greatest role of his career. He said that Rodgers and Hammerstein had asked him to play Emile de Becque opposite Doris Day as Nellie Forbush in the film version of *South Pacific*. But, said Lamas, Merman—who was a part owner of *Happy Hunting*—refused to release him from his contract.

The final performance of *Happy Hunting* was gratefully approached by both stars. Merman and Lamas looked forward to the last scene in which she joined him onstage and they marched arm-in-arm to the rear of the stage, their backs to the audience.

Lamas was delivering his final lines when he heard a commotion in the wings. He noticed the wardrobe woman working frantically on Ethel's black sequined tube dress. As often happened during a show's run, Ethel had gained weight, and the dress would not zip up the back. Her bare back was visible.

She could wait no longer, and she edged onstage to join Lamas. "Don't turn me around!" she said desperately under her breath.

"Why not?" he asked innocently.

"You sonofabitch, don't push me!" she muttered.

They came to the end of the song, and she eyed him nervously. In a sweeping gesture, he removed his white suede overcoat and draped it over her shoulders. Then he marched her to the rear of the stage as the curtain descended. The audience's applause was joined by that of the cast and crew who had been watching Ethel's predicament from the wings.

"You bastard!" Ethel snarled. "I'll never forgive you as long as I live."

14.

Gypsy

Ethel Merman's return to Broadway had a salutary effect on her marriage. Six seemed to like her more as a musical comedy star than as mistress of a Colorado mansion. Despite the misery with Fernando Lamas, Ethel felt happier back in New York, close to her parents, who were beginning to display the symptoms of age. Ethel did not want to suffer the shame of another broken marriage. She realized that both Ethel and Bobby had come to consider Bob Six their father, especially after Bob Levitt's suicide. In time, both children began using Six's name, though they were never adopted by him.

After the close of *Happy Hunting*, Ethel returned to Colorado, which she still considered home. She was repeatedly on the move, however, appearing in television variety shows as the guest of Dinah Shore, Perry Como, Frank Sinatra and others. Then one day in 1958 she heard about a new show that was being designed especially for her: *Gypsy*.

The show was based on a book by Gypsy Rose Lee about her life and notorious career as America's most famous stripteaser. She had written vividly about her early struggles in small-time show business and especially about her ferocious stage mother, Rose Hovick. David Merrick, who had swiftly become the most prolific and successful producer on Broadway, bought the rights to *Gypsy: A Memoir* as the basis for a musical.

Merrick assigned Betty Comden and Adolph Green to create a book and Jule Styne to write the music. Comden and Green seemed enthusiastic about the project, but when they became involved in writing the movie script for *Auntie Mame* they dropped out. A year passed, then Merrick joined forces with Leland Hayward to reactivate *Gypsy*, for which they engaged Ethel Merman as star.

The producers hired Arthur Laurents to write the book, Jerome Robbins to direct. Cole Porter was asked to write the songs, but declined due to failing health. Irving Berlin said he didn't feel like writing songs for a stripteaser's saga. Carolyn Leigh and Moose Charlap auditioned songs but were not accepted.

Hayward and Merrick sounded out Stephen Sondheim, who had written the lyrics for *West Side Story*. Sondheim was interested, but only if he could write both lyrics *and* music.

"No," said Merman, who felt she had suffered because of relatively inexperienced songwriters for *Happy Hunting*. "I want Jule Styne to write the music. He knows my style, and he writes great show tunes." Although he had never written a show for her, Ethel knew Styne from her Fox days, when he had been her vocal coach. He had produced the television version of *Anything Goes*.

After delicate negotiations, a collaboration was forged between the newcomer Sondheim and the Broadway veteran Styne, composer of *High Button Shoes, Gentlemen Prefer Blondes* and *Two on the Aisle*.

In his pursuit of a plot line for *Gypsy*, Laurents became more and more fascinated by the figure of Rose, the mother. The real story, he concluded, was not Baby Louise, who became Gypsy Rose Lee, or Baby June, who became June Havoc, but their demonic, single-minded mother. But would Ethel Merman play such a role?

Laurents met Merman for the first time over dinner at Sardi's. The playwright warned: "This woman could be considered a monster, and I want to know how far you're willing to go."

"I'll go as far as you want me to," Ethel assured him. "I've been waiting for years to play a real, dramatic role."

The *Gypsy* project faced a major problem: June Havoc. She

was feuding with her sister and resented the attention being paid to Gypsy. She refused to sign a release allowing herself to be portrayed. "Don't worry, she'll sign," assured Merrick, and Laurents proceeded to write his script with Baby June as a principal character.

Jule Styne and Stephen Sondheim approached their collaboration with foreboding. Sondheim was still resentful that Merman had not allowed him to write the music as well as the lyrics, and he feared Styne was an old-style songwriter, aiming for a hit tune rather than songs that would embellish the plot and characters. Styne realized that Sondheim represented the brash new generation in the theater and he feared that the younger man would try to impose his own ideas on the songs.

They collaborated splendidly. As the script was being written, Sondheim consulted with Laurents, who explained what he needed musically, scene by scene. Sondheim related this to Styne, who devised the music. Then Sondheim added the words.

Sondheim and Styne clashed on only one major issue. Like all veteran songwriters, Styne had a trunkful of tunes that had been discarded from previous films or shows for various reasons. Styne offered some of them for use in *Gypsy*. Sondheim vigorously objected. "All of the songs must be *new*, written especially for this show," he insisted.

Styne acquiesced, until Jerome Robbins came to his rescue. Robbins, who had directed *High Button Shoes*, remembered a song Styne had written with Sammy Cahn, "Betwixt and Between." It had been dropped from *High Button Shoes*, and Robbins suggested the melody might work as a rousing number to end the first act. Sondheim wrote a lyric, lengthening the title music, and the result was the hit song of *Gypsy:*

You'll be swell, you'll be great,
Gonna have the whole world on a plate!
Starting here, starting now,
Honey, everything's coming up roses!

Styne also reached into his trunk for "You'll Never Get Away from Me," which he had first written for a Marilyn Monroe movie, then used in the television special "Ruggles of Red Gap." Sondheim was furious when he learned, long after *Gypsy* had opened, that he had set lyrics to another Styne retread.

Ethel Merman recalled hearing the *Gypsy* music for the first time at the Manhattan garden apartment of Ruth Dubonnet, close friend of Jule Styne.

"Rodgers and Hammerstein were there, everybody was there, and we sat around the floor while Jule played the score. I burst into tears. I had a pretty good idea that night that it was going to be a hit, because you feel like that. It was like that when Cole Porter played 'I Get a Kick Out of You' and 'Anything Goes' and 'Blow, Gabriel, Blow.' You have a feel for a song, whether it's going to be good or bad."

That evening Styne did not play "Rose's Turn," the climactic song of *Gypsy*, because it hadn't taken shape yet. From the beginning, Arthur Laurents had diagrammed a final song in which the character of Mama Rose would be exposed to the audience. Styne and Sondheim had made a few attempts at the number, but none pleased Jerome Robbins. With rehearsals beginning, Merman complained that she exited after each of her songs. She had no chance to stop the show in her patented manner and stand out there and bask in the adoration of the New York audience.

"I wanted to give Ethel something big," Styne recalled in *Jule: The Story of Composer Jule Styne*, "and I went over it carefully with Laurents. In my mind, I wanted to review her life musically, a rough thing to do. At that moment, Rose was saying, in effect, the children don't need me anymore but, by God, they better understand what I contributed. It was her turn to tell everyone that they were what she'd made them. It was rather easy to say in words but to say it musically is more difficult."

He completed his task, and Sondheim added the words. Robbins gave his approval, and at eleven o'clock that night at the Amsterdam Theater he stopped rehearsal. Styne sat down to the piano and Sondheim stood on the half-dark stage to sing "Rose's Turn."

It starts with Rose's customary bravado: "Here she is, boys! Here she is, world! Here's Rose!" Her supreme self-confidence rises to a crescendo with a series of assertions, "Mama's talkin' loud, Mama's doin' fine, etc." Suddenly her assurance begins to crumble as she realizes her daughters, whom she has protected and promoted with the ferocity of a she-wolf, will be leaving her. For Rose it would be "Thanks a lot and out with the garbage." Then her spirit returns, and she proclaims that from now on it's going to be Rose's turn.

When Sondheim shouted the last defiant words, *"For me!"* Ethel rushed stage-center to embrace him and Styne, tears streaming down her face. "It's a goddammed aria!" she exclaimed.

Ethel had told Laurents she would go as far as he wanted her to, but she reneged. Sondheim relates that the lyrics of "Some People" was "an angry quatrain for Rose, directed at her father, culminating in her telling him to go to hell. Ethel said to me that her public would be alienated if they heard her tell her father to go to hell." The passage was eliminated.

The role of Herbie, Rose's long-suffering boyfriend, required an actor who would be sympathetic to Rose but strong enough to argue with her. Numerous names from Hollywood and Broadway were considered. Robbins was intrigued with Jack Klugman, who had wide experience in nonmusical plays.

"I can't sing," Klugman declared, but Robbins was not dissuaded. He sent Klugman a vocal coach, but when the actor auditioned again, he showed no improvement. He auditioned for three weeks, always with the same uncertain baritone.

One morning at the Amsterdam Theater, Jack Klugman faced the final audition. The decision makers were present: Robbins, Hayward, Styne, Sondheim. Also Merman, who would sing the duet "Small World" with Klugman. "If she belts it," he warned Robbins, "I'm gonna walk out."

Robbins asked Ethel to hold down the volume, and for once in her life she did (she always sang the same in either rehearsal or performance: loud). "She sang so softly, so un-Mermanly," Styne recalled, "that her voice cracked."

The nervous Klugman and the muted Merman sang the duet with a special poignancy that touched their listeners:

> *Funny, you're a stranger who's come here,*
> *Come from another town.*
> *Funny, I'm a stranger myself here—*
> *Small world, isn't it?*

Klugman fled from the audition, convinced that he had failed. Robbins telephoned him at home with the news that he had won the role of Herbie. The other major role, Louise (Gypsy), went to a willowy young actress named Sandra Church.

Rehearsals went forward even though the producers had not solved the legal problems posed by June Havoc. She had asked for changes in the script, including a rewrite of the Mama Rose character to make her more of a villainess. Laurents refused, and the stalemate continued. David Merrick, himself a lawyer, suggested the libel laws could be skirted by naming the younger daughter Baby Claire. That caused confusion with members of the cast. In rehearsals and later in Philadelphia performances, half of them called her Baby Jane and half Baby Claire.

It became apparent that *Gypsy* was far too long, and after considerable wrangling between Robbins and Laurents, cuts were made. The show was ready to go on the road.

The "gypsy" runthrough—the final rehearsal for the benefit of the chorus people (known in the theater as gypsies) as well as the rest of the cast—was held at the Winter Garden Theater on the Sunday afternoon before departure to Philadelphia. Members of the company were allowed to invite friends, and the producers themselves asked well-known members of the Broadway community. The Winter Garden was jammed, word having circulated that *Gypsy* was something special.

The stage was bare, the scenery had already been shipped. The only musicians in the pit were a pianist, a bass player and a drummer. Jerome Robbins moved the scenery—a chair here, a bench there—and explained to the audience what the sets and costumes would look like. "Now this is where Rose and the girls come out in coats made out of blankets," he announced.

Ethel Merman wore a smart beige suit, the rest of the cast wore capris, sweat suits, the usual rehearsal attire. The players didn't go to their dressing rooms after exiting from the scene; they sat against the back wall or stood on the sides of the stage. When she wasn't performing, Ethel leaned against the proscenium arch, arms folded, assessing the proceedings as if she was seeing them for the first time.

With stage waits and Robbins' explanations, *Gypsy* lasted more than three hours. The audience was enraptured throughout. When Ethel finished "Rose's Turn," the crowd erupted in cheers.

"It was the most thrilling performance I have ever seen in the musical theater," says Carole Cook, then an aspiring singer and actress.

Miss Cook adds: "I watched Ethel as she stood at the side of the stage and studied the other scenes. She had a reputation for eliminating any showstoppers except her own. There were two in *Gypsy:* Paul Wallace's 'All I Need Is the Girl' and the strippers' 'You Gotta Have a Gimmick.' Wallace's number didn't even fit in the show; it was more like a night club act. I thought surely both of those would be eliminated. But they weren't."

"I was worried, too," Paul Wallace recalls, "because I thought Ethel would object. But from the first audition she encouraged me. When I was nervous before opening, she told me, 'Honey, if they could do what you do, they'd be up here.' "

Ever the perfectionist, Jerome Robbins continued tinkering with *Gypsy* during rehearsals at the Shubert in Philadelphia. Each number was honed and polished until the director gave his final approval. A problem number was Sandra Church's strip, in which she was to portray Gypsy Rose Lee's emergence as a burlesque performer. It was watched disapprovingly by Gypsy Rose Lee herself.

George Eells, then a reporter for *Look* magazine, remembers sitting in the rear of the Shubert Theater with Gypsy and Ethel as they observed Church's performance.

"It isn't right," Gypsy muttered. "No zip, no zing."

"My God, nobody knows how to do it better than you," Ethel said. "Why don't you show 'em?"

"Oh, no," Gypsy replied. "They don't want me to interfere."

"Gypsy," said Ethel, "you're the only gentleman here!"

Opening night at the Shubert extended long past midnight. The audience seemed confused and disappointed. If the show was about Gypsy Rose Lee, where were the stripteases and dancing girls? And what kind of an Ethel Merman show was this, anyway? After being dressed so smartly in *Call Me Madam* and *Happy Hunting*, she made her entrance in a moth-eaten coat, carrying a huge handbag and a small, mangy dog.

The entrance itself was totally un-Mermanlike. Always she had been brought onstage amid fanfare and anticipation. This time she came down the center aisle of the darkened theater during rehearsal of a kiddie revue and bawled, "Sing out, Louise—sing out!"

The Philadelphia reviews reflected the confusion of the audience. Robbins and Laurents began making more cuts, and Jack Klugman's only solo was among the casualties. All of Merman's numbers remained, and she was beginning to realize how strenuous *Gypsy* would be.

Jule Styne visited her dressing room every night after the end of Act I. He found her exhausted, head in hands, unable to make conversation. But when the cue came for her second-act entrance, she strode onstage with customary energy. One night she complained to Styne, "Hey, I want to tell you something. This is a hard show to do every night."

The warring sisters came to Philadelphia to inspect *Gypsy*. "You made me cry," exclaimed Gypsy Rose Lee to Ethel. "I still don't like it," June Havoc told David Merrick. But she also didn't like having her identity erased and substituted for with Baby Claire. She signed the release.

Late in life, Merman related an incident during the Philadelphia tryout to interviewer David Galligan: "We were playing around Easter time, and Jule Styne decided to have a Seder. You know I'm not Jewish; a lot of people think I am, but I'm not. I didn't know anything about a Seder, except I knew the food would be lousy. I mean, I wasn't accustomed to eating that kind of food.

"On the way to wherever the Seder was, I went to a delicatessen and bought a ham and cheese sandwich on rye bread. I put it in my purse and took it to the Seder. Well, we were all sitting at this long table and everybody was starting to eat. So I reached in my purse and took out my ham and cheese sandwich, unwrapped it and took a bite.

"Jule says, 'Ethel, what are you eating?' I said, 'I'm eating the ham and cheese sandwich I bought; what do you mean, what am I eating?' He said, 'You can't eat that!' I said, 'Why not?' He said, 'Because it has to be blessed.' I went like this [making the sign of the cross] and I started to eat."

"What this town has needed is Ethel Merman. What Miss Merman has needed is a good show. We got her and she got it last evening, when *Gypsy* opened at the Broadway Theater," John Chapman began his review in the *Daily News*.

"What a comedienne! What a trouper! What a star!" Robert Coleman marveled in the *Daily Mirror*. "To see our wonderful Eth is like watching the heartbeat of show business."

Walter Kerr in the *Herald Tribune* called *Gypsy* "the best damn musical I've seen in years." Better than all of the other elements of the show put together, he added, was Ethel Merman—"a brassy, brazen witch on a mortgaged broomstick, a steamroller with cleats, the very mastodon of all stage mothers."

(The producer had guaranteed that Kerr would see the climactic "Rose's Turn." Stephen Sondheim comments: "The only memory I have of opening night in New York is that of Walter Kerr going up the aisle before the end of the show and David Merrick preventing him from leaving the theater until it was all over." A replay of Michael Todd and *Something for the Boys*.)

Even the *Times*' Brooks Atkinson, who had long found Ethel Merman too earthy for his taste, conceded that she "would not permit *Gypsy* to be anything less than the most satisfying musical of the season."

He added that Miss Merman, "her pipes resonant and her spirit syncopated, struts and bawls her way through it triumphantly. Ever since *Annie Get Your Gun,* it has been obvious that she is an actress in addition to being a singer. . . . Not for the first time in her fabulous career, her personal magnetism electrifies the whole theater. For she is a performer of incomparable power."

Small wonder that when the critics assembled a month later to vote their awards for the 1958–59 season, Ethel's was selected the best performance by an actress in a musical. But when the Tony Awards were announced, the winner was Mary Martin for *The Sound of Music.* Convinced that *Gypsy* represented her best work ever, Ethel was stung by the snub. Publicly, however, she professed not to care: "How are you going to buck a nun?"

Ethel had been so confident of the success of *Gypsy* that she'd taken a year's lease on an apartment in the Park Lane Hotel. Under terms of her contract, she was entitled to miss a performance on the night of June 3, 1959. That was the date of Ethel, Jr.'s graduation from Cherry Creek High School, and her mother and brother flew all night to arrive in time for the ceremony. Bob Six was also present, and during the brief period of family felicity, Merman almost convinced herself that the marriage could be saved.

After the graduation, Ethel again flew all night to resume the grueling role of Mama Rose back in New York. Matinee days were the worst. She refused to spare herself in the afternoon performance, charging full-throttle until the final, defiant, "For me, for me, for me, for me, *for me!*"

"My head would be down, my hands would go down," Ethel recalled. "Milton [Rosenstock, the conductor] would be in the pit, and he'd look up and whisper, 'We have to do this again tonight.' I felt like saying, 'It's all right for you—you don't have to open your mouth.' "

15.

Troubles

In August of 1959, Ethel Merman came off the stage after "Rose's Turn" with a strange sensation in her throat. She figured it was a slight strain from having done two shows that Saturday, and she accompanied members of the company to a jazz joint. The sensation persisted in the morning, and she consulted a throat doctor. After years of punishment, the Merman larynx had broken a blood vessel. Ethel would have to drop out of *Gypsy* for a week.

That was the beginning. Just as Ethel Merman had reached the peak of achievement in her matchless Broadway career, she began suffering a series of embittering personal setbacks that shadowed her nature for the rest of her life.

Her Broadway hit prompted NBC to schedule a television special, "Ethel Merman on Broadway." Ethel was especially pleased that the show would be produced by her great friend and former accompanist-arranger, Roger Edens, now a producer of musicals at MGM.

"Ethel Merman on Broadway" was a flop, both in audience ratings and with reviewers. Too much was crammed into one hour, and viewers were left satiated.

The biggest cause of Ethel's distress was her steadily eroding relationship with Bob Six. On social and family occasions, they were on cool but civil terms. In private they engaged in shouting matches. She was suspicious of his lengthy absences, though he maintained that his travels were entirely to benefit Continental Airlines.

During Ethel's Christmas break from *Gypsy,* she and Six fulfilled a promise to take young Ethel and Bobby to Montego Bay in Jamaica. Merman entertained a faint hope of reconciliation, but it was extinguished several weeks later when she learned of at least one reason for her husband's travels.

"The sonofabitch is keeping a broad in Honolulu!" she exclaimed to her friend Betty Bruce.

Scorned and betrayed, Merman reacted on a Vesuvian scale, especially when news of Six's perfidy reached the gossip columns. Her fingers pounding the typewriter keys, she fired off a "Dear Robert" letter that signaled the end to the marriage.

Ethel began drinking more. Never before or during a performance; her professionalism would not allow that. But after the show and on nights off, she allowed herself more than was usual for her, not just her customary champagne, but vodka. And when she drank too much, she inevitably became abusive, lashing out at close friends.

She now carried the protection of her well-earned turf onstage to an almost paranoid level. She accused Sandra Church of playing with her pigtails during "Everything's Coming Up Roses," a curious reprise of Merman's dispute with Paula Laurence in *Something for the Boys.* Sandra was always trying to undermine her, Ethel claimed.

Ethel had befriended Paul Wallace, and she seemed pleased when he started dating young Ethel, who was visiting from Colorado. One night at "21," Ethel was entertaining her daughter and Wallace. Merman had consumed several cocktails and suddenly turned to Wallace: "You sonofabitch, you're flashing your eyes when I do my lines." She slapped him across the face.

Both Wallace and young Ethel were shocked. Merman never apologized, but a few days later she handed Wallace a handsome wallet with $50 inside. "Always keep it filled," she said.

Young Ethel visited with her mother in New York, but she

made it clear that her life was in Colorado. She would be entering Colorado College at Colorado Springs in the fall of 1960, and she talked excitedly about courses she wanted to take. Although she had never expressed much interest in her mother's profession, Ethel thought she might take some acting courses. Since she loved animals, she considered becoming a veterinarian. "Or maybe I could be a teacher," she said. "I can't wait to start college."

At Colorado College, young Ethel fell in love with a good-looking sophomore from Wayne, Pennsylvania, William Geary. In September of 1960, Geary, who was twenty-one, announced to the press that he and Ethel Merman Six had been secretly married on May 6 in Juarez, Mexico. Ethel was four months pregnant at the time of the announcement. She dropped out of school to await the baby.

Merman at first was upset by the abruptness of the marriage, but Ethel sounded so happy over the telephone that her mother softened. After all, hadn't she married Bob Levitt under similar circumstances?

For months Merman had wanted to rid herself of the marriage to Bob Six, but *Gypsy* interfered. Finally at Christmas she had a week's vacation, and she followed the same procedure she had used to divorce Bob Levitt. She flew to El Paso, crossed the border to Juarez and with the aid of her attorney, Paul O'Dwyer, obtained an uncontested divorce.

Ethel hurried on to Colorado Springs for Christmas with her daughter and new son-in-law. She was pleased to find Bill Geary a personable and responsible young man and was delighted to see that her daughter seemed serenely happy as wife and expectant mother. Although the baby was due in two months, young Ethel busied herself for hours in the kitchen to prepare a full-course Christmas dinner. "That's something your old lady could never do," Merman admitted.

Then it was back to New York and *Gypsy*. Ethel was relieved that she had eliminated Bob Six from her life. Or had she? Could she really erase the stinging realization that she had been used and that as soon as her usefulness had been exploited she was discarded for a younger, more attractive woman? She never forgave Six, who later married Audrey Meadows, Jackie Gleason's ever-patient wife, Alice, in television's "The Honeymooners."

Ethel found solace in playing Mama Rose, whose life in curious ways paralleled her own: three husbands, two children, single-mindedness of purpose. She consoled herself that with *Gypsy* she had created her greatest role, one that was indelibly Merman. Surely when the movie was produced, no studio would dare cast anyone else.

With a July vacation from *Gypsy,* Ethel embarked on her first grand tour of Europe, accompanied by Bobby and Benay Venuta. The two women had been friends since Benay replaced Ethel in *Anything Goes.* A slender blonde who was as outspoken as Ethel, Benay had known a varied career as singer and actress, interrupted by marriages to film producer Armand Deutsch and Fred Clark, the actor.

Bobby was eager to partake of the treasures of European history, and he found a ready companion in Benay, herself an accomplished painter. Ethel wasn't interested. She enjoyed visiting the cafés and night clubs but drew the line at museums and cathedrals.

"Why can't you be like Benay?" Bobby pleaded with his mother. "We're going to the Sistine Chapel today. Don't you want to see it?"

"No, thanks," Ethel replied. "Bring me a brochure."

After returning to *Gypsy,* Ethel made appearances for the presidential campaign of Richard Nixon. But on January 20, 1961, she flew to Washington to entertain at the inaugural balls for John F. Kennedy.

On February 20, Ethel Merman Geary gave birth to a seven-pound, five-ounce daughter who was named Barbara Jean. Merman took another break from *Gypsy* to visit her granddaughter. "Call me Grandma," Ethel announced to the press.

At loose ends—her marriage dissolved and her children grown—Ethel told David Merrick she would be willing to undertake the first national tour of her career. In Chicago and Toronto she was greeted by enthusiastic, capacity audiences. In San Francisco, the reception approached delirium.

The applause started as soon as the raucous voice shouted from the darkness: "Sing out, Louise!" The noise grew as she walked down the aisle and onto the stage. For minutes the cast and orchestra waited as the waves of applause and cheers continued for the woman in the tattered, oversize coat.

"I've never seen anything like it," Ethel told a reporter. "They greet me like that every night. Not just here in San Francisco. But everywhere I've been. I tell you, those people who say theater is dead have a surprise coming if they get out of New York and see the warmth and enthusiasm of audiences in this country of ours. They're so appreciative that you bring them a play. Particularly if you bring them the genuine article, not a carbon copy."

Ethel expected the opening of *Gypsy* in Los Angeles to be a special triumph, a smashing return to the film community that had alternately sought and rejected her. She asked her mother and father to come to California so they could share her triumph.

Then the crushing news: Jack Warner had decided to cast Rosalind Russell in the film version.

"That sonofabitch!" Ethel exploded. "How dare he let anyone else play Rose! And Rosalind Russell, for crissake. The broad can't even sing."

Ethel became convinced that the whole thing was a plot perpetrated by Russell's producer-husband Frederick Brisson. She believed that Brisson had bought the film rights to the play *A Majority of One* and sold them to Warner Brothers with his wife as star—with the proviso that she also star in *Gypsy*.

"That's nonsense," Rosalind Russell wrote in her posthumously published autobiography, *Life Is a Banquet*. "It would have been a nice husbandly act if he'd done it, but he hadn't."

Miss Russell stated the facts as she knew them: Jack Warner had bought *A Majority of One* and sought her as star. She argued she was miscast as a Jewish housewife and that the role should be played by Gertrude Berg, who created it on Broadway. Warner countered that Miss Berg had flopped in a movie and he needed a film name. He used the same argument for *Gypsy:* Merman had failed in *There's No Business Like Show Business,* hence *Gypsy* required a recognizable movie personality.

Ethel's bitterness over losing the movie lead overshadowed the triumph of the Los Angeles opening. Among the many celebrities who poured backstage to congratulate her was Mervyn LeRoy, who had been assigned to direct Rosalind Russell in *Gypsy*. LeRoy asked Ethel to join his party and she replied pointedly, "No, thanks, I'm going out with *friends.*" As a parting shot, she added: "If she can't handle the songs, don't hesitate to call."

Mitzi Gaynor, who had become a close friend during *There's No Business Like Show Business,* understood Ethel's unhappiness and planned a dinner party in her honor. Guests included Jack and Mary Benny, George Burns and Gracie Allen and other friends and admirers of Ethel.

Late in the evening at Mitzi's party, Ethel stood at the piano as Roger Edens accompanied her. For an hour she sang all of her hit songs, seemingly in defiance of a Hollywood that had denied her the chance to play her greatest role.

Jerry Herman retains a vivid memory of the telephone call in 1961 between David Merrick and Ethel Merman.

At fourteen, Herman had been profoundly influenced by Ethel Merman. His parents took him to a matinee of *Annie Get Your Gun*, and afterward the boy sat down to the piano and played five of the Merman songs from memory. From then on he wanted to write scores for Broadway shows, an ambition he realized years later with *Milk and Honey*.

"Let's do a new show for Ethel Merman," proposed David Merrick following his success with *Gypsy*. Jerry Herman was thrilled to be writing for the star who had long been his idol. He composed the songs and Michael Stewart wrote the book for a musical version of Thornton Wilder's play *The Matchmaker*.

Herman reported to Merrick's office with the news that he was ready to play the score for Merman. The producer telephoned Ethel and began his pitch: "Ethel, I've got a great new show for you. . . ." Suddenly Merrick's face fell.

"Are you sure?" he asked. He listened grim-faced, then concluded, "Well, I'm terribly disappointed, Ethel." He put down the telephone and said to Herman, "She won't do it. She doesn't want another Broadway show."

The thirty-year love affair between Ethel Merman and the Broadway theater was over.

"I've had it," she told her friends. "I've done fourteen goddam shows and what have I got to show for it? Three busted marriages and two kids I never had enough time for. When other dames were starting to enjoy an evening with their families, I had my dinner on a tray so I could get to the theater on time. Weekends in the country? Forget it! Well, I'm through with the theater. From now on I'm living for Ethel."

She kept her word. There would never again be another new Ethel Merman musical.

16.

Ethel and Ernie

"I was then offered a part in Stanley Kramer's *Mad, Mad, Mad, Mad World,*" Groucho Marx wrote to Nunnally Johnson in 1962. "Two weeks later I received word they were replacing me with Ethel Merman. I know show business is a strange profession but . . . However, I later saw Merman one night and realized she would be ideal for the part. She has enough balls to get to first base without a hit."

If the role had indeed been planned for Groucho Marx, it had been significantly altered to fit Ethel Merman. She was cast as the shrewish mother-in-law of Milton Berle in a big-budget comedy produced and directed by Kramer.

After a career of socially significant dramas, Kramer decided to make a film with laughs as well as a theme. Greed was the topic of *It's a Mad, Mad, Mad, Mad World*, with teams of comics frantically searching for a hidden supply of stolen cash. Spencer Tracy was the perpetrator of the hunt; the comics included Mickey Rooney, Milton Berle, Phil Silvers, Buddy Hackett, Dick Shawn, Jonathan Winters, Jimmy Durante, Buster Keaton and Joe E. Brown.

Merman had worked with comics, but never in such great number. "Naturally they all wanted to pull their gags on the great Merman," Kramer recalls, "but they only succeeded once."

Most of the film was shot in the desert near Palm Springs,

where the cast was housed in a plush hotel. One day Ethel was sitting beside the pool, waiting for a car to take her to Los Angeles for dental work. Milton Berle and Phil Silvers, who had learned the name of her dentist, were seated nearby.

"How bad was it, Milton?" Silvers asked.

"I wanna tell you, it was murder," Berle replied. "What that guy did to my teeth, only Hitler should have happen to him."

"That bad, huh?"

"I'm telling you, that Dr. ________ is a butcher!"

Ethel looked up suddenly. "What's that? You know Dr. ________?"

"Oh, you know him, Ethel?" Berle said.

"Yeah. He's doing some work on me today."

"I wouldn't worry about it, dear. I'm sure you'll have better luck than I did."

Ethel was apprehensive on the long drive to the dentist's office. Only when he proved to be utterly gentle did she realize she'd been had.

Berle, she realized, had instigated the plot, and she planned her own revenge. One day the entire cast was seated at lunch under a long tent. Ethel was conversing with Silvers while Berle sat five chairs away.

"Look, Phil," Ethel remarked in matter-of-fact tones, "I don't give a damn about billing. I'm just happy that it will read '. . . and Ethel Merman.' "

"What? What's that?" Berle said with alarm. "I thought it was agreed that the billing would be alphabetical."

"Oh, that's for you comics," Ethel replied airily. "My agents worked out a special deal."

After frantic calls of protest to his agents, Berle discovered that Merman had turned the tables and played one on him.

Berle recalls another incident during the filming of *Mad World:* "We were playing a scene in which Ethel orders me out of the car and starts beating me with her carrying bag. Stanley said, 'Action!' and she started hitting me over the head. And I'm getting hurt! The blows kept coming, and I was saying, 'Stop it, Mama! Stop it!'—fortunately I didn't say 'Ethel'—and my cries were real.

"Finally Stanley said, 'Cut! Print!' and I said, 'Get me an ambulance, I'm hurt.' I asked Ethel, 'What have you got in that bag?' She said, 'Oh, my God! The script girl said I wasn't wearing all that heavy costume jewelry in the previous scene, so I put it in the bag.'

"I developed a big lump on my head that never went away. Every time I saw Ethel after that, I said, 'Feel what you did to my head.' "

When Ethel Merman lost the *Gypsy* movie to Rosalind Russell, she fired her MCA agents, blaming them for not securing the role for her. Milton Pickman became her manager. A veteran studio executive who had been assistant to Harry Cohn at Columbia Pictures, he had started his own talent agency.

"No more Broadway shows," Ethel instructed him.

"Okay, then let's go for the big dough," he proposed. "Las Vegas, Lake Tahoe, concerts. That's where you can clean up."

Pickman booked Merman into the Flamingo Hotel in Las Vegas at $40,000 a week. Judy Garland, Mitzi Gaynor, Roger Edens and other Hollywood friends arrived for the opening, and they led the cheering for Ethel's performance. But the engagement was not a success, either for the casino owners or for Merman. She failed to attract the bigtime gamblers on whom casinos depended, and to ordinary tourists Ethel Merman was merely a half-remembered name.

After the long years of enjoying the rapt attention of Broadway audiences, Ethel was irritated by Las Vegas crowds. They included noisy families of tourists, disgruntled losers at the tables, hustlers on the make with showgirls. Not Merman's cup of tea.

The Ethel Merman Show toured tents and outdoor arenas in the eastern United States during the summer of 1963 with disappointing results. Says Pickman: "The show always did a big opening weekend, then business for the rest of the week was poor. The problem seemed to be that Ethel Merman was a big star in New York, but not in the rest of America."

Merman returned to California to appear on the television shows of Lucille Ball, Red Skelton and Judy Garland. Her frequent escort on social occasions was Ernest Gann, the author of aviation novels, most notably *The High and the Mighty.* On the evening of November 30, 1963, Gann and Ethel attended a dinner party at the home of her close friends, Temple and Joe Schribman. Among the guests was Ernest Borgnine.

He had been an unlikely candidate for film stardom, a big, ham-handed man with a broad, homely face. He spent ten years in the Navy, then followed his mother's suggestion to take acting lessons after World War II. He played minor roles in the theater, went to Hollywood and was typed as a heavy, notably as Fatso Judson in *From Here to Eternity.* As the lovelorn butcher in *Marty,* he won the Academy Award as best actor of 1955.

A casualty of his stardom was Rhoda Kemins, the pharmacist's mate he had met and married while both were in the Navy, mother of their daughter Nancy. Borgnine, the son of Italian immigrants, next married the Mexican actress Katy Jurado, and the clash of their Latin temperaments made news from the Sunset Strip to the Via Veneto. They were separated by the time Borgnine met Ethel at the home of the Joe Schribmans.

Ernest Borgnine was a passionate man, and on that November evening he chose Ethel Merman as the object of his passion. He telephoned her the following day.

"My daughter saw you in *It's a Mad, Mad, Mad, Mad World* and thought you were terrific," Borgnine said. "Would you have dinner with her and me?"

Ethel was hesitant but flattered. She agreed to the dinner, and Borgnine began calling her for dates alone. When she returned to New York for a singing engagement at the Plaza Hotel, his calls continued. During the Christmas break in his television series, "McHale's Navy," he flew to New York to propose marriage.

No man had ever given Ethel such a rush before, and she was overwhelmed by the dynamic actor who proclaimed that he was crazy about her. Ethel was fifty-four at the time, and worried that she was no longer attractive to men. Ernie was ten years younger, and although he was not conventionally handsome, he could still attract women who were younger and more beautiful than Ethel. But he wanted *her.*

On the day after Christmas, Ethel told him, "Yes, I'll marry you." She was as astonished by her reply as he was.

"Great!" Borgnine responded. "Let's tell it to the world!"

On the following day, newspapers headlined the startling news: ETHEL MERMAN TO WED ERNEST BORGNINE.

"I'm certainly happy, and I think Miss Merman is, too," Borgnine commented. "What can I say? It just happened."

"I can't believe it, I'm in love!" said Ethel as she snuggled close to Ernie for photographers. "I've never been in love—really in love—before. For the first time in my life I feel protected, I have a feeling of security. I wouldn't believe it, but it's true."

Ernie had met and been approved by Ethel's parents and by her son, home for Christmas from his theater arts studies at Carnegie Tech. Ethel telephoned the news to her daughter in Colorado. The wedding would be held at a place convenient for the families, said Ernie, possibly in California. It would have to be delayed for six months; his divorce from Katy Jurado would not be final until June.

The jubilant Borgnine returned to California to resume filming of "McHale's Navy." On his first day back with the company, comedian Joe Flynn held aloft a headline announcing the engagement and crowed: "I get the pick of the litter." Ernie was furious and wouldn't speak to him for months.

Many of Ethel's friends were appalled by the prospect of her marriage to Borgnine. Among them was Benay Venuta, who accompanied Ethel to London for the recording of an album.

"Ethel, you don't even *know* Ernest Borgnine," Benay argued. "You don't know what kind of a man he is. I saw Katy Jurado at a party in New York. She told me, 'You should warn your friend Ethel Merman about Ernest Borgnine.' "

"Oh, she's just jealous because I got him," Ethel replied. "He loves me. I'm going to marry him, move to California, bring Mom and Pop out there, and get myself a television series. That'll be the perfect life for me."

Having experienced three swift weddings, Ethel enjoyed the leisure of a six-month engagement. She left for California, where

Lucille Ball gave her a bridal shower attended by Gypsy Rose Lee, Vivian Vance and other Hollywood pals. And she and Ernie engaged in a series of mid-continent rendezvous.

"For about six months, Ethel didn't want to work," recalls her manager, Milt Pickman. "I had trouble reaching her, and I couldn't figure out why. Later I found out she was meeting Ernie on weekends when he got off work from 'McHale's Navy.' They stayed at the Ambassador East in Chicago, the Roosevelt Hotel in New Orleans and other well-known hotels in other cities. Amazingly, they managed to remain incognito."

Ethel received a work offer she couldn't resist: a movie comedy produced by Ross Hunter and starring James Garner, Angie Dickinson, Dick Van Dyke, Elke Sommer and Carl Reiner, who also wrote the script. Ethel wore a series of gaudy costumes in her role as Madam Coco. She lived with a number of nubile young women in what was obviously a bordello but could not be termed that because of the film industry's censorship code.

"When this picture came up, Ernie said it was too good to turn down," Ethel told me on the set of *The Art of Love*. "But now I hardly have a minute to take care of the wedding, and what details!"

Fortunately, she had already arranged for her wedding dress in New York, and she described it for me: "It's chiffon in three shades of yellow, with a beige slip underneath so you don't really know which shade you're seeing. It's street-length, very full, with a tight waist, stiff bodice and scooped neckline edged in seed pearls. The sleeves are puffy and full-length with seed pearls around the cuff, which is tight. Then I'll wear a yellow veil that just covers the eyes, with a ring of seed pearls around the top."

She went on to tell how she and Ernie wanted a small wedding, but that it just seemed to grow. Her parents were coming out from New York, young Ethel would fly in from Colorado Springs and Bobby would take time out from his studies at Carnegie Tech. Ernie had invited all of his buddies from "McHale's Navy." "I know," said Ethel, "because I addressed all the envelopes."

Meanwhile she was moving her furniture into Ernie's house: "He said to move out anything of his that I wanted to, and I took him at his word. I brought out all of my paintings, and now his living room looks like the Museum of Modern Art. I don't know where we're going to put all the stuff."

She made it clear that she had no intention of becoming a Beverly Hills housewife: "I'll work when I want to. Ernie has said many times—and I use his words—that a talent like mine shouldn't be hidden. I'll do some television and play my night club act here and there, but I won't do another Broadway show. No, sir. That wouldn't make sense for our marriage."

The wedding took place in the garden of Borgnine's house on June 27, 1964, with Ethel's family and a few close friends in attendance. Milt Pickman was best man, his wife Kay matron of honor. As Pickman drove Ethel to the reception at Chasen's restaurant, she asked him, "Who's paying for this party?"

"Who do you think is paying?" Pickman replied.

"You're ducking me."

"Well, Ethel, it's customary for the parents of the bride to pay for the wedding and reception."

"You mean my mother and father are expected to pay?"

"That's right."

"And who's going to pay them?"

"You are."

Ethel and Ernie entered Chasen's Chestnut Room together and were cheered by the guests, who included Bob Hope, Milton Berle, Gypsy Rose Lee, Lucille Ball and Jack Benny. Also the raucous crew from "McHale's Navy": Tim Conway, Carl Ballantine, Gary Vinson, Gavin McLeod, etc.

Ernie escorted his bride through the throng, beaming at her in admiration. To Ethel's old friends, she seemed extraordinarily demure. After a champagne toast, guests urged Ethel to sing.

"Oh, no," she said. "Not at my own wedding reception."

"Come on," Ernie urged. "I've never heard my baby sing."

She shot him an annoyed glance. "You haven't?" Ethel said. She obliged by singing "I Got Rhythm," delighting her listeners by placing special emphasis on the line "I got my man—who could ask for anything more?"

Ernie had planned a honeymoon to the Orient, paid for by American Express for which he had made a personal appearance.

First, Ethel had to complete three final days of work on *The Art of Love*. Then Milt Pickman drove the newlyweds to Los Angeles International Airport and wished them a happy honeymoon.

On the following day, Pickman lifted a ringing telephone receiver and was greeted with the apoplectic voice of Ethel Merman. She unleashed a string of expletives, all directed at her new husband, Ernest Borgnine. Then he came on and made similar comments about his bride. Both said they were returning immediately to California.

"Calm down," Pickman urged. "If you came back now, it'll make the papers and you'll both be embarrassed. Take the flight to Tokyo. Maybe you'll feel different by the time you get there."

After one night in Japan, Ethel and Ernie took the return flight to Los Angeles.

Pickman was waiting when they arrived. Ethel stormed off the plane in a rage, Ernie followed fifty feet behind, looking just as angry. Ethel began cursing Borgnine to Pickman, who tried to calm her.

"I'm not going to that bastard's house; I don't want to be under the same roof with him," she ranted.

"I don't think that's a good idea," the manager counseled. "You don't want to be in a position of desertion."

For one tortuous week, Ethel Merman and Ernest Borgnine coexisted in a warlike atmosphere, then Ethel moved into the Beverly Hills Hotel and ordered her attorney to draw up divorce papers. The next thorny matter: what to do with the wedding presents.

Milt Pickman and Mel Tucker, Borgnine's business manager, arbitrated the negotiations, dividing the list of donors between Ethel's friends and Ernie's friends. Ethel was unrelenting. When a gift-giver was a mutual friend, she insisted, "I know him better than Borgnine does."

Ross Hunter, producer of *The Art of Love*, had presented the Borgnines with an expensive glass bar cart that had been sold to him as "one of a kind." While shopping at the same store months later, Hunter came across the same cart. Ethel had returned it for a refund.

On August 6, news of the separation of Ethel Merman and

Ernest Borgnine appeared in the Los Angeles newspapers. "I have nothing to say, absolutely nothing," Ethel told a reporter. "I don't mean to be rude—but nothing." On the set of "McHale's Navy," Ernie Borgnine remarked, "No comment. Ask my wife."

In November, Ethel appeared in Santa Monica Superior Court to seek a divorce. She declared that she and her husband had quarreled over the maid employed at his house: "I objected strenuously to this woman, but Mr. Borgnine refused to fire her. Mr. Borgnine said he did not intend to change his mode of living, and if I didn't like it, I could lump it." The divorce was granted.

What happened between Ethel and Ernie? Neither of them would talk about it. One of Ethel's favorite jokes was the one about Chapter XXVIII of her second autobiography, *Merman.* The chapter is titled "My Marriage to Ernest Borgnine." It is a blank page.

Obviously there was a clash between two tremendous temperaments.

The Borgnine debacle tinctured Ethel Merman's life with bitterness and disillusion. She would have dalliances thereafter, but never again would she give her vulnerable heart to a man.

A few years later, she expressed her disillusion to Edith Efron of *TV Guide:*

"My last experience—which I won't go into—well, marriage doesn't last. You go into it, you think it will be wonderful. And *pow!* it blows up. A lot of men are Jekyll and Hydes. They're one thing before the conquest—and another thing afterwards. Men are always looking around. They're looking at the young ones with the mini-skirts. I'd rather be single than live like that. They all cheat.

"It's a terrible feeling. Haven't I got enough to hold somebody? An attractive gal walks in the room—bzzzz, all the men *look* and *talk.*

"I'd rather not be married. It would break my heart."

17.

Death in Colorado

Work seemed like the best antidote, and Ethel Merman told Milt Pickman to keep her as busy as possible. He booked her for an engagement at the Hilton Hotel in Sydney, Australia, and Roger Edens agreed to leave his producing duties to go along as her accompanist. Ethel's brassy style was well received by the Australians, just as she had won over the English earlier in 1964 during an engagement at London's Talk of the Town night club.

Returning to the United States, Ethel volunteered to join Ross Hunter on a fourteen-city tour to help promote *The Art of Love*. It was a hectic schedule, with interviews at every stop and four appearances daily at theaters. The promotional effort couldn't prevent the movie's failure, however, and *The Art of Love* ended Merman's film career.

When Ethel wasn't appearing on television variety shows or playing night clubs, she traveled. Bobby was nineteen and eager to see the world, so Ethel took him on a three-and-a-half-week tour around the world, visiting Japan, Hong Kong, Thailand, India, Russia and Finland.

Early in 1966, Irving Berlin called Ethel with an intriguing suggestion: Would she like to appear in *Annie Get Your Gun* exactly twenty years after its first production? Ethel was totally opposed to returning to Broadway in a new musical. Berlin explained that the *Annie* revival would play a limited run at the New York State Theater. Ethel said yes.

No matter that she would be playing the girlish Annie Oakley at the age of fifty-eight. Or that her leading man, Bruce Yarnell, was thirty years younger. Ethel plunged into the revival with customary gusto, disregarding Broadway wise guys who dubbed the show *Grannie Get Your Gun*.

When Ethel arrived at the New York State Theater on opening night, she gazed up at the marquee and froze. ANNIE GET YOUR GUN it read, nothing more. She tramped backstage and bawled for the stage manager.

"I'm not going on," she announced. "What the hell is happening? Why isn't my name on the marquee?"

The stage manager explained that traditionally the theater did not list performers on the marquee, only titles.

"I don't give a fuck for tradition," Ethel replied. "If 'Ethel Merman' isn't above the title, you don't get Ethel Merman. Now run along and tell the producers to go fuck themselves." A hastily painted sign permitted the opening night to proceed.

Ethel Merman had been absent from the Broadway theater for six years, and the newspaper critics welcomed her back joyfully.

"Little Sure Shot is older, but she is also more mellow," said the *Times*. "Most important, the pipes sound true, if not quite as loud, as they ever did. And that implacable, straightforward thrust towards a comic situation can't be stopped by anything—neither time nor a first-night audience whose love threatened to turn the show into a noisy devotional service."

For the revival Berlin had written a new song, "Old-Fashioned Wedding," a counterpoint number along the lines of "You're Just in Love," and it stopped the show in the middle of the second act. The libretto was tightened by eliminating the secondary love story and hence the song "Who Do You Love, I Hope." The five-week engagement was so successful that Ethel agreed to play another eight weeks.

The revival cast of *Annie* included Harry Bellaver, repeating his role as the original Sitting Bull, Jerry Orbach as Charlie Davenport and Benay Venuta as Dolly Tate, the role she had played in the movie. Venuta and Merman had been friends for thirty years, but *Annie* marked the first time they had appeared together.

"I was able to see close up how Ethel operated," Venuta remarks. "Some musical performers go through a ritual of preparation before a performance. Ethel came to the theater and cleared her throat. That was her preparation.

"One thing shocked me. As a courtesy, I always stopped by her dressing room to say hello before the performance. When it came time to start the show, she said to me, 'Let's go face the assholes.' "

When Milt Pickman returned to the film business, Tom Korman became Merman's agent. One of his first bookings for her was the prestigious Palmer House in Chicago. Ethel opened during Lent, in the midst of a fierce storm. When she swept onto the Palmer House floor, she faced an audience of twenty-eight people. Korman was sitting at a ringside table with invited guests, including the actress Eleanor Parker. The agent could tell that Ethel was seething as she belted out her songs. She became more incensed as the spotlight started to wander. The electrician was drunk.

Ethel didn't return for a bow after the final number. Korman warily escorted his guests to the Merman dressing room. His fears grew as he heard Ethel's heels clicking back and forth on the dressing room floor. He knocked on the door and it swung open to reveal the furious Merman. Korman began, "Ethel, I'd like you to meet—"

"That fucking spot man!" Ethel ranted. "Fire the sonofabitch."

Reflecting on his years as Merman's agent, Korman says, "Ethel could eat people alive if she felt she had been badly treated. But afterward she would be cool and businesslike. She was a two-calls-a-day client. She had to know that you were there and thinking of her, but she never asked, 'What have you got for me today?' She didn't *need* to work, as some actors do."

Ethel wanted to work in television, and Korman hustled her roles in the Marlo Thomas series "That Girl," "The Lucy Show" with Lucille Ball and the comic-strip adventure "Batman." Next came "Tarzan."

"Ethel Merman in 'Tarzan?' " said Ron Leif, Tom Korman's partner.

"Yeah," said Steve Shagan, who was producing the "Tarzan" series. "NBC wants a two-parter, and my star, Ron Ely, wants to ride a horse. So I'm putting together a two-hour show with Ethel Merman in Africa singing hymns to a bunch of hippies who have dropped out, plus Tarzan on horseback."

"Sounds crazy, but send me a script, and I'll show it to Ethel."

Ethel loved the script, and she flew to California to confer with Shagan. He telephoned her room in the Beverly Hills Hotel and said he would meet her in the Polo Lounge. "Okay, sweetie," she said, "I'll be wearing a white dress with a white carnation." As if I needed help to identify Ethel Merman, the producer mused.

She arrived and enthused over the script, adding that she knew the perfect hymns to use. "I'll be the first one on the set, and I'll know my lines, I promise you," said Ethel. "Just one thing: Can I have another take if I feel I need it?"

"Of course," said Shagan. "Film is the cheapest part of the budget."

"Then you got me, sweetheart!"

The bizarre script was filmed in Durango, Mexico, and Ethel made no complaint, despite the primitive housing and native meals. She even joined the film crews in revelry at the Bucket of Blood saloon. Other movie companies were working near Durango, and among those in the saloon were Sean Connery, Anthony Quinn and John Huston. All listened raptly as Ethel Merman sang "I Got Rhythm" at one o'clock in the morning to the accompaniment of a Mexican guitar.

Young Ethel had become a source of deep concern for her mother. She had seemed like such a happy girl, devoted to her son and daughter and to her husband. But Ethel had evidenced signs of emotional instability. At times young Ethel wanted nothing more than to be a wife and mother, and she devoted her days to cooking and housework. Then, deciding she wanted to pursue her mother's profession, she submerged herself in campus play productions.

Ethel had completed two and a half years of college when Bill graduated and moved the family to Los Angeles. She became increasingly serious about wanting to pursue an acting career, and her mother made sporadic attempts to assist her. When Merman played *Call Me Madam* at the Valley Music Theater in the San Fernando Valley, she directed the producers to hire young Ethel for the role of the ambassador's secretary.

At times young Ethel seemed to resent her mother's efforts to help her. She detested being called Ethel, Jr. and became incensed when she was compared to her mother. When they appeared together on the "Tonight Show," she became so vitriolic that Johnny Carson cut the interview short. The two Ethels had a shouting match in the dressing room afterward.

"I'll never amount to anything in show business because my mother is a star," Ethel complained to friends. "That's the way it is. I don't have a chance."

Her depression became severe, her behavior more erratic. In February of 1967, Bill Geary obtained a divorce and custody of the children. Ethel underwent medical treatment and appeared to be making progress with her emotional problems under the supervision of a psychiatrist. With her doctors' encouragement, she returned to Colorado with the intention of resuming her college education.

In August of 1967, Ethel telephoned Bill Geary and asked if the children could visit her for a couple of weeks before the start of the fall semester. Geary agreed.

"Do you think that's wise?" Benay Venuta asked Merman. "Do you really think little Ethel is well enough to take care of the children?"

"I don't know," Merman said worriedly. "But what can I do? I'm only the grandmother."

Barbara Jean, who was six, and Michael, five, accompanied

their mother to Green Mountain Falls, a resort near Colorado Springs.

Mrs. Jerry Friesen, a tourist from North Newton, Kansas, was sitting in her car in front of the motel at 9:30 on the morning of August 23 when a little girl ran up to her. "I can't wake my mama up and she's turning blue," the girl cried.

Mrs. Friesen accompanied the girl to the cottage and found a young woman in a nightgown, curled up on the couch. She summoned the local fire department, but attempts to resuscitate Ethel Six Geary failed. A coroner arrived and estimated that she had died at midnight, apparently of an overdose of tranquilizers and barbiturates. Several bottles of drugs were found in the cottage, along with empty vodka bottles.

Bill Geary's sister-in-law came from Colorado Springs to identify the body and claim Barbara Jean and Michael. Bill telephoned the dreadful news to Ethel Merman in New York. She resolved immediately to fly to Colorado. She telephoned Benay Venuta and asked, "Will you go with me?" "Certainly, Ethel," Benay replied.

The fastest way to reach Colorado was to fly to San Francisco. Ethel and Benay were met there by Bobby, who was accompanied by a doctor. Ethel was hysterical, and the doctor gave her a sedative for the flight to Denver. When the party arrived in Colorado Springs, Ethel could not bring herself to view her daughter's body. "I want a lock of her hair," she said. "Would you cut it for me, Benay?"

Benay agreed, but Bill Geary told her, "You don't want to see Ethel the way she is now. I'll do it for you."

Bobby assumed responsibility for the funeral arrangements. Ethel's agents, Tom Korman and Ron Leif, also flew to Colorado Springs to console her. "I don't see how she can come out of this," said Korman.

"She'll make it," said Leif. "She's a strong lady."

By the time the agents had arrived, Ethel had recovered from the initial shock and was numbly observing the rituals of a family tragedy. The funeral was held in Colorado Springs, and young Ethel's ashes were installed in a mausoleum at the Evergreen Shrine of Rest.

Dr. Raoul Urich, coroner of El Paso County, reported that Ethel Six Geary, age twenty-five, had died from an overdose of tranquilizers, barbiturates and other drugs not identified. Traces of alcohol were also found.

"I feel certain the death was accidental," the coroner told a reporter from the Denver *Post*. "Persons who take barbiturates and tranquilizers develop a kind of somnolence. They have a tendency in their drowsy state to forget they have taken a drug and give themselves another dose. I think this is what happened here."

To the end of her life Ethel Merman was haunted by reports that her daughter had been a drug addict and a suicide.

"Ethel was *not* on hard drugs," Merman insisted again and again. "She was taking *medication*—drugs that had been prescribed by doctors to help treat her condition. She was not a doper. Her death was *accidental*, not a suicide. The coroner said so. She left no note, she wasn't despondent. She was happy to have the kids with her. She certainly wouldn't invite them to visit her and then kill herself, knowing they would discover her body. Never! And Ethel had just bought a horse. She loved to ride. Why would she buy a horse if she was contemplating suicide?"

The legend would not die. The 1984 obituaries for Ethel Merman in both the *New York Times* and the Los Angeles *Times* reported that her daughter had been a suicide.

18.

A Merman Portrait

For a time Ethel Merman was inconsolable. Back in New York, friends trooped to her Park Lane apartment and found a mother overwhelmed by grief, blaming herself for failing to help her daughter find the tranquility she so desperately needed. Ethel went daily to St. Bartholomew's Church to light candles for the soul of Ethel, Jr. and to pray for understanding.

Help came from an unexpected source: a small journal called *The Daily Word*, published by the Unity School of Christianity in Unity Village, Missouri. It had been sent to her by Mary Dayton, a Beverly Hills real estate woman with whom Ethel had formed a warm friendship. Published monthly, *The Daily Word* contained inspirational quotations for each day of the year.

"Mary, *The Daily Word* is terrific!" Ethel telephoned her friend. "I can't tell you how much it has helped me since Little Ethel passed away. I read it every day. I'm even pasting some of my favorites in a notebook so I can review them."

Ethel continued the practice for the rest of her life. Whenever Mary Dayton was distraught over the loss of an escrow or another mishap, Ethel instructed, "Read your *Daily Word*, goddammit! You sent it to me. Read it!"

A photograph of Ethel, Jr. remained beside her mother's bed, along with the lock of hair. Also a framed quotation from *The Daily Word:*

> *The light of God surrounds me.*
> *The love of God enfolds me.*
> *The power of God protects me.*
> *The presence of God watches over me.*
> *Wherever I am, God is.*

At first Ethel could not contemplate singing before an audience. Friends persuaded her that work would be the best escape from her grief, and she made an appearance on the Ed Sullivan television show. She gradually accepted other engagements, and she discovered she could hide her sorrow though she could never remove it.

There was plenty of work to be found: television guest appearances, concerts, revivals of *Call Me Madam.* Ethel rejoined Richard Eastham and Russell Nype to perform the show in three theaters-in-the-round in California during 1966. In 1968, they played *Call Me Madam* in Florida.

When Merman arrived at the theater in Fort Lauderdale, she found six musicians in the pit. "Is this the orchestra?" she inquired testily. Informed that it was, she said, "I want nine pieces, minimum." She got them.

On the evening of the Fort Lauderdale opening, Richard Eastham stopped by Ethel's dressing room and found her weeping, her face stained with mascara. On her makeup table was a local newspaper, opened to an interview with Ethel Merman. It stated that she had suffered the suicides of her second husband and her daughter.

"How can they print that?" Ethel sobbed. "I told the reporter that little Ethel's death was an accident, that she would never have taken her life with the children there. How can they print such things?"

Eastham could not console her, and he expected there would be no performance that night. He was wrong. Ethel played Sally Adams without missing a note or neglecting a laugh.

Call Me Madam was sought by outdoor theaters in Kansas City and St. Louis during the summer of 1969. When Eastham was asked to repeat his role as Cosmo Constantine, he was informed that Russell Nype would receive equal pay and billing with him.

"What the producers pay Russell is their own business," Eastham replied, "but the billing does affect me. I can't allow it."

"That's the way Ethel Merman wants it," he was told.

Eastham telephoned Merman to inquire if she had indeed requested the billing change. "Of course not," she replied edgily. "Why would you think I'd make such a demand?"

Merman, Eastham and Nype played *Call Me Madam* in Kansas City and St. Louis with the billing as before, but the damage had been done. Merman had pronounced Eastham guilty of disloyalty for believing that she would interfere in a billing matter. She treated him perfunctorily onstage and refused to speak to him offstage. Her friendship with Eastham and his wife, which had been extraordinarily warm, had ended. She never spoke to them again.

Such would be the pattern with Ethel Merman in her later years. If a friend, no matter how close, offended Ethel by word or deed, that person was written out of Ethel's life forever. Rarely did she relent.

Betty Bruce and Ethel had been buddies since *Something for the Boys*, sharing a passion for bawdy humor. The friendship began to show strains when Bruce replaced one of the strippers in *Gypsy* and Ethel accused her of upstaging. One night at a party, both women had been drinking, and Bruce felt constrained to warn her friend about a musician with whom Ethel was having a fling.

"He's no good," said the tipsy Betty Bruce. "He told me he doesn't really like you. He just goes out with you because you're Ethel Merman."

The Merman-Bruce friendship was frozen in time for five years, until Betty Bruce was dying of cancer. Ethel reconciled with her old friend, and she paid half of the funeral expenses.

Another entertainer who had attracted notice in a Merman

show became friendly with Ethel, who considered the young woman her protégée. The protégée became a star and seemed faintly condescending once during an appearance with Ethel. Thenceforth Ethel referred to her as "that bloodsucker."

The Merman "shit-list" grew longer. It included onetime close friends, columnists, business associates, restaurants and even countries. A real or imagined slight, a casual remark, a thoughtless gesture—anything could incite her hostility. Merman herself was sometimes the cause of the estrangement, especially when she was drinking.

"After five drinks, Ethel could become a monster," remarks one of her managers. Her acquaintances learned to escape from Ethel when she was in that condition, lest they became victims.

Benay Venuta once gave a party in honor of Donald Stannard, who had launched a costume jewelry business. Benay invited many of her show business friends, including Ethel Merman. Also present was Earl Wilson, the New York *Post* columnist, and his wife. Midway through the party, Ethel cornered the hostess and snapped, "You never would have gotten Earl Wilson to come if I weren't here."

Benay stared at her friend in astonishment. "What are you talking about?"

"He'd never come to a party just for you," Ethel insisted.

"Ethel, for God's sake, I've known Earl and Rosemary for thirty years! They've come here many times."

"You're a goddam liar. I'm sick of your using me." Ethel turned on her heel and left.

Benay never displayed her anger at Ethel's behavior, but for two years she offered only a polite "Hi, Ethel" when they met. Finally Ethel insisted her old friend come to the apartment for a Chinese dinner one evening. Ethel reheated the take-out food and served it to Benay. "That was her way of saying she was sorry," Benay theorizes.

Ethel often took an immediate and unreasoned dislike to individuals and rarely did she change her opinion. This applied even to small children. Of the two children of Temple Texas and Joe Schribman, Ethel adored Owen and distrusted Trudy.

One night at the Schribman house, Ethel awakened Owen, who was two years old, and entertained him by singing all her songs from *Gypsy*.

With Trudy it was different. Ethel never played with the little girl and seldom talked to her. Once, when some of the Schribmans' party guests posed for a group photograph, Trudy made the mistake of standing in front of Ethel. "Back up, honey," Ethel said tartly. "Nobody upstages your aunt Ethel."

George Eells noted a Merman characteristic: "Most diners in a Chinese restaurant share their dishes. Not Ethel. She always ordered the dishes she liked, and she shared them with no one."

Her spirit of competition was ever present, even in small ways. Attending a party at the home of Bob Kaufman, Ethel excused herself for a visit to the bathroom. While using the facilities, she looked up and saw a wall decoration, an old *Theater Arts* magazine with a portrait of Sylvia Sidney, another Kaufman friend. The next day Kaufman received a lobby poster from *The Art of Love* showing Ethel in her madam costume. "Hang this in your bathroom," she instructed.

Ethel was devoted to Madeline Gaxton, calling her every day on the telephone no matter where she was. When they traveled together, Ethel always grabbed both their traveling bags and carried them through air terminals. "I'm balanced this way," said Ethel, barging her way through the crowd.

"I feel like a Chinese lady," commented Mrs. Gaxton.

"What do you mean?" Ethel asked.

"I'm in back of you all the time."

"You'll catch up."

Ethel Merman at sixty was little changed from the big-voiced young woman who bowled over Broadway during the Depression. She never forgot Astoria. Even though she hobnobbed with the Rockefellers and the Duke and Duchess of Windsor, her best friends, she said, were still Martha Neubert and Alice Welch, who went to school with her, and Josie Traeger, a co-worker at the Bragg-Kliesrath Corporation. Whenever she wearied of the theatrical world, Ethel went to Astoria to play anagrams with her old friends.

"They're real people," Ethel explained to her friend Benay Venuta.

"What are we—unreal?" Benay Venuta demanded.

Nobody was more devoted to her parents than Ethel, observes Temple Texas, who started as press agent for Merman during *Gypsy* and became one of her closest friends. "In fact, I think Ethel cared more about her parents than about her own children."

Perhaps, some may argue, that was because children can be rebellious and questioning, while Agnes and Edward Zimmermann were the most adoring of parents. They gloried in Ethel's career, attended every triumph, consoled Ethel in times of trial. Edward Zimmermann unfailingly clipped every news item and review about his daughter and pasted them in scrapbooks.

Ethel telephoned her parents every day whenever she traveled. As they began to feel the symptoms of age, Ethel moved them into the hotel apartment above hers.

Merman always lived in a hotel, first the Park Lane, then the Berkshire. She liked the convenience of a hotel—especially the room service. "I can't cook," she proclaimed, "and I sure as hell am not going to learn at this late date."

She had the kitchens removed from both hotel apartments, leaving only a refrigerator. She was delighted, however, to learn of the convenience of a toaster oven and bought one. When she wasn't going out to dinner, she heated her favorite dish: chicken frankfurters.

For dinner parties, she served drinks and canapés, then took her guests to one of her favorite eateries, usually a steak house or a Chinese restaurant. Almost invariably, she ordered steak or chicken. Fancy dishes did not entice her.

Ethel was fanatical about paying for meals herself and sometimes devised elaborate ruses to ensure that she received the bill. She became emphatic if someone else tried to buy the dinner. She examined each bill with care and sent it back if she detected an overcharge. Always she paid 15 percent of the total, no more, no less, and she excluded the tax in her calculation.

During her heavy drinking period, Merman consumed large

quantities of vodka. She had an interlude of favoring banana daiquiris, which she mixed herself and tried to foist on friends. When hard liquor threatened her health, she switched to wine, always Almadén Chablis.

"When Ethel was hostess of a French wine tasting at the '21' Club," Temple Texas recalls, "she brought along her own bottle of Almadén Chablis. 'You don't think I'm going to drink that other stuff, do you?' she said."

Ethel often drank too much on social occasions, growing louder and more abusive, but she never touched a drop before a performance. That was part of the Merman code.

When considering David Merrick's offer to take over the late run of *Hello, Dolly!*, she agreed to see Pearl Bailey in the show one night. Tom Korman took her to dinner before the performance and was surprised when she ordered a ginger ale.

"Later I realized what she was thinking," Korman says. "Pearl Bailey made a habit of inviting performers onstage with her at the curtain call, and Ethel didn't want to drink before working. Sure enough, Pearl brought Ethel onstage, and they sang a couple of songs together. Afterward Ethel and I went out and got bombed."

Ethel was insatiable in her appetite for Rabelaisian stories. Whenever she heard a new dirty joke, she roared with laughter and immediately repeated it to her network of telephone correspondents. She listened gamely to their jokes too, but often retorted, "Oh hell, I heard that one three weeks ago."

José Ferrer, who had only a fleeting acquaintance with Ethel, remembers encountering her once at a rather formal reception in a palatial Manhattan residence. As Ferrer was descending the curving, marbled double stairway, Merman was ascending the other side.

"Hey, Joe," Ethel shouted, "did you hear the one about the Polack who was so dumb he thought Fuck-king and Suck-king were a couple of Chinese cities?"

"No, I hadn't, Ethel," said Ferrer, continuing on his way with dignity.

Ethel was equally relentless with risqué greeting cards. She hunted them in stationery stores in New York and Los Angeles, as well as other cities where she appeared, and was constantly seeking new ones. Her favorites were those that seemed like normal greeting cards but had an unexpected punch line when the card was opened. For example, a card received by Richard Eastham: "Help bring love to the world. . . . Fuck someone today."

Despite her fondness for bawdy humor, Ethel Merman remained surprisingly puritanical in some respects. The lifelong Episcopalian and Republican was appalled by the new freedoms exercised by the youth of the 1960s. The hippie movement, the drug culture, the sexual revolution—all were subjected to Ethel's scorn. She couldn't understand why young people would behave so abominably. And she certainly had no taste for their rock music.

Ethel also deplored what was happening to the Broadway theater, of which she had been the temple goddess. She abhorred the license of *Hair* and *Oh, Calcutta!* After seeing *Chicago*, she complained to her friend Rose Marie: "You know what some broad says right at the beginning? She says, 'I gotta pee'! Can you imagine that in a musical? Jeez, that ain't Broadway."

Years later she refused to attend *Sweeney Todd.* Her comment: "Who wants to see a show about a guy who cuts up people and bakes them in pies?"

Her friends were amazed when Ethel commented once about having seen a recent opera. Merman and opera? The two seemed antithetical, yet Ethel was fascinated by certain operatic singers, first Lily Pons, later Joan Sutherland. Robert Gardiner, Ethel's concert manager and a devotee of opera, took her to *Macbeth, Rigoletto* and other attractions at the Metropolitan. "Ethel loved to hear the singing," he recalls. "She wouldn't get up from her seat between the acts."

Gardiner introduced Ethel to opera people at parties on his roof garden. He was surprised to see her and singer Sherrill Milnes locked in amused conversation. Gardiner discovered later they were exchanging dirty jokes.

Ethel had no interest in other cultural or intellectual pursuits.

She read magazines only if they contained pictures. Except for *The Daily Word* and other works of inspiration, she never read books. Her only pastime was needlepoint, which she pursued single-mindedly in dressing rooms, at parties, on planes. On one "red-eye" flight to California, Ethel was unable to sleep at dawn and decided to bring out her needlepoint. She raised the window shade for better light to work by.

"Lady, I'm trying to sleep," grumbled the man sitting next to her. "Would you lower the shade?"

"Go find yourself another seat, brother," Merman replied. "I'm working."

A friend considered it typical of Merman that in all her years of doing needlepoint, she always employed only one basic stitch.

Ethel's great passion was gossip. She loved to hear the latest rumors about the show biz crowd, and she functioned as a clearing house for information. She spent hours on the telephone: If the person on the other end could offer neither the latest gossip nor dirty jokes, Ethel's conversation was perfunctory—especially on expensive long-distance calls.

Realizing her sense of thrift, Ethel's friends learned not to expect lavish gifts from her. When she gave a present, it was usually small but thoughtful. Some friends suspected she maintained a closet of unwanted gifts that she recycled as presents to others.

Ethel detested the public obligations of stardom. She cringed under the onslaught of adoring fans and dispensed autographs grudgingly and with little grace. At the end of dinner once with friends in a Manhattan restaurant, she donned the oversized pink sunglasses she wore in the daytime. "Why on earth do you wear those?" Tony Cointreau asked. "With these on, nobody recognizes me," she declared. As she made her way out of the restaurant, the other diners rose and applauded Ethel Merman.

She took pride in never having hired a secretary. Ethel was a prodigious correspondent, pounding out single-spaced letters on a script typewriter. As a writer of thank-you notes, she was almost as thorough as Joan Crawford. On every out-of-town letter envelope she typed the words *Fly Me*, continuing the practice long after the postal service abandoned the air-mail designation.

Early in her career, Ethel Merman had learned how to look her best: piled-up hair and high heels to add height; low-cut dresses and high skirts to accent her best features, bust and legs. She never changed.

"She had beautiful legs, and she liked to show them," says Dorothy Strelsin, a longtime friend. "She wore short skirts and often swung around so the legs would be revealed. She loved shoes, wore only pumps with high heels to make her legs prettier."

Her clothes were high fashion, often purchased at a bargain. She discovered a clever way to augment her wardrobe. Whenever she appeared for a television special, she remarked, "Gee, I don't have anything I can wear." She was allowed to shop for a dress at the company's expense. Invariably when the special had been completed, she was allowed to keep the dress.

The Merman walk was unique. With each stride she flicked the side of her dress, giving her a jaunty, self-confident look while incidentally showing off the Merman legs.

The few close friends that Ethel had were women: Dorothy Strelsin, Benay Venuta, Temple Texas, Madeline Gaxton, Mary Dayton, the chums from Astoria. After four divorces—the last two particularly humiliating—Ethel had grown wary of men. She worked with them, sometimes flirted with them, exchanged dirty jokes with them—but she rarely trusted them.

She had been hurt too many times, and she was vigilant not only for herself, but for her friends. At a cast party after the premiere of a Broadway show featuring her friend Rose Marie, Ethel—like many of the guests—got drunk. Rose Marie introduced the man she intended to marry, and Ethel congratulated them both, declaring she would sing "Oh Promise Me" at their wedding. When she left the party, Ethel turned to the fiancé and said with a smile, "That's my baby. If I hear that you harmed one hair of her head, I'll cut your balls off. Good night."

Despite her frequent ferocity, some of Ethel's close friends theorize that she was basically a shy person.

Ethel Merman shy?

"Absolutely," argues Temple Texas. "She was completely honest and totally shy. If my husband and I gave a party for her, it had to be *her* guest list. She was never comfortable among strangers. Once she dropped in at our Christmas party. There were about thirty people, and Ethel didn't know them. She spent her time with Owen and Trudy, our children, and then she left."

It is a bold theory, yet others who saw her close up have also suggested that behind all the swaggering bluster of Ethel Merman was an uncertain, woundable woman named Ethel Agnes Zimmermann.

"Ethel definitely was shy," Benay Venuta testifies. "Whenever we went to a big party together, she always said, 'You go in first.' She always felt uneasy in a crowd.

"She was shy about visiting her old boyfriend, Walter Annenberg, when she and I went to London for the *Annie Get Your Gun* revival album. Walter was ambassador to Great Britain, and I sent a note that we were coming. He replied with his phone number and a date to visit him at his private residence.

"Ethel was terribly nervous about seeing him. 'Gee, will he remember me?' she said. 'What will his wife say?' As soon as we walked in, Walter said, 'Hiya, Cupcake'—that was his pet name for her—and he told his wife, 'I had such a love affair with this woman!' "

Considering the fact that Ethel introduced the show business anthem and remained its most frequent singer, there was surprisingly little show business in her personal life. Many of her friends were from entirely different fields of endeavor. Unlike most high-powered performers, she never evidenced the compulsion to be constantly "on." And the business aspects of her work failed to interest her, except when they directly affected her own career.

She never felt the need to be seen at parties and premieres. Carole Cook once asked Ethel if she had attended a recent New York affair that had been crowded with entertainment stars.

"Oh, no," Ethel replied, "I'm not *that* kind of show business."

19.

Good Times, Bad Times

Ethel's last Broadway show was *Hello, Dolly!*, which Jerry Herman and Michael Stewart had written for her in 1963. With Carol Channing as star, the show had enjoyed tremendous success. The producer, David Merrick, had kept *Hello, Dolly!* on Broadway by introducing a succession of Dolly Levis: Ginger Rogers, Betty Grable, Martha Raye, Pearl Bailey, Phyllis Diller and Bibi Osterwald.

Year after year, Merrick tried every possible strategy to induce Merman to assume the role. Year after year, she said no.

Finally in early 1970 she consented to star in *Hello, Dolly!* for a three-month period in the seventh year of the run. "I understand that Jerry Herman wrote a couple of songs for me, but they weren't used in the show," she said.

"That's right," said Merrick. "They were the kind of song that only Merman could do."

"I wanna hear 'em," she said.

Ethel went to the West 10th Street carriage house of Jerry Herman, and the songwriter told her how seeing *Annie Get Your Gun* had inspired him to pursue a career in musicals. The meeting was off to a good start. Admittedly nervous, Herman played and sang "Love, Look in My Window" and "World, Take Me Back."

"I can handle 'em," Ethel said confidently.

Since the original director, Gower Champion, was in California, the Merman version of *Hello, Dolly!* was staged by his assistant, Lucia Victor. Rehearsals went smoothly; as always, Ethel submitted to direction, as long as it didn't conflict with her principles of how best to present herself. Nothing was eliminated to make room for the two new songs; ten minutes were simply added to the running time.

Opening night for Ethel Merman in *Hello, Dolly!* came on March 28, 1970. David Merrick and his press department gave it all the trappings of a Broadway premiere: First-string critics were invited, and the St. James Theater was jammed with Merman fans, many of them homosexuals. As with Judy Garland and other stars, Ethel Merman in her later years attracted a vociferous following in the gay community and became a favorite subject of female impersonators.

When Merman made her entrance as Dolly Levi, the ovation was thunderous, not only from homosexuals who saw her as a kind of superwoman, but from Broadway theater fans who considered her an icon. Predictably, their outpourings irritated the critics.

"They stand up and scream on the first number," wrote Walter Kerr in the *Times*, "they stand up and scream louder on the second and by the time she gets to the 'Hello, Dolly!' number they don't bother to sit down between notes. I'd like to make a deal with them. Equal time for Miss Merman."

Jerry Herman watched the show from the back of the theater, waiting for the reaction to the two new songs.

"Both of them stopped the show cold," he remembers. "It's easy to stop a show with a big, rousing number and a chorus behind you. But she did both songs alone on the stage. After she sang 'World, Take Me Back,' I ran backstage and found her in the wings. She was ecstatic. 'I told you! I told you!' she said."

At the finale, the audience rose once more, and the noise was deafening. Ethel stood center-stage, eyes brimming with joyful tears, face beaming. The curtain descended and rose a dozen times before her followers would leave the theater. Later, flanked by her agents Ron Leif and Tom Korman, Ethel strode into Sardi's for another standing ovation. Merman was back, and all was well with Broadway.

The critics reflected that feeling, and for the final time they exercised their skills in analyzing Ethel Merman's unique hold on a Broadway audience.

"My God, what a woman she is," Walter Kerr marveled. "Her comic sense is every bit as authoritative, as high-handed really, as her singing voice. At the very opening, as she's offering one of her calling cards to a horse, she makes the gesture with such confidence that you expect the horse to take the card. . . .

"Merman is odd. She has won love by never asking for it. She does what she does, on her time and in her tempo, and it's up to you to decide when you want to come around. Everybody's come around by this time, and there she still is, cocky, chin tilted, half-dollar eyes sprouting sunburst black lashes, power flowing from her that will still light the town when Con Edison fails."

Ethel was so pleased by the reception of her Dolly that she agreed to extend the engagement by six months, allowing the show to surpass *My Fair Lady* as the longest-running musical in Broadway history.

Merman's forty-year reign, from *Girl Crazy* to *Hello, Dolly!*, had ended. She had been a star throughout that time, from the innocent entertainments of the Depression to the glittery crowd-pleasers of the war years to the superhits of *Annie Get Your Gun* and *Call Me Madam*, then the sharp-edged new kind of musical, *Gypsy*. Ethel Merman had devoted two-thirds of her life to the Broadway theater. No more. "From now on, I'm living for Ethel," she declared with all the fervor of Mama Rose.

The 1970s did not bring the tranquility Ethel had hoped for. Her parents' health became a constant concern. Agnes Zimmermann had grown frail, and although her husband remained sturdy, his eyesight was diminishing. After the end of the *Hello, Dolly!* run, Agnes had a heart attack that incapacitated her. Ethel hired a full-time nurse to care for her parents.

Two young English producers, Barry Brown and Fritz Holt, came to Ethel with a proposal. They wanted to revive *Gypsy* in London, then bring it back to Broadway. Here was a chance to play a show in London for the first time, and in her best role.

"I can't do it," she replied. "My mother is too ill. I can't leave her, nor my father."

"We'd be willing to fly both your parents to London and provide the best of care," said one of the producers.

"No, it would be too much of a strain on both of them."

In 1973 Agnes Zimmermann suffered a massive stroke. Ethel and her father went to Roosevelt Hospital every day for eight months, even though Agnes didn't recognize them. Unwilling to leave New York for singing engagements, Ethel decided to volunteer at the hospital. Every week she served as a saleswoman in the gift shop, a practice she was to continue for years. Some customers recognized her, some didn't, and she found great amusement in their reactions.

On January 14, 1974, Agnes Gardner Zimmermann died. Ethel took her ashes to Colorado Springs, where they were placed beside those of Ethel, Jr.

Even though her mother's death had been expected, Ethel was desolated by it. She talked often now of Mom and Little Ethel and how she would one day be reunited with them in heaven. "You do believe that I'll see them again, don't you?" she asked a journalist friend.

"Don't ask me that, Ethel," he replied. "I'm not really a believer when it comes to such things."

"Then I feel sorry for you," she snapped.

Edward Zimmermann was at first confused by the loss of the woman who had been virtually inseparable from him for more than fifty years. But, with the help of Ethel's constant attention, he learned to adjust. Confident that he was in the hands of a good caretaker—the same woman who had cared for Agnes Zimmermann—Ethel began accepting offers for appearances again.

Ethel's relations with her son Bobby were ambivalent throughout the 1970s. She was fiercely devoted to him, far more than she had ever been to Ethel, Jr. Bobby had studied stagecraft at

Carnegie Tech and at the prestigious American Conservatory Theater in San Francisco, where his mother once gave a one-woman benefit concert.

"Bobby's a genius at lighting," Ethel bragged, and he sometimes supervised the lights on her appearance tours. But despite her offers to use her considerable influence to get him jobs—or perhaps because of them—he rarely was employed. He preferred to travel, investigating the philosophies of the world.

During a concert tour, Ethel sat in her hotel suite watching a quiz show on daytime television. The master of ceremonies posed a question to a contestant: "Larry Hagman, who plays J.R. on 'Dallas,' is the son of an equally famous woman who is a star on Broadway. What is her name?"

"Ethel Merman," replied the contestant.

"Haw!" exclaimed Merman. "My son doesn't even have a job!"

Ethel couldn't understand Bobby's adoption of the casualness of his generation. She once complained to a friend: "Bobby came to my apartment in a sheepskin coat, with hair down to his shoulders, and *she* was with him. This was some broad who was already married. He wanted to stay, but I told him he wasn't going to sleep with a married woman under my roof." Yet at other times mother and son were exceptionally close, and Bobby always arrived to console Ethel in times of tragedy.

Ethel was pleased when Bobby fell in love with Barbara Colby, an actress he had met at the American Conservatory Theater. Ethel and Barbara formed an immediate rapport. Being an actress, Barbara could understand and sympathize with Ethel's drive and self-centeredness. As a mother, Ethel saw Barbara as a compassionate, talented and sound-thinking woman who could offer Bobby the stability he needed.

An actress of exceptional range, Barbara Colby was well respected in theater circles on both coasts. She had made her off-Broadway debut in *Six Characters in Search of an Author*. Her first Broadway play was *The Devils*, with Anne Bancroft and Jason Robards. In Los Angeles she became a member of the Center Theater Group at the Mark Taper Forum, appearing in *Father's Day, Murderous Angels, Afternoon Tea* and other new plays. Her stage accomplishments led to a number of television roles.

Barbara Colby and Robert Levitt were married in 1972. They separated two years later. Ethel was furious with Bobby, blaming him for failing to make the marriage work. Her warm relationship with Barbara didn't change. (Many of Ethel's friends believed that Barbara had taken the place of Ethel, Jr. in her affections.)

Finally, at the age of thirty-seven, Barbara Colby appeared on the brink of a career breakthrough. She had made a good impression on "The Mary Tyler Moore Show," appearing as a cellmate when Mary found herself in jail. Barbara was signed to a contract for a featured role in a new series, "Phyllis."

Then, the terrible night of July 24, 1975.

Ethel had come to Los Angeles for a television special. She and Rose Marie had attended *Wonderful Town* at the Music Center downtown, then returned to the Beverly Hills Hotel. As soon as Ethel entered the room, the telephone rang. Ethel's face grew white as she listened. "Oh, my God, no!" she cried.

"What is it, Ethel?" Rose Marie said.

"It's Barbara. She's been murdered."

The killing appeared to have been random and senseless. Barbara Colby and an actor friend, James Kiernan, had concluded a yoga class at a studio near Culver City. As they walked to their car, a light-colored van drove up, and one of the occupants fired two bullets. Barbara was killed immediately; Kiernan died ninety minutes later at a hospital. The assailants were never found.

"What can I do?" Ethel wailed.

"There's nothing you can do," said Rose Marie. "The police are taking care of everything."

"Stay with me. I can't bear to face this alone."

"I'll stay with you, Ethel."

Others arrived to console Ethel the following day, and they found her surprisingly calm. Mary Dayton offered Valium, but Ethel said, "I don't need that stuff. I'll be okay."

Barbara had been a member of a sect that followed a mystic Indian philosophy, and a memorial service was held in a shrine in Santa Monica. When Ethel arrived, she was dismayed to find an incense-filled place with barefooted people sitting on the floor. They faced a wooden casket with a photograph of the sect's guru above it.

The sect did not believe in death, and one speaker after another remarked that Barbara's spirit had merely risen to another plane. Finally it was Ethel Merman's time to speak.

"I don't know what this shit is all about," she said. "All I know is, I can't get up in the morning and get Barbara on the telephone, and I'm goddamned mad about it."

Always she responded with anger, lashing out at the multiple injustices perpetrated on her. As the years passed, she grew indignant over the sorrow that her daughter had inflicted on her. "How could she do that to me?" demanded Merman, never conceding any guilt over young Ethel's troubles.

20.

Angry Years

On a sunny Saturday afternoon in mid-July, Ethel Merman floated lazily on a rubber raft in the swimming pool of her friend Bob Kaufman in East Hampton. Eyes closed, luxuriating in the warmth, she seemed totally at ease, a rare condition for Ethel Merman. Suddenly she roused and called, "What time is it?"

The startled Kaufman replied, "It's two o'clock, Ethel. Why do you ask?"

She smiled smugly. "I was just thinking of all those poor bastards who right at this moment are putting on their makeup, changing into costumes and getting ready for a goddam matinee!" She closed her eyes and resumed her silent floating in the placid pool.

On September 23, 1974, *Gypsy* returned to Broadway, this time with Angela Lansbury as star. It was the production that Ethel Merman had declined to join in London. The show and Miss Lansbury had been cheered by London critics and audiences, and the reaction was the same in New York. Some reviewers preferred the new version to the Merman *Gypsy* of fifteen years before.

Predictably, Merman was angry.

Angela Lansbury recalls: "Ethel figured Rose was her private property, and I had no right to play the role. She told people that, although she was always cordial to me when we met. I can understand why she was upset. Critics made comparisons between her and me, which was unfair because we had our own interpretations of the role. Also, I got the Tony and she didn't, although she richly deserved it.

"It disturbed me that she was resentful, because I admired her so. I thought she was great doing 'Heat Wave' in *Alexander's Ragtime Band,* which I saw as a kid in England. And Ethel Merman in *Annie Get Your Gun* was the greatest performance I have ever seen in the theater. It inspired me to attempt a career in musicals."

Ethel found a good deal else to be angry about. She was incensed when Tom Korman presented her with an offer to play a recurring role in the television series "The Odd Couple." The agent thought Ethel would be pleased, since she had been urging him to find a television role for her.

"They want me to play Jack Klugman's aunt?" Ethel exploded. "Goddammit, he was my leading man in *Gypsy!* Why the hell should I play his aunt? It's insulting."

Korman relayed her objections to the series producers, and he returned with a different proposal: Ethel could play Klugman's older sister. "Absolutely not!" she decreed.

Ethel refused another opportunity to appear on a popular television show. Impressed by Ethel's portrayal in *It's a Mad, Mad, Mad, Mad World,* the writers of "The Danny Kaye Show" proposed a sketch in which Merman would portray the comedian's mother. Kaye relished the idea of appearing with his longtime friend, and he was pleased with the sketch the writers concocted. Ethel was not. She returned the script with a curt refusal, angering Kaye and infuriating the writers. The role was taken by Kaye Ballard.

The unhappy truth was that Ethel Merman could have passed for Jack Klugman's aunt or Danny Kaye's mother. She was now in her sixties, and the years had been unkind to her. In earlier years her face, while lacking real beauty, had a bright, fresh pertness that radiated across the footlights. Now the eyes had lost their sparkle, and added flesh blurred her features. While not as stout as an opera diva, she had acquired a thickness that dieting could not erase.

And the voice. Something had happened to that unflawed clarion. The volume was as great as ever, but the long notes had developed a vibrato, a wavering that produced a caricature of the great Merman voice. It may have been caused by the emotional stress of personal tragedies, the aging process, or simple rebellion of long overworked vocal cords. The tremolo disturbed longtime fans and made young listeners question the validity of the Merman legend.

"The wavering was bothersome, but Ethel was always true to pitch," says Marty Pasetta, who directed her in several television specials.

"She was a perfectionist. She wanted to know everything: where the camera would be, where the cut would come. In later years it was difficult shooting her because of her looks. She was aware of it and said, 'Don't shoot too tight.'

"One thing she could not do: hold back on the vocal. I tried to explain to her, 'Ethel, we have microphones, mixers, and transmitters that can do anything; you don't have to belt.' But she said, 'That's not what I'm all about. What I do is me. That's what I am.' "

In rehearsal or performance, her delivery was the same. One day she rehearsed "Before the Parade Passes By" in Pasetta's office. When she finished, applause came from an office two doors away.

In 1975, Ethel Merman added a new phase to her career: concerts. It began in May when Arthur Fiedler invited her to appear with the Boston Pops. The concert was warmly received by Pops patrons, and the PBS broadcast brought offers from symphony orchestras for benefit appearances.

"I love it," she told a *New York Times* reporter. "I get mail from teenagers and from senior citizens, a lot from people who weren't even around when I started. They come to see me, to see what the hullabaloo is all about. I've done it in every city in every kind of house. The biggest was the Hollywood

Bowl with one hundred and fourteen men behind me. It was terrific."

She explained how she prepared for concerts. She rehearsed with the orchestra, humming along "to get the phrasing and the stops. I read music so nobody puts anything over on me. . . . What I have to go through is the stage movements. I don't stand in one spot, I take up the whole stage. So I see how it looks—stage-right, stage-left. We mike the stage, and it's done."

She made it sound easy, but those who were close to Ethel knew how meticulous she could be. After her body mike failed during a Pittsburgh concert, she insisted on a contract clause in future appearances: She would be equipped with two body mikes, both with new batteries. Specifications for lighting were also spelled out in the contracts.

"Ethel would call me two or three times a day during the two weeks before a concert," recalls Robert Gardiner, who became her concert agent in 1975. "Usually she found some reason for coming down on me. That was a form of nerves, I believe, even though she claimed to be totally nerveless about appearances.

"She abstained from alcohol for a week before a concert. She told me: 'I'm a human being; I'm not infallible. If I make a mistake—forget a lyric or miss a bridge—I don't want to blame it on wine.'"

Merman had been eased into the concert field by Eric Knight, who had become her conductor for night club and other appearances in 1963. Classically trained, Knight had helped make the connection with the Boston Pops and introduced Merman to Gardiner. In concerts she always introduced him as "Eric Knight, my right arm."

"In rehearsals and in performances, Ethel's speeches were always the same; she never varied," says Knight. "The songs were always the same, so I never had to look at her, except to observe her foot movements."

"She was the greatest actress in the world," observes Gardiner. "Onstage she simply radiated happiness; her smile could light up the world. Offstage she was an entirely different woman. She gave vent to her hostilities, ranting against what she considered injustices to her. When she said no, it was permanent. Once she made a decision, she closed the door irrevocably.

"It was all business with Ethel. She didn't want to know about your problems or anybody else's. I tried to give her warmth, but it was impossible. She was simply unapproachable."

As her conductor for eighteen years, Eric Knight traveled with Merman to England, Australia and all over the United States and Canada. In the early years there were good times, often punctuated by the Merman humor. During her engagement at the Talk of the Town in London, Ethel was intrigued by the British words for certain musical notes, including "crotchet" and "quaver." When a trumpeter sounded a wrong note, she cracked, "What's wrong—does he have a quaver in his crotchet?"

During a meal in a midwestern restaurant, Merman and Knight were being served by a waitress who was all aflutter in the presence of a star. "Migawd," muttered Ethel, "she's like a fart in a bottle."

"After the Borgnine affair, Ethel became much more private," Knight remembers. "She grew more demanding, more difficult to handle. I was willing to listen, obey and swallow my pride. As I began to do things with my own career [as a conductor], she didn't want to hear about it. . . . I could never express myself on a day-to-day basis. She could, I couldn't."

In late 1976, Ethel Merman and Mary Martin were asked to appear at a joint concert to benefit the Theater and Music Collection of the Museum of the City of New York. Ethel agreed enthusiastically. Mary was reluctant; she had undergone throat surgery and was unsure of her voice. But she was persuaded.

The concert was scheduled for May 15, 1977, and a single ad in the *New York Times* sold out the seats, which ranged up to $250. The producer was Anna Sosenko, who had masterminded the career of Hildegarde for twenty-two years.

Ethel began preparing for the concert months in advance. Since both she and Mary had appeared in *Hello, Dolly!* a duet was planned with the two stars wearing the red spangled costumes of the show's finale. Miss Sosenko proposed borrowing Dolly Levi gowns from the David Merrick office.

"Are you kidding?" Ethel said indignantly. "You're asking Mary and me to wear secondhand outfits? We're stars. You'll have to make new costumes."

"But Ethel, this is a benefit," Miss Sosenko argued. "We're trying to hold the expenses."

"Hey, you're getting Mary and me free, aren't you? Make the costumes." The new costumes added $2,500 to the budget.

The Broadway Theater was available for a week before the concert, and Mary Martin asked for extra rehearsals because of her uncertainty about her voice. When Ethel heard about it, she demanded extra rehearsal time, too.

"How are we getting to rehearsals?" Ethel asked.

"The museum has a taxi service that will be at your disposal," said Miss Sosenko.

"A taxi service! Whaddaya think we are—a couple of chorus girls? Get us limos." The limousines added another $2,200 to the show's cost.

Donald Saddler directed the concert. The entrance was designed to overwhelm, and it did. The two stars crashed through two paper hoops to the music of "Send in the Clowns," Merman in the frowzy furs of Mama Rose, Martin in the oversize sailor suit of Nellie Forbush.

The love feast continued for three hours, cheers resounding to the roof of the Broadway Theater. The critics were equally jubilant the next day. After a lifetime of love letters to Ethel Merman, Walter Kerr managed to find new ways to describe her genius:

". . . at the Broadway she was an itch that couldn't be scratched, a brushfire claiming a whole mountainside, a pop and snap and a crackle that kept her rocking from side to side like a metronome on wheels, slipping without warning into a fiercely infectious jig-step for 'Doin' What Comes Natur'lly,' throwing her substantial but untamable body around as easily as she tossed breathless key-shifts to the winds, and—I guess I still don't believe it—unleashing 'Everything's Coming Up Roses' like a freshly tapped gusher with a sound soaring high in the air, straight up and off and into eternity. Incredible."

* * *

Ralph Edwards had been warned that Ethel Merman might prove a difficult subject for "This Is Your Life," that the hard-boiled Queen of Broadway might resent the intrusion on her privacy and disparage the entire proceedings, as had Lowell Thomas in a memorable telecast. Nevertheless, in 1977 Edwards put his researchers to work and began devising a ruse to surprise Merman with the re-creation of her life story.

Jerry Herman was enlisted as part of the plot. He told Ethel: "I'm going out to Hollywood to appear on 'The Merv Griffin Show,' and I'd love to have you go with me and sing the two songs I wrote for you in *Hello, Dolly!*" Ethel, who relished appearances on television talk shows, quickly agreed.

Among the other guests on the Griffin show was Ralph Edwards, who was asked how he managed to surprise the subjects of "This Is Your Life." He explained that he placed them in normal situations, then sprang his surprise.

"For instance, I could say, 'Merv Griffin, This Is Your Life,' " Edwards suggested. "Or I could say, 'Jerry Herman, This Is Your Life.' But what I'm really going to say is, 'Ethel Merman, Queen of Musical Comedy, This Is Your Life!' "

The hard-boiled queen collapsed. Edwards had planned to continue his show immediately, moving across the hall to his own studio. Ethel was weeping so steadily that the proceedings had to be delayed several minutes until she could compose herself.

She wept throughout the show as her friends paraded from behind the curtain: Josie Traeger from the Astoria days; Benay Venuta, her best friend from show business; Perle Mesta, the inspiration for *Call Me Madam;* Temple Texas, her onetime press agent; pianist, Goldie Hawkins. When Bill Geary brought on Ethel's grandchildren, Barbara Jean and Michael, the tears flowed without ceasing.

One of the conspirators in setting up the surprise was George Eells, who was then collaborating with Ethel on her autobiography. Ethel had no hesitation about issuing a second autobiography, arguing that *Who Could Ask for Anything More?* had been merely a series of magazine articles. Besides, that was published in 1955, and she had done a lot of living since then.

Eells had interviewed Ethel Merman many times while covering the Broadway scene for *Look* magazine and had written well-received biographies, notably *The Life That Late He Led,* concerning Cole Porter.

"People told me if I helped set up 'This Is Your Life,' it would be the end of my friendship with Ethel," Eells recalls. "But she always thanked me for it. She never thanked me for the book we did together. She always had the star's attitude that she deserved what she got."

When Eells undertook the autobiography with Merman, he was also warned, "She'll chew you up and spit you out." Eells found her to be sentimental and cooperative, though with certain areas of obstinacy.

The literary agent, Gloria Safier, first offered the project to E.P. Dutton. The publishers expressed interest but first wanted a sample of Merman's reminiscences, perhaps a couple of hours on tape.

"They want us to audition, huh? Get us another deal," Merman instructed the agent. "We're stars. We don't audition."

A contract was concluded with Simon and Schuster, and Ethel began her collaboration with Eells. The reputedly tough lady proved to be remarkably tender, particularly in reference to her family. She was charitable in discussing most of her fellow performers, though she had an unexplained antagonism toward Carol Channing. Said Merman: "*Dolly!* was a foolproof part. Look how many women have done it—even Betty Grable!"

Ethel displayed little charity toward husbands three and four. At first she agreed to discuss what happened after the wedding to Borgnine. Then a friend gave her the idea of leaving a blank page for the chapter "My Marriage to Ernest Borgnine." Eells argued that would be cheating the reader. "I think it's a great stunt," she replied. Executives of Simon and Schuster tried to dissuade her but failed.

Ethel was tireless in promoting the book, appearing on every national television talk show, traveling from city to city and uttering quotes that delighted interviewers.

In Boston she was asked if she had sent a copy of her book to Fernando Lamas. "Why should I send him a book when I wouldn't send him a postcard?" she replied. "He knows what I think of him."

In Atlanta she told of a man who buttonholed her while she was autographing books in Macy's New York store: "He claimed I met him forty-five years before. He said his mother told him I'd peered into his baby carriage in Central Park and said, 'What a beautiful baby!' I felt like answering, 'I wish I could say that today.' But I kept that to myself."

In San Francisco she commented: "Some of my best friends are homosexuals. Everybody knew about J. Edgar Hoover, but he was the best chief the FBI ever had. A lot of people have always been homosexual, so now they are coming out of the closet. To each his own. They don't bother me, I don't bother them. . . . It's not anybody's business what people do. If they want to be gay, let them be gay."

In Chicago she complained: "They write songs nowadays that are not singable. They write a score that nobody can hum and nobody can sing. Berlin, Porter, Gershwin . . . [today's songsmiths] don't write their kind of real, down-to-earth, commercial tunes any more." The only new song she had found to sing in her concerts, she said, was "What I Did for Love" from *A Chorus Line*.

In Minneapolis she deplored the state of the Broadway musical: "Last Saturday night I saw *Dancin'*. It's not really dancing. It's bumps and grinds, hootchy-kootchy. If I had seen one more dame open her legs . . . I kept wondering when the dancing was going to start."

Late in 1977, Edward Zimmermann told his daughter, "I'm lucky, Ethel, to be ninety-seven and still have all my marbles." But he was blind and beset with physical ills, and when he died on December 22, Ethel felt relief as well as sadness. There was no extended period of mourning, as there had been after her mother's death. Even though Ethel had always felt closer to her father, she recognized that he had lived too long.

Now Ethel had only Bobby—plus the grandchildren, whom she saw in California as often as possible. Relations between Ethel and her son had improved, partly because they seldom saw each other. Bobby had been traveling the world, and although Ethel complained because he wouldn't settle down, their reunions were always warm and loving.

In the late 1970s, Ethel acquired a new agent, Gus Schirmer. He was a member of the music publishing family, with wide experience as a producer and agent in many areas of show business. He booked her for television game shows, which she enjoyed, a telethon in Honolulu, a "Love Boat" musical and numerous specials.

"Get me a series, Gus," Ethel urged her agent. "I want to settle down in one place for a change."

In 1977, Merman appeared in a pilot film for a situation comedy, "You're Gonna Love It Here." To her disappointment, CBS decided not to place the show on the fall schedule.

In 1979, she made a brief but memorable appearance in the hit movie *Airplane!*

"Off the wall!" exclaimed Ethel, employing her favorite expression when she heard about her role in the film, a far-out satire of airplane-disaster movies. In one flashback scene, the fighter pilot-hero finds himself in a mental ward with other battle-scarred veterans. The fellow in the next bed, he explains to his sweetheart, is so deranged "he thinks he's Ethel Merman." Whereupon Ethel Merman rises from the bed and sings a few bars of "Everything's Coming Up Roses."

Jerry Zucker, one of the three writer-directors, remembers: "Unlike some of the cameo actors we dealt with, Merman was totally cooperative. 'What do you want me to do?' she asked. 'Where shall I move?' It was only two hours' work, but she insisted on her own hairdresser. When she arrived, she had the familiar Merman beehive. Which made us wonder why she needed a hairdresser." She was paid $1,500 for the job.

Ethel joined the Now Generation with *The Ethel Merman Disco Album*. It was the brainstorm of Kip Cohen, a vice president of A & M Records, who figured to cash in on the 1979 craze for disco music by combining the new beat with Broadway's most famous belter.

"Off the wall!" Ethel cried once more. She had visited Studio 54, Manhattan's citadel of disco, and although she didn't take part in the dancing, she found the music invigorating. She was pleased that Peter Matz, with whom she had worked on television specials, would arrange the songs and conduct for her.

Matz sent her cassette tapes of the piano-rhythm tracks, and Ethel sang to them over and over again, her standard method of learning new arrangements. She continued practicing the numbers on the airplane to California. "The man next to me thought I was going bananas," she said afterward. "I think he was ready to jump out the window."

Ethel rehearsed for hours in Matz's office while he accompanied her on the piano. He explained that disco featured long introductions, supposedly to allow patrons to reach the dance floor when the chorus began. "Just let me know what the last eight bars will be," said Ethel.

Miraculously, the bothersome vibrato was gone. The old Merman voice rang out as strongly as ever, and the long note on "I Got Rhythm" was sustained and pure. She also sang "Alexander's Ragtime Band," "I Get a Kick Out of You," "There's No Business Like Show Business" and her other trademark songs.

Ethel was convulsed when she arrived at the A & M recording studio to find the employees wearing T-shirts stamped ETHEL BOOGIES. The record company's star, Donna Summer, visited the studio and told Ethel, "If I'm the Queen of Disco, you're the Disco Diva."

Kip Cohen told a reporter that Ethel was "the nicest, most down-to-earth, unpretentious lady in the world, but the speed with which she works is amazing. She's a real pro."

Nevertheless, despite the efforts of both A & M and Ethel to promote the album, it failed. As Peter Matz explains, "It was released at the very moment the disco craze ended. Ethel was terribly disappointed, because she felt she had done some of her best work. So did I."

In 1980, Sylvia Fine Kaye telephoned Ethel with an offer to appear with numerous other musical stars on a special television broadcast about the Broadway musical. Mrs. Kaye was producing and narrating the show for the Public Broadcasting System.

"I warned her that the job would pay only $1,000 because we were operating on a Public Broadcasting budget," Mrs. Kaye recalls. "Ethel was cool until I told her we planned to reproduce three numbers from *Anything Goes* exactly as they were done in the original production—costumes, scenery, everything. 'No kidding, Syl, the costumes exactly as before?' she said. When I told her that was right, she said she'd do it."

Ethel appeared for rehearsal precisely at nine in the morning, in full makeup and dressed as if ready to perform. The other performers straggled in late, wearing jeans and other rehearsal gear. Ethel was scheduled to sing "You're the Top" with Rock Hudson, who would be doing the William Gaxton part. When they met, Hudson was astounded to notice that Ethel was trembling. "Imagine," he says, "the great Merman as nervous as I was! But as soon as we started working together, we got along fine."

Mrs. Kaye had planned to intersperse the numbers with impromptu conversation. Ethel balked at anything spontaneous. "I'll talk," she said, "but I want to know what you're going to ask me." Mrs. Kaye acquiesced and briefed Ethel on the questions.

Something curious happened at dress rehearsal. The production was flowing smoothly until Mrs. Kaye began to question Ethel between numbers.

"Let's stop right there," Ethel insisted. "What the hell is going on?"

"What's the matter, Ethel?" Mrs. Kaye asked.

"I wanna know what the fuck you're trying to do, throw me a curve or something?"

"But this is what we've already rehearsed."

"I swear on my mother's grave, I never heard that question before."

Mrs. Kaye was perplexed. She suggested moving on to Ethel's next number, "Anything Goes." Ethel looked at the script and said, "I've never seen these lyrics before."

A break was called in the rehearsal. Mrs. Kaye was alarmed

by Ethel's color, and she suggested to Gus Schirmer that a doctor be called. Ethel absolutely refused. She did agree to be treated by a physical therapist Mrs. Kaye knew.

Shortly before the taping, Mrs. Kaye found Ethel in her dressing room, fixing her hair and reading the script while undergoing massage by the therapist. "Oh, I know these lyrics," Ethel said, throwing down the script. Her performance was letter-perfect, as always.

While in California, Ethel paid a visit to Jimmy Durante. The comic genius, Ethel's co-star in *Red, Hot and Blue!* and *Stars in Your Eyes,* had suffered a stroke in 1972. His career ended, he rarely left his home on Beverly Drive. Only a few of his old-time pals visited him.

"I'm going to see Jimmy," Ethel announced to Temple Texas. Together they drove the few blocks from the Beverly Hills Hotel to the Durante house, where they were greeted by his wife, Marge. She warned the visitors they would be shocked by Jimmy's appearance.

Ethel drew in her breath when she saw him. The eyes were dim, the mouth slack, the face devoid of its once-great exuberance. Ethel concealed her shock and started talking.

"Jimmy, do you remember when you and Hope used to pounce on me in my dressing room at the Alvin?" she said. "Oh, what a couple of bastards you were! And how I loved it! We didn't have any songs together, you and me, in *Red, Hot and Blue!* But we did in *Stars in Your Eyes.* You remember this one?"

She sang the melody of "It's All Yours" in a voice that rattled the windows. She talked about appearing with Clayton, Jackson and Durante at Les Ambassadeurs and how she had to leave the engagement because of her inflamed tonsils. She sang her early night club songs and "I Got Rhythm" and "Moonshine Lullaby."

For one hour she sang and told jokes and reminisced. And Jimmy heard nothing. She held his hand, she stroked his face—but no flicker of recognition appeared in the faded eyes. The performance was witnessed by Marge, Temple and the male nurse with tear-filled eyes, but Ethel never gave up. After she sang the last song, she kissed Jimmy and said, "I'll come back and see you again, honey."

Only when Ethel and Temple were driving back to the hotel did Ethel allow herself to cry. Then she sobbed so uncontrollably that Temple pulled the car to the curb. "Oh, God, poor Jimmy!" Ethel cried. "Why should it happen to him?"

On May 10, 1982, more than fifty years after her Broadway debut in *Girl Crazy,* Ethel Merman appeared in concert at Carnegie Hall. It was another benefit for the Museum of the City of New York produced by Anna Sosenko. Ethel began preparations five months beforehand, selecting her gown and testing the sound system. She returned four times to check out the sound and on the morning of the concert rehearsed with the American Symphony Orchestra, which would accompany her. Ethel always insisted on rehearsals in the morning before a performance; the afternoon might be too late to make necessary changes.

Merman came strutting onto the Carnegie Hall stage, flipping her skirt to show the still-lovely legs. Adoring New Yorkers yelled and cheered until Ethel quelled them so she could sing.

She began with "I'm Just a Lady with a Song." When she sang the line "If you find my songs are right for you, I'll stay and sing all night for you," the audience accepted her proposal with cheers. After "Gee, But It's Great to Be Here," she chatted for a few minutes. She even cited the old joke: "How do you get to Carnegie Hall? You gotta practice!"

"My son Bob and I were figuring out my share of the punch line," she remarked. "By adding up the hours—the *hours*—that I have spent practicing over on Broadway to get here tonight. You know what—I kid you not—you know what it comes to? Six years. . . ."

The songs poured forth, each one greeted with a wave of grateful recognition. "Natur'lly" and "Hostess" and "Cherries" and "Rhythm" and "Smoothie" and "De-Lovely" and "Buddies" and "Roses." All with the grace notes that never changed: the slides, the holds, the phrasing ("bore me terrrr-IF-ically, too"). And of course "Show Business," an even greater closing song than "You're a Grand Old Flag."

One more time the critics tried to come to terms with Merman. Clive Barnes composed his *Post* review in the form of an unabashed love letter:

"Not everyone *liked* your voice, you know," Barnes wrote. "In fact, I don't think *anyone* really *liked* your voice. It was a voice the happy majority—blissfully including me—love, and a mealy-eared, frost-bitten minority hate.

"People often suggest you belt out songs, Ethel, but you know, belt is really too coarse a word for what you do. Your voice—incidentally, what do you do to keep it in such pristine condition, give it a larynx-lift or something?—is incisive rather than loud. It has very few grace notes, and incredibly rhythmic inflections but very little actual melodic coloring. . . . Your voice is also very thrilling—it raises my emotional temperature, it makes my feet tap and feel bellicosely happy—you must have been great at selling war bonds."

The concert, at which Ethel was presented the Pied Piper Award by ASCAP president Hal David, was an unquestioned triumph. It would be the last appearance in New York City by Ethel Merman.

21.

Last Curtain

Late in 1982, Ethel Merman was dining at Maxwell's Plum with Benay Venuta, her friend of almost fifty years. They had known months, even years of estrangement, but always they reconciled.

As they began their dinner, Benay noticed a familiar-looking couple at a table nearby. "Who *is* that?" she asked.

"That's Block and Sully, stupid," Ethel replied. Jesse Block and Eve Sully, a famous husband-and-wife act in vaudeville, had appeared with Ethel in the 1934 film *Kid Millions*.

"My God, I thought they were dead," said Benay.

"Haw! They're probably saying the same thing about us!"

Now in her mid-seventies, Ethel was aware of the onrush of time. The inexplicable mental lapse on the PBS special had disturbed her. "I keep repeating myself," she complained to Madeline Gaxton. "I don't like that."

Ethel's friends were always astonished when she'd open her bedroom closet and say cheerfully, "There's Mama and Papa and Little Ethel." Norwegian marble urns contained the ashes of Agnes and Edward Zimmermann and Ethel Merman Geary, the ones Ethel had loved most. She made no secret that she had obtained the ashes from their resting places.

In May of 1982, she told a reporter: "I dream about my mother, my dad and my daughter a lot. I see them all the time in my dreams, just as I know I'll see them in after-life. Sometimes I see their presence here. That's why it's a wonderful feeling to have the ashes with me. If something nice happens, I go in and tell them about it. On their birthdays I sing 'Happy Birthday' and at Christmas, the carols." To make the family complete, she eventually acquired the ashes of Bob Levitt, the only husband she regretted losing.

With many of her friends and business associates, Ethel now seemed unreasonable, and, at times, uncontrollable. Her conductor, Eric Knight, suggests that her erratic behavior—and her subsequent illness—may have stemmed from a 1980 accident.

Ethel and Knight had gone to Hamilton, Ontario, for a television special, "The Jack Jones Show." The performance continued satisfactorily until the finale, when streamers showered down on members of the cast. As a joke, one of the performers wrapped streamers around Ethel. When she tried to take a step, her legs became entangled and she fell on her face with a sickening thud.

"She remained still, and the curtains were pulled," Knight remembers. "I ran to the stage and found her still dazed. She was taken to a hospital, but she wouldn't stay. She flew back to New York the next day, wrapped in bandages, eyes blackened."

Her temper flared on a trip to Monte Carlo later that year. Incensed because Knight brought his wife along, she wouldn't speak to him all week. Finally she told him: "I think you took advantage of me." After the performance she directed her wrath at Robert Gardiner. And on the flight back to New York, she excoriated the concert manager over imagined misdeeds.

Ethel became equally difficult with friends, alienating many of them irretrievably. Russell Nype finally broke off relations with her "because I got tired of trying to deal with a twelve-year-old mind." Ethel had long been a friend of Goldie Hawkins, a gifted pianist who operated a Manhattan night spot she frequented. When Goldie invited her to drop in one evening, Ethel muttered to a friend, "Why is he inviting me? I always go to his place on my own. He must be trying to use me." A business proposal came up during the evening, and Ethel was incensed. Goldie Hawkins was banished from her life.

She became increasingly suspicious and resentful of Eric Knight. Instead of introducing him at concerts as "my right arm," she began to ignore him. When the omission seemed glaring at the Carnegie Hall concert, she said offhandedly, "Oh, yes, I forgot to introduce my conductor, Eric Knight." It was the last time they worked together.

Robert Gardiner, however, patiently continued dealing with Merman's unreasonableness. A proposal was made for a concert version of *Girl Crazy* at Carnegie Hall with the two original cast members, Ethel Merman and Ginger Rogers. Ethel agreed, but she insisted on first billing. Realizing that Ginger would not submit to lesser billing, Gardiner suggested offsetting the names, a practice originated to placate superstars in the same movie:

GINGER ROGERS
ETHEL MERMAN

"I never heard of such a thing," Merman bawled. "My name is on the left, hers is on the right. That's the way it's gonna be."

Gardiner found a concert ad in which the names of Zubin Mehta and Luciano Pavarotti were offset. "See—if they can do it, you and Ginger can," her agent suggested. "You gotta be nuts," Merman replied. "It's my way or no way." The impasse continued. The concert was postponed indefinitely.

Ethel maintained a hectic schedule, and even a painful sciatic nerve condition did not prompt her to cancel an appearance. Basso Jerome Hines came to her Roosevelt Hospital room to rehearse "You're Just in Love," which they were scheduled to sing at an opera benefit in Washington, D.C. Ethel wrote to Max Showalter on January 28, 1983, that she didn't remember performing at the benefit because she had been heavily medicated with Valium and Demerol. But she did remember that she and Hines had to repeat the song because of the ovation.

She wrote Showalter that the severe pain had gone, and she was leaving in five days for concerts in San Jose, California, and in Lakeland, Daytona and Orlando, Florida.

Ethel had turned seventy-five on January 16, 1983, though she claimed to be four years younger. It was a time of reconciliation for her. Relations with Bobby were more stable than they had ever been, and Ethel was reaching out to friends she had alienated during her drinking days.

Ethel Merman and Mary Martin had known each other since 1938, when Mary made her Broadway debut singing "My Heart Belongs to Daddy" in *Leave It to Me*. Though their daughters attended each other's birthday parties, Merman and Martin worked too steadily to become real friends. The Broadway crowd suggested there was a rivalry between the two, and that seemed credible after Merman's crack, "How can you buck a nun?" Then there was her reputed comment: "Mary Martin's okay—if you like talent."

Nevertheless, the two stars remained cordial whenever they met socially. Mary and Richard Halliday, her husband, once invited Ethel to visit their Brazilian farm. Ethel declined politely, but she told friends, "Can you imagine me going to that godforsaken place without a doctor in a thousand miles? They gotta be crazy. Off the wall!"

In 1982, Mary asked Ethel to appear on "Over Easy," her PBS television series offering advice to people of mature years. "I've got an idea for a song we could do," said Mary. "We could sing, 'Anything I Can Do, You Can Do Better.' " Ethel loved the idea, and she made plans to fly to San Francisco, where the program was taped.

Ethel went directly from the airport to Mary's house, and they began rehearsals immediately. For two days they practiced with Mary's accompanist until both stars were satisfied. The studio audience was electrified by the sight of Ethel Merman and Mary Martin singing and clowning their way through "Anything I Can Do, You Can Do Better." Ethel was so exhilarated that she decided to remain for a couple of days so she and Mary could visit.

"Do you remember," Mary said, "when I rehearsed *Annie* in *your* theater, the Imperial? We had the dress rehearsal the day before our company was supposed to leave for Dallas. You and the whole New York company came, and I just about died. You sat down front and you had on white gloves. I could see you clapping and I could hear your laugh. But I wanted to shoot you. Why did you wear those white gloves?"

"I wanted you to see them," Ethel replied.

"Yes, but I couldn't *hear* them!"

For two days, Ethel and Mary went shopping, prowled Chinatown, dined together. At one point, Mary asked, "Did you really say 'Mary Martin's okay—if you like talent'?"

"Of course not," Ethel insisted. "A press agent dreamed it up."

Mary Martin remembers: "When Ethel left San Francisco, she told me, 'I can't remember ever having a better time in my life.' This just thrilled me to death. She was a funny one. She could be very down, very morose. Then you see the other side—very up, very cheerful. That's the way she was that time in San Francisco."

News of the Merman-Martin performance reached Hollywood, and they were asked to perform at the Academy Awards ceremonies the following spring. They would be the stars of a tribute to Irving Berlin, and both were eager to participate. Then in September of 1982, Mary was severely injured in a traffic accident that killed her manager, Ben Washer, and injured Janet Gaynor so seriously that she later died.

Ethel telephoned San Francisco General Hospital day and night to inquire about Mary's condition. Finally she was told that Miss Martin would recover but faced a long period of convalescence. Howard W. Koch, who was producing the Academy Awards show, asked Ethel to perform the Berlin tribute alone. She agreed.

In March of 1983, Mary Martin was recuperating at her Palm Springs home when she received a telephone call from Merman: "Honey, I'm coming out to do the Oscar show, then I'll be down to see you the next day. We'll have a ball together."

On March 26, Ethel Merman wrote a chatty letter to her friend Mary Dayton in Los Angeles. It was full of news about her activities: she had just returned from Florida, where she had sung concerts and presented scholarships at the Burt Reynolds Theater in Jupiter; future plans included three Carnegie

Hall concerts at which she and Ginger Rogers would sing their songs from *Girl Crazy*, then Ethel was to sing "I Got Rhythm" on the Tony Awards telecast.

Ethel also wrote that she was scheduled to sing "Show Business" in a tribute to Irving Berlin on the Oscar telecast. She would have to take the midnight "red-eye" flight to Washington that night because she was scheduled to attend a dinner at the White House the following evening. Hence she had to cancel the visit to Mary Martin in Palm Springs.

On the morning of April 7, Ethel packed her suitcases in her apartment at the Hotel Surrey, where she had moved when the Berkshire was converted to condominiums. As always, everything was compartmentalized and labeled, so she could immediately reach anything she needed at her destination.

She telephoned some of her closest friends to inform them of her plans. "I'll be home on Wednesday, and I'll call you as soon as I get in," she told Madeline Gaxton. She told the same thing to Tony Cointreau, scion of the liqueur family, who noticed something disturbing. During the past year, Ethel had habitually reversed words and phrases, always correcting herself and saying "I'm all right." But on that day when she transposed a phrase, she said, "I'm all right"—and made the same mistake all over again.

Ethel glanced at her watch. Two o'clock, time to leave. As she lifted the telephone to order the bag pickup, the thunderbolt flashed inside her brain.

She staggered and fell to the floor.

"Hello? Hello? Miss Merman?"

Ethel could hear the telephone operator's voice, but she couldn't answer. She opened her mouth and only gargled sounds emerged. She was confident that the operator would understand her desperation and send someone to rescue her. But the door! It had four locks and a steel bolt, precautions Ethel felt necessary after thieves stole her entire jewelry collection in 1970.

It might take an hour to break down the door, she realized.

Slowly, painfully, she crawled along the floor until she reached the door and pulled herself up to release the locks.

At Roosevelt Hospital, doctors surmised that she had suffered a stroke. But tests uncovered something else: a brain tumor.

On April 11, Mary Martin, watching the Academy Awards telecast, waited expectantly for the Irving Berlin production number. No Ethel.

"That's strange," Mary said worriedly. "Ethel never misses a show. Something must be wrong."

In the beginning, it was reported that Miss Merman had been unable to keep the Academy Awards engagement because of a bad cold. Even her closest friends were unaware of the gravity of her condition. Like Mary Martin, many of them were perplexed when they didn't see Ethel on the Oscar show. Bobby told a few of them how ill his mother really was. They found it incredible that Ethel's dynamism should suddenly be quelled. To Gus Schirmer, who had spoken to her three or four times a day for years, "the silence was deafening."

On April 15, Ethel underwent four hours of surgery. The news was released that the operation had been for a brain tumor and that she appeared to be recovering. The hospital received calls from Bob Hope, Van Johnson, Mary Martin and other celebrities, as well as Merman fans. President Reagan tried three times to call and was disconnected each time. Finally he reached a hospital administrator. The President told the press: "I'm very happy that she is in satisfactory condition and that she's apparently come through the operation and is resting comfortably. I want to send her flowers."

In truth, the surgeons had discovered the tumor to be inoperable.

For weeks Ethel remained at Roosevelt Hospital, unable to speak or walk. She had been cheered by thousands of cards and letters, including one from President and Mrs. Reagan. Mary Martin, still recovering from her car accident, sent a telegram that made Ethel smile: "DEAR ETHEL—ANYTHING I CAN DO YOU CAN DO BETTER. LOVE, MARY."

In May, Miss Martin was well enough to accept a White House invitation. On the way to Washington, she stopped in New York to see her old friend. She remembers:

"They gave me her room number, but I thought it was a mistake when I looked inside. No hair, just a mound of flesh, bloated from the medicine. I thought it was a man. But I went to the desk, and they said, 'No, that's where she is.' I went back to the room, and the nurse, who apparently had been looking out the window, said, 'She knows you're here.'

"I nearly died; I wasn't prepared for it. I went over and took her hand. Her nurse had dyed her fingernails bright red, something feminine for her to see. [Ethel] looked at me a long time and smiled. I said, 'Did you get my telegram?' Then she started to cry.

"I decided I wasn't going to cry, so I just started to talk and talk and talk. She began to smile and laugh, and she tried to get words out. Finally she said, 'I . . . can't . . . walk.' I said, 'Yes, you can. You *have* to.' She said, 'But I can't . . . it . . . hurts.' I said, 'Of course it hurts, but you *have* to walk. You have to get out of that bed and get on the walker. You have to do it every day. Me, I couldn't stand up straight. I had to bend over to walk—one . . . two . . . it was murder. Will you promise me you will?' She said, 'Yes, I will . . . If you can do it . . . I can do it.' "

Bobby telephoned Mary the next day: "It's like night and day. Mother *asked* to get up, she *asked* for the walker, she's starting to talk better. It's amazing."

By July, Ethel's condition had improved enough for her to return to her apartment at the Surrey. Dorothy Strelsin, a wealthy friend who lived a block away, visited almost every day, often bringing her meat loaf, a Merman favorite. Madeline Gaxton was a frequent visitor as well. She brought Ethel a wig; when Ethel complained about it, Mrs. Gaxton had her hairdresser restyle it.

During her first weeks at home, Ethel remained optimistic about the future. She told Gus Schirmer: "Don't make any bookings until December."

Her energies weakened, however, and her speech grew more

labored and indistinct. Visitors from California were shocked by her appearance. John Green, who had accompanied Ethel on the piano at the Palace and had conducted her triumphant concert at the Hollywood Bowl in 1979, came with his wife, Bonnie.

"We're praying for you, Ethel," said Mrs. Green. "We know it's all going to come back."

"No . . . it isn't," Ethel said haltingly. "It's . . . finished."

Says Green: "We got the impression that Ethel was no longer fighting, that she didn't want to linger the way she was."

All of the visitors were impressed by how attentive and loving Bobby was. All of the quarrelsome years between mother and son were erased. "Where's my Bobby?" Ethel often cried, and he appeared immediately. She gained comfort from his presence, holding his hand for hours in the darkness. He protected her, screened visitors, advised them on the best time to see her, kept her from growing tired. He also managed to keep the seriousness of her illness from the press.

Wracked by pain and frustration, Ethel sometimes raged at her son, accusing him of past transgressions. Bobby waited patiently for the mood to subside.

Ethel could not understand what had happened to her. She had never known any serious illness; nothing had ever slowed her down for long. Her mind seemed as alert as ever, yet she couldn't express herself. Sometimes the words came out right, then they'd be gibberish. Over and over again she wailed, "But I'm so young!" And in her mind she was.

A regular visitor was Tony Cointreau. He remembered how Ethel had often told of singing her first song, "He's Me Pal," for the troops at Camp Yaphank and Camp Mills. He had a small pillow made for her with the song's title spelled out in needlepoint. When Ethel saw it, she began to cry, and she held the pillow next to her cheek. Suddenly she began to sing, her voice articulating the lyrics she had learned sixty-five years before:

He's me pal,
He's me pal,
He's the very best friend that I know.

His heart's full of love
As the heavens above,
He drives away sorrow and woe.

The decline continued inexorably, her recognition of people fading. Old friends came to hold her hand and tell her stories, not knowing whether she comprehended. Benay Venuta related an anecdote about her and Ethel told repeatedly by gypsies (chorus people), the tale becoming more embellished with each telling.

The actual incident happened after a performance of the *Annie Get Your Gun* revival. Ethel had finished dressing and was adjusting a fox hat before leaving the theater. "You know, dear," said Benay, "you're supposed to wear it with your hair tucked underneath." Ethel replied, "No, I like to have some hair showing; it gives a softness to the face."

As Ethel lay in bed staring blankly, Benay continued: "Now the way the gypsies tell it, you and I got into a screaming argument about a turban. We continued shouting as we went out to the limousine and you turned and said, 'Fuck off, I like a little softness about the face.' "

Benay waited for Ethel's response. At first there was none, then her lips began to move and she muttered, "Assholes."

One night *There's No Business Like Show Business* was being shown on television. Bobby turned on the set in front of his mother's bed. She never recognized herself on the screen.

On January 15, the day before Ethel's seventy-sixth birthday, Mary Martin paid a visit to the apartment. Bobby had warned her beforehand that his mother's condition had worsened, but Mary was still not prepared for the shock.

Mary recalls: "I went out and bought the wildest robe I could find, really crazy. I walked into the room and put the robe in front of her, expecting she would see it. She opened her eyes and—no recognition. Nothing.

"Bobby and the nurse left, and I held her hand for an awful long time, just talking to her to see if eventually she'd come out of it, or make any sign of recognition. She'd go to sleep, then waken, then go to sleep again. Finally I decided this wasn't going to work, so I started to leave.

"As I pulled my hand away, she opened her eyes. She recognized me and—I can't even describe it—this *wail* came out. She went 'Oooooooooooooo' at the top of her lungs. No words. Just that terrible sound."

Death came on February 15, 1984. Bobby instructed the funeral establishment to give the press no details of the cause of death nor of the memorial services, declaring only that the body would be cremated. Only a few close friends and entertainment figures were invited to the funeral at St. Bartholomew's Church, where Ethel had worshiped from the beginning of her Broadway career. The only flowers on the altar were seventy-six roses, one for each of her years.

The obituary writers took up the longtime challenge of defining the Merman magic.

Time: "Her brassy and absolutely clear singing inspired metaphors like 'a chorus of taxi horns,' but words never quite captured its unique qualities."

New York Times: "Her delighted customers knew that when the 'belter' strode onstage, turned her round eyes on them, raised her quizzical eyebrows and opened her wide mouth, they would get full value wherever they sat. She needed no hidden microphones. Equally important, they knew that when they bought tickets to a Merman show—usually well in advance—she would be there, her face beaming, strong arms churning, regardless of snowfall or flu epidemic. Her health was as legendary as her toughness and outspokenness."

Newsweek: "One by one, the irreplaceables of the century are going—Louis Armstrong, George Balanchine, Ethel Merman. . . . She was the greatest musical-comedy performer of her time, maybe anyone's time. She had a quality that can never again spring spontaneously into being—call it classicism, call it Olympian simplicity, call it God's untaintable socko, but call it Merman."

Radio stations played records of Merman belting "I Got Rhythm" and her other hits. Television channels broadcast *Call Me Madam* and *There's No Business Like Show Business*. But, as in her lifetime, no mechanical medium could convey her mesmerizing hold on a live theater audience.

The Merman estate amounted to less than her friends had expected, considering Ethel's thriftiness and the high earnings during her Broadway career. Its worth was estimated at $800,000, most of it bequeathed to her son and two grandchildren. The will directed that her personal effects be sold.

An auction was held at Christie's East in New York City on October 15, 1984, raising $120,310. Old friends were there to bid for cherished items. Dorothy Strelsin bought a Dufy painting. Ethel's attorney, Raymond Katz, won the bidding for a gold bracelet with charms depicting the classic Merman roles, a gift for his wife. Benay Venuta bought back the painting she had done of Ethel as Mama Rose, for donation to the Museum of the City of New York. Three letters and a telegram from President Reagan brought $1,300, a framed letter from Dwight Eisenhower $450, the prop rifle from *Annie Get Your Gun* $1,500.

On February 20, 1984, a long black car rode slowly down Broadway. Inside was Robert Levitt, Jr. and with him was an urn carrying his mother's ashes. The car swung past the Alvin, the Imperial, the Broadway, the Majestic—the great old houses that had rung with the Merman voice. Then, a minute before curtain time, all of the shining marquees dimmed their lights in final remembrance of the star who outshone all others.

APPENDIX A Theater Appearances

Title	Premiere	Theater	Perfor-mances	Songwriters	Merman Songs	Others in Cast
Girl Crazy	10/14/30	Alvin	272	Ira and George Gershwin	"Sam and Delilah," "I Got Rhythm," "Boy, What Love Has Done to Me!"	Willie Howard, Ginger Rogers, Allen Kearns, William Kent
George White's Scandals (11th Edition)	9/14/31	Apollo	202	Lew Brown, Ray Henderson	"Life Is Just a Bowl of Cherries," "Ladies and Gentlemen, That's Love," "My Song," "The Good Old Days"	Rudy Vallee, Everett Marshall, Willie and Eugene Howard, Ray Bolger, Ethel Barrymore Colt
Humpty Dumpty	9/26/32	Nixon (Pittsburgh)	Closed in tryout	Nacio Herb Brown, Richard Whiting		Lou Holtz, Sid Silvers, Eddie Foy, Jr., J. C. Nugent
Take a Chance	11/26/32	Apollo	243	Nacio Herb Brown, Richard Whiting, Vincent Youmans	"I Got Religion," "Rise 'n Shine," "You're an Old Smoothie," "Eadie Was a Lady"	Jack Haley, Sid Silvers, June Knight, Jack Whiting, Mitzi Mayfair

APPENDIX A Theater Appearances

Title	Premiere	Theater	Performances	Songwriters	Merman Songs	Others in Cast
Anything Goes	11/21/34	Alvin	420	Cole Porter	"I Get a Kick Out of You," "You're the Top," "Anything Goes," "Blow, Gabriel, Blow," "Buddy, Beware"	William Gaxton, Victor Moore, Bettina Hall, Vivian Vance
Red, Hot and Blue!	10/29/36	Alvin	183	Cole Porter	"Down in the Depths on the 90th Floor," "You've Got Something," "It's De-Lovely," "Ridin' High," "You're a Bad Influence on Me," "Red, Hot and Blue!"	Jimmy Durante, Bob Hope, Lew Parker, Vivian Vance, Grace and Paul Hartman
Stars in Your Eyes	2/9/39	Majestic	127	Arthur Schwartz, Dorothy Fields	"This Is It," "A Lady Needs a Change," "Just a Little Bit More," "I'll Pay the Check," "It's All Yours"	Jimmy Durante, Richard Carlson, Tamara Toumanova, Dan Dailey, Jr.

Du Barry Was a Lady	12/6/39	46th Street	408	Cole Porter	"When Love Beckoned," "Come On In," "But in the Morning, No," "Give Him the Oo-La-La," "Katie Went to Haiti," "Friendship"	Bert Lahr, Betty Grable, Charles Walters, Ronald Graham, Benny Baker
Panama Hattie	10/30/40	46th Street	501	Cole Porter	"Visit Panama," "My Mother Would Love You," "I've Still Got My Health," "Let's Be Buddies," "I'm Throwin' a Ball Tonight," "Make It Another Old-Fashioned, Please," "You Said It"	James Dunn, Phyllis Brooks, Rags Ragland, Betty Hutton, Arthur Treacher, Joan Carroll, Pat Harrington, Frank Hyers
Something for the Boys	1/7/43	Alvin	422	Cole Porter	"Something for the Boys," "When We're at Home on the Range," "Hey, Good-Lookin'," "He's a Right Guy," "The Leader of a Big-Time Band," "There's a Happy Land in the Sky," "By the Mississinewa"	Paula Laurence, Bill Johnson, Betty Bruce, Betty Garrett, Allen Jenkins

APPENDIX A Theater Appearances

Title	Premiere	Theater	Performances	Songwriters	Merman Songs	Others in Cast
Annie Get Your Gun	5/16/46	Imperial	1,147	Irving Berlin	"Doin' What Comes Natur'lly," "You Can't Get a Man with a Gun," "There's No Business Like Show Business," "They Say It's Wonderful," "Moonshine Lullaby," "I'm an Indian, Too," "I Got Lost in His Arms," "I Got the Sun in the Morning," "Anything You Can Do"	Ray Middleton, William O'Neal, George Lipton, Harry Bellaver, Marty May

Call Me Madam	10/12/50	Imperial	644	Irving Berlin	"The Hostess with the Mostes' on the Ball," "Washington Square Dance," "Can You Use Any Money Today?" "Marrying for Love," "The Best Thing for You Would Be Me," "Something to Dance About," "You're Just in Love"	Paul Lukas, Russell Nype, Galina Talva, Pat Harrington
Happy Hunting	12/6/56	Majestic	412	Harold Karr, Matt Dubey	"It's Good to Be Here," "Mutual Admiration Society," "Mr. Livingstone," "This Is What I Call Love," "A Newfangled Tango," "The Game of Love," "Happy Hunting," "I'm a Funny Dame," "Just Another Guy"	Fernando Lamas, Virginia Gibson, Gordon Polk, Gene Wesson, Estelle Parsons

APPENDIX A Theater Appearances

Title	Premiere	Theater	Performances	Songwriters	Merman Songs	Others in Cast
Gypsy	5/21/59	Broadway	702	Jule Styne, Stephen Sondheim	"Some People," "Small World," "Mr. Goldstone, I Love You," "You'll Never Get Away from Me," "Everything's Coming Up Roses," "Together Wherever We Go," "Rose's Turn"	Jack Klugman, Sandra Church, Paul Wallace, Lane Bradbury
Annie Get Your Gun (revival)	9/28/66	New York State	78	Irving Berlin	Original score, plus "Old-Fashioned Wedding"	Bruce Yarnell, Jerry Orbach, Benay Venuta, Rufus Smith, Harry Bellaver
Hello, Dolly!	(Merman opened) 3/28/70	St. James	(Merman performances) 210	Jerry Herman	"I Put My Hand In," "World, Take Me Back," "Motherhood," "Dancing," "Love, Look in My Window," "Before the Parade Passes By," "Hello, Dolly!" "So Long, Dearie"	Jack Goode, Russell Nype, June Helmers, Danny Lockin

APPENDIX B Feature Films

Title	Distributor	Release Date	Director	Others in Cast
Follow the Leader	Paramount	10/12/30	Norman Taurog	Ed Wynn, Ginger Rogers, Stanley Smith, Lou Holtz
We're Not Dressing	Paramount	4/26/34	Norman Taurog	Bing Crosby, Carole Lombard, George Burns and Gracie Allen, Leon Errol, Ray Milland
Kid Millions	United Artists	10/17/34	Roy Del Ruth	Eddie Cantor, Ann Sothern, George Murphy, Jesse Block, Eve Sully, Burton Churchill, Warren Hymer
Strike Me Pink	United Artists	1/14/36	Norman Taurog	Eddie Cantor, Sally Eilers, Harry Parke, William Frawley, Brian Donlevy
Anything Goes	Paramount	2/5/36	Lewis Milestone	Bing Crosby, Charles Ruggles, Ida Lupino, Grace Bradley, Arthur Treacher, Margaret Dumont
Happy Landing	20th Century–Fox	1/22/38	Roy Del Ruth	Sonja Henie, Don Ameche, Cesar Romero, Jean Hersholt, Billy Gilbert
Alexander's Ragtime Band	20th Century–Fox	5/28/38	Henry King	Tyrone Power, Alice Faye, Don Ameche, Jack Haley, Jean Hersholt, John Carradine

APPENDIX B Feature Films

Title	Distributor	Release Date	Director	Others in Cast
Straight, Place and Show	20th Century–Fox	9/28/38	David Butler	Ritz Brothers, Richard Arlen, Phyllis Brooks, George Barbier
Stage Door Canteen	United Artists	5/12/43	Frank Borzage	Cheryl Walker, Lon McCallister, plus guest stars Alfred Lunt, Lynn Fontanne, Tallulah Bankhead, Helen Hayes, Katherine Cornell, Katharine Hepburn, Gypsy Rose Lee, etc.
Call Me Madam	20th Century–Fox	3/12/53	Walter Lang	Donald O'Connor, Vera-Ellen, George Sanders, Billy De Wolfe, Helmut Dantine, Walter Slezak
There's No Business Like Show Business	20th Century–Fox	12/8/54	Walter Lang	Donald O'Connor, Marilyn Monroe, Dan Dailey, Johnny Ray, Mitzi Gaynor, Richard Eastham, Hugh O'Brian
It's A Mad, Mad, Mad, Mad World	United Artists	11/7/63	Stanley Kramer	Spencer Tracy, Milton Berle, Sid Caesar, Buddy Hackett, Mickey Rooney, Dick Shawn, Phil Silvers, Terry-Thomas, Jonathan Winters, Edie Adams, etc.
The Art of Love	Universal	5/6/65	Norman Jewison	James Garner, Dick Van Dyke, Elke Sommer, Angie Dickinson, Carl Reiner
Airplane!	Paramount	7/11/80	Jim Abrahms, David Zucker, Jerry Zucker	Robert Hays, Julie Hagerty, Kareem Abdul-Jabbar, Lloyd Bridges, Peter Graves, Leslie Nielsen Robert Stack

Acknowledgments

The author is grateful to the following for recounting their memories of Ethel Merman: June Allyson, Lucille Ball, Milton Berle, Ray Bolger, George Burns, Tony Cointreau, Carole Cook, Mary Dayton, Richard Eastham, George Eells, José Ferrer, Robert Gardiner, Madeline Gaxton, Mitzi Gaynor, John Green, Flo Haley, Jerry Herman, Bob Hope, Dolores Hope, Rock Hudson, Ross Hunter, Van Johnson, Robert Kaufman, Sylvia Fine Kaye, Jane Kean, Ruby Keeler, Eric Knight, Howard W. Koch, Tom Korman, Stanley Kramer, Angela Lansbury, Ron Leif, Artie Malvin, Mary Martin, Peter Matz, Don Mischer, Russell Nype, Donald O'Connor, Jerry Orbach, Marty Pasetta, Richard Perry, Milt Pickman, Johnny Ray, Florence Rome, Cesar Romero, Rose Marie, Walter Scharf, Gus Schirmer, Joseph Schribman, Temple Texas Schribman, Steve Shagan, Max Showalter, Stephen Sondheim, Dorothy Strelsin, Florence Sundstrom, Rudy Vallee, Benay Venuta, Paul Wallace.

Special thanks to Miles Kreuger, Anna Sosenko and Maurice Zolotow.

These facilities were invaluable for research: UCLA Theater Arts Library; Academy of Motion Picture Arts and Sciences; Library of the Performing Arts, Lincoln Center; Museum of the City of New York; Central Library, Los Angeles.

Especially helpful were the two Merman autobiographies, *Who Could Ask for Anything More?* (with Pete Martin) and *Merman: An Autobiography* (with George Eells).

Other books consulted include: *The Life That Late He Led: A Biography of Cole Porter* by George Eells; *Notes on a Cowardly Lion* by John Lahr; *Have Tux, Will Travel* by Bob Hope (with Pete Martin); *Call Me Lucky* by Bing Crosby (with Pete Martin); *Musical Stages* by Richard Rodgers; *A Valuable Property: The Life Story of Mike Todd* by Michael Todd, Jr. and Susan McCarthy Todd; *The Nine Lives of Mike Todd* by Art Cohn; *Getting to Know Him: A Biography of Oscar Hammerstein II* by Hugh Fordin; *Bob Hope: A Life in Comedy* by William Robert Faith; *Marilyn Monroe* by Maurice Zolotow; *Broadway's Greatest Musicals* by Abe Laufe; *Broadway* by Brooks Atkinson; *Josh* by Josh Logan; *Groucho* by Hector Arce; *Dancing in the Dark* by Howard Dietz; *Jule: The Story of Composer Jule Styne* by Theodore Taylor; *Two on the Aisle* by John Mason Brown; *No People Like Show People* by Maurice Zolotow; *My Heart Belongs* by Mary Martin; *Irving Berlin* by Michael Freedland; *"Mister Abbott"* by George Abbott; *Life with Lindsay and Crouse* by Cornelia Otis Skinner; *Lyrics on Several Occasions* by Ira Gershwin; *The Theater in Spite of Itself* by Walter Kerr; *George Gershwin: His Journey to Greatness* by David Ewen.

Scores of magazine and newspaper articles contributed to this biography. Most of the important ones are mentioned in the text.

Index